THE BEATLES
201 • CHORD SONG BOOK

score

Intro.

제 2차세계대전으로 폐허가 된 영국에서 탄생한 리버풀 출신의 밴드 비틀즈.

그들의 일대기와 음악들은 팝 역사상 누구와도 비교할 수 없는 대단한 사건이었다고
생각합니다. 소녀들의 열광적인 지지를 받는 락앤롤 스타에 머무르지 않고 끝없는
변화를 거듭하여 음악적 스펙트럼을 방대하게 넓혀 나가며 불후의 명곡들을 남겼으며,
그 시대의 문화 전반에 걸쳐 수많은 족적과 이야깃거리를 남겼습니다.

팝 역사상 최고의 송라이팅 파트너로 알려진 폴 매카트니와 존 레논. 그리고 조지
해리슨과 링고 스타의 곡들을 들여다 보면 '초보자에게 어렵지 않지만 숙련자에겐
쉽지 않은' 묘한 매력을 가진 곡들이 많습니다. 심플하지만 탁월한 멜로디 감각과
가사들은 어째서 그토록 많은 사람들이 비틀즈의 음악을 사랑하는가 하는 질문에
스스로 고개를 끄덕이게 만듭니다.

1963년의 Please Please Me 부터 1970년 Let It Be 까지의 정식 앨범들의 수록곡들,
싱글 커트된 곡들과 B-side 곡 그리고 초기의 미발매 앨범들의 가사와 코드를 정리하여
Song Book의 형태로 한 권의 책에 담았습니다. 더불어 비틀즈의 인기만큼이나 셀 수
없이 많은 비틀즈 관련 자료들을 원곡과 비교 대조하고 한곡 한곡 직접 연주해보며
최대한 정확한 가사와 코드들을 담으려 많은 노력을 기울였습니다. 부디 비틀즈와
그들의 음악을 사랑하시는 분들에게 즐겁고 유용한 자료가 되길 바랍니다.

책을 보시기 전에

* 기타의 스탠다드 튜닝을 기준으로 하고 있지만 연주 하시기전 각 페이지의 상단에 기재된 튜닝(조율) 또는
카포(Capo)위치를 숙지하시기 바랍니다.

* 조지 해리슨이 연주했던 시타르가 사용된곡, 오케스트라와 협연한곡, 또는 당시 녹음 환경에 따라
A440(Pitch Standard)에 맞지 않는 곡들이 다수 포함되어 있습니다. 튜닝기의 피치 조정 기능으로 기타의
조율을 미세하게 조정하시기 바랍니다.

* 밴드 내에서 기타 두대의 연주외에 베이스 또는 그외 추가 악기들의 음들을 감안하여 코드를 표기
하였으므로 기타 이외의 악기로 코드를 참조하여 연주해도 무방합니다.

* 가사에서 영국식 철자 표기를 따랐습니다.

THE BEATLES Discography

Please Please Me

22 March 1963
Parlophone PMC 1202 (mono)
Parlophone PCS 3042 (stereo)

I Saw Her Standing There
Misery
Anna (Go To Him)
Chains
Boys
Ask Me Why
Please Please Me
Love Me Do
PS I Love You
Baby It's You
Do You Want To Know A Secret
A Taste Of Honey
There's A Place
Twist And Shout

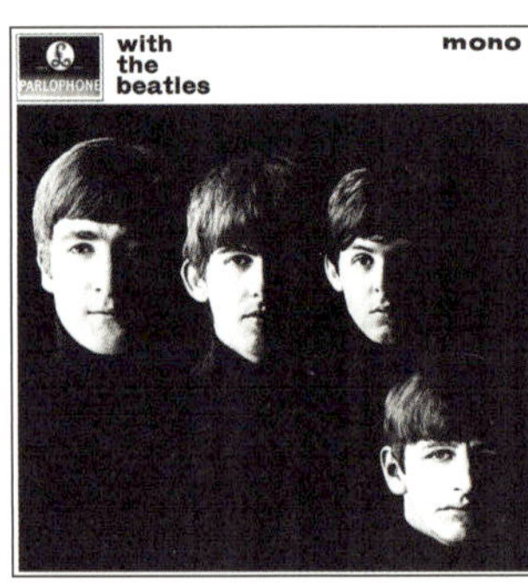

With The Beatles

22 November 1963
Parlophone PMC 1206 (mono)
Parlophone PCS 3045 (stereo)

It Won't Be Long
All I've Got To Do
All My Loving
Don't Bother Me
Little Child
Till There Was You
Please Mister Postman
Roll Over Beethoven
Hold Me Tight
You Really Got A Hold On Me
I Wanna Be Your Man
Devil In Her Heart
Not A Second Time
Money (That's What I Want)

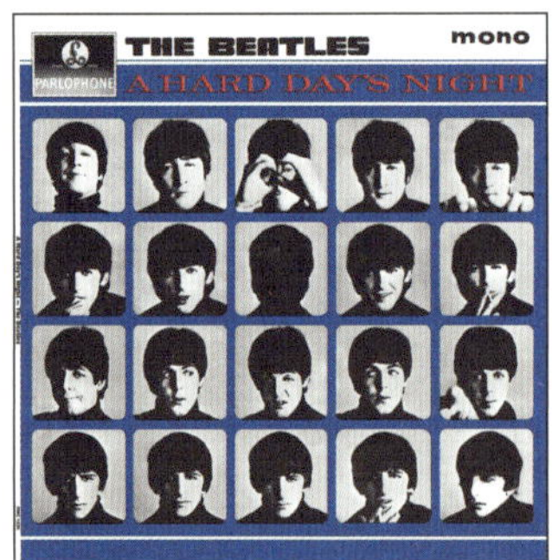

A Hard Day's Night

10 July 1964
Parlophone PMC 1230 (mono)
Parlophone PCS 3058 (stereo)

A Hard Day's Night
I Should Have Known Better
If I Fell
I'm Happy Just To Dance With You
And I Love Her
Tell Me Why
Can't Buy Me Love
Any Time At All
I'll Cry Instead
Things We Said Today
When I Get Home
You Can't Do That
I'll Be Back

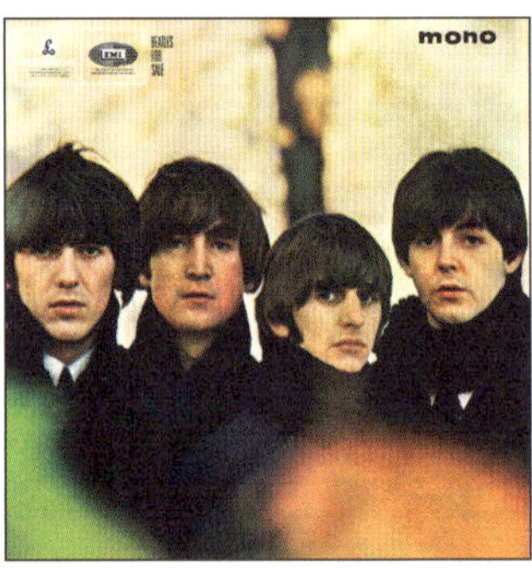

Beatles For Sale

4 December 1964
Parlophone PMC 1240 (mono)
Parlophone PCS 3062 (stereo)

No Reply
I'm A Loser
Baby's In Black
Rock And Roll Music
I'll Follow The Sun
Mr Moonlight
Kansas City/Hey-Hey-Hey-Hey!
Eight Days A Week
Words Of Love
Honey Don't
Every Little Thing
I Don't Want To Spoil The Party
What You're Doing
Everybody's Trying To Be My Baby

Help!

6 August 1965
Parlophone PMC 1255 (mono)
Parlophone PCS 3071 (stereo)

Help!
The Night Before
You've Got To Hide Your Love Away
I Need You
Another Girl
You're Going To Lose That Girl
Ticket To Ride
Act Naturally
It's Only Love
You Like Me Too Much
Tell Me What You See
I've Just Seen A Face
Yesterday
Dizzy Miss Lizzy

Rubber Soul

3 December 1965
Parlophone PMC 1267 (mono)
Parlophone PCS 3075 (stereo)

Drive My Car
Norwegian Wood (This Bird Has Flown)
You Won't See Me
Nowhere Man
Think For Yourself
The Word
Michelle
What Goes On
Girl
I'm Looking Through You
In My Life
Wait
If I Needed Someone
Run For Your Life

Revolver

5 August 1966
Parlophone PMC 7009 (mono)
Parlophone PCS 7009 (stereo)

Taxman
Eleanor Rigby
I'm Only Sleeping
Love You To
Here, There And Everywhere
Yellow Submarine
She Said She Said
Good Day Sunshine
And Your Bird Can Sing
For No One
Doctor Robert
I Want To Tell You
Got To Get You Into My Life
Tomorrow Never Knows

Sgt Pepper's Lonely Hearts Club Band

1 June 1967
Parlophone PMC 7027 (mono)
Parlophone PCS 7027 (stereo)

Sgt Pepper's Lonely Hearts Club Band
With A Little Help From My Friends
Lucy In The Sky With Diamonds
Getting Better
Fixing A Hole
She's Leaving Home
Being For The Benefit Of Mr Kite!
Within You Without You
When I'm Sixty-Four
Lovely Rita
Good Morning Good Morning
Sgt Pepper's Lonely Hearts Club Band (Reprise)
A Day In The Life

The Beatles (White Album)

22 November 1968
Apple PMC 7067-7068 (mono)
Apple PCS 7067-7068 (stereo)

Back In The USSR
Dear Prudence
Glass Onion
Ob-La-Di, Ob-La-Da
Wild Honey Pie
The Continuing Story Of Bungalow Bill
While My Guitar Gently Weeps
Happiness Is A Warm Gun
Martha My Dear
I'm So Tired
Blackbird
Piggies
Rocky Raccoon
Don't Pass Me By
Why Don't We Do It In The Road?
I Will
Julia

Birthday
Yer Blues
Mother Nature's Son
Everybody's Got Something To Hide Except Me And My Monkey
Sexy Sadie

Helter Skelter
Long, Long, Long
Revolution 1
Honey Pie
Savoy Truffle
Cry Baby Cry
Revolution 9
Good Night

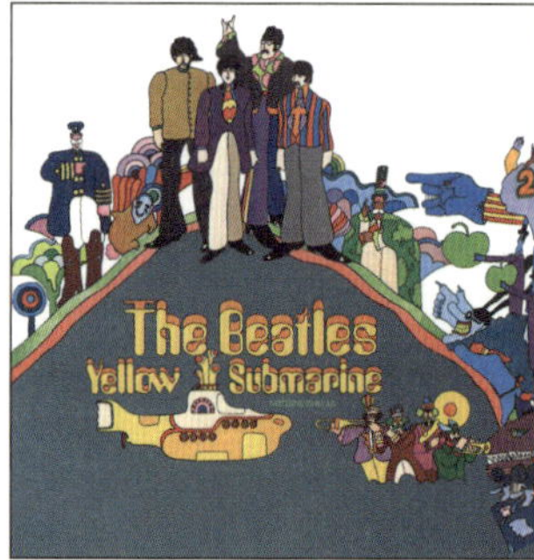

17 January 1969
Apple/Parlophone PMC 7070
(mono)
Apple PCS 7070 (stereo)

Yellow Submarine
Only A Northern Song
All Together Now
Hey Bulldog
It's All Too Much
All You Need Is Love
Pepperland
Sea Of Time
Sea Of Holes
Sea Of Monsters
March Of The Meanies
Pepperland Laid Waste
Yellow Submarine In Pepperland

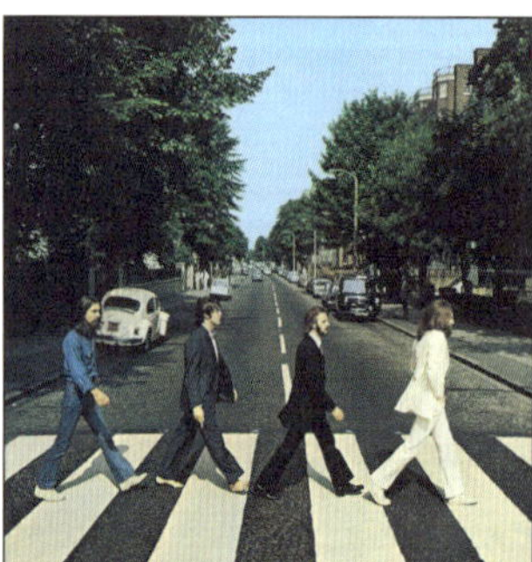

Abbey Road

26 September 1969
Apple PCS 7088

Come Together
Something
Maxwell's Silver Hammer

Oh! Darling
Octopus's Garden
I Want You (She's So Heavy)
Here Comes The Sun
Because
You Never Give Me Your Money
Sun King
Mean Mr Mustard
Polythene Pam
She Came In Through The Bath-
room Window
Golden Slumbers
Carry That Weight
The End
Her Majesty

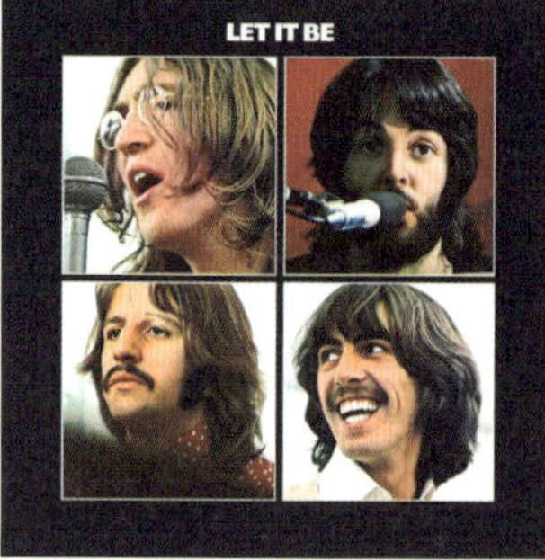

Let It Be

8 May 1970
Apple PCS 7096

Two Of Us
Dig A Pony
Across The Universe
I Me Mine
Dig It
Let It Be
Maggie Mae
I've Got A Feeling
One After 909
The Long And Winding Road
For You Blue
Get Back

Magical Mystery Tour

19 November 1976 (LP)

22 September 1987 (CD)
Parlophone PCTC 255 (LP)
Parlophone CDP 7 48062 2
(CD)

Magical Mystery Tour
The Fool On The Hill
Flying
Blue Jay Way
Your Mother Should Know
I Am The Walrus
Hello, Goodbye
Strawberry Fields Forever
Penny Lane
Baby You're A Rich Man
All You Need Is Love

(1–2) 컬렉션, 라이브, 박스세트
등 (이미지 없음)

A Collection Of Beatles Oldies
9 December 1966
Parlophone PMC 7016 (mono)
Parlophone PCS 7016 (stereo)

She Loves You
From Me to You
We Can Work It Out
Help!
Michelle
Yesterday
I Feel Fine
Yellow Submarine
Can't Buy Me Love
Bad Boy
Day Tripper
A Hard Day's Night
Ticket To Ride
Paperback Writer
Eleanor Rigby
I Want To Hold Your Hand

**The Beatles At The Holly-
wood Bowl**

6 May 1977
EMTV 4

Twist And Shout

She's A Woman
Dizzy Miss Lizzy
Ticket To Ride
Can't Buy Me Love
Things We Said Today
Roll Over Beethoven
Boys
A Hard Day's Night
Help!
All My Loving
She Loves You
Long Tall Sally

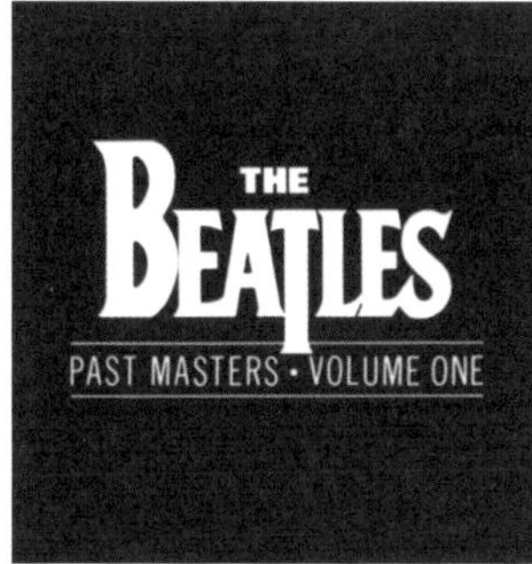

Past Masters Volume One

7 March 1988
Apple/ Parlophone CDP 7
90043 2

Volumes One and Two released
as a single collection on 9 September 2009

Love Me Do
From Me To You
Thank You Girl
She Loves You
I'll Get You
I Want To Hold Your Hand
This Boy
Komm, Gib Mir Deine Hand
Sie Liebt Dich
Long Tall Sally
I Call Your Name
Slow Down
Matchbox
I Feel Fine
She's A Woman
Bad Boy
Yes It Is
I'm Down

Past Masters Volume Two

7 March 1988
Apple/ Parlophone CDP 7
90044 2

Volumes One and Two released
as a single collection on 9 September 2009

Day Tripper
We Can Work It Out
Paperback Writer
Rain
Lady Madonna
The Inner Light
Hey Jude
Revolution
Get Back
Don't Let Me Down
The Ballad Of John And Yoko
Old Brown Shoe
Across The Universe
Let It Be
You Know My Name (Look Up
The Number)

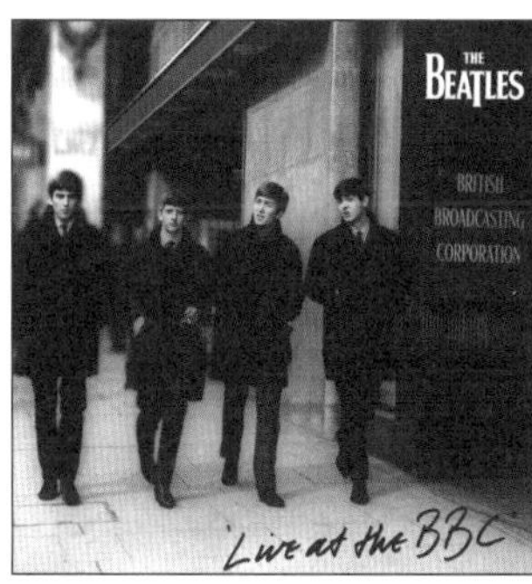

Live At The BBC

30 November 1994
Apple/Parlophone CDPCSP
726

Beatle Greetings (Speech)

From Us To You
Riding On A Bus (Speech)
I Got A Woman
Too Much Monkey Business
Keep Your Hands Off My Baby
I'll Be On My Way
Young Blood
A Shot Of Rhythm And Blues
Sure To Fall (In Love With You)
Some Other Guy
Thank You Girl
Sha La La La La! (Speech)
Baby It's You
That's All Right (Mama)
Carol
Soldier Of Love
A Little Rhyme (Speech)
Clarabella
I'm Gonna Sit Right Down And
Cry (Over You)
Crying, Waiting, Hoping
Dear Wack! (Speech)
You Really Got A Hold On Me
To Know Her Is To Love Her
A Taste Of Honey
Long Tall Sally
I Saw Her Standing There
The Honeymoon Song
Johnny B Goode
Memphis, Tennessee
Lucille
Can't Buy Me Love
From Fluff To You (Speech)
Till There Was You
Crinsk Dee Night (Speech)
A Hard Day's Night
Have A Banana (Speech)
I Wanna Be Your Man
Just A Rumour (Speech)
Roll Over Beethoven
All My Loving
Things We Said Today
She's A Woman
Sweet Little Sixteen
1822! (Speech)
Lonesome Tears In My Eyes
Nothin' Shakin'
The Hippy Hippy Shake
Glad All Over
I Just Don't Understand
So How Come (No One Loves
Me)
I Feel Fine
I'm A Loser
Everybody's Trying To Be My
Baby
Rock And Roll Music
Ticket To Ride
Dizzy Miss Lizzy
Kansas City/Hey Hey Hey Hey!
Set Fire To That Lot! (Speech)
Matchbox

I Forgot To Remember To Forget
Love These Goon Shows
(Speech)
I Got To Find My Baby
Ooh! My Soul
Ooh! My Arms (Speech)
Don't Ever Change
Slow Down
Honey Don't
Love Me Do

Anthology 1

21 November 1995
Apple/Parlophone CDPCSP
727

Free As A Bird
Speech: John Lennon
That'll Be The Day
In Spite Of All The Danger
Speech: Paul McCartney
Hallelujah, I Love Her So
You'll Be Mine
Cayenne
Speech: Paul
My Bonnie
Ain't She Sweet
Cry For A Shadow
Speech: John
Speech: Brian Epstein
Searchin'
Three Cool Cats
The Sheik Of Araby
Like Dreamers Do
Hello Little Girl
Speech: Brian Epstein
Besame Mucho
Love Me Do
How Do You Do It
Please Please Me
One After 909 (Sequence) / One
After 909
Lend Me Your Comb
I'll Get You
Speech: John
I Saw Her Standing There
From Me To You
Money (That's What I Want)

You Really Got A Hold On Me
Roll Over Beethoven
She Loves You
Till There Was You
Twist And Shout
This Boy
I Want To Hold Your Hand
Speech: Eric Morecambe and
Ernie Wise
Moonlight Bay
Can't Buy Me Love
All My Loving
You Can't Do That
And I Love Her
A Hard Day's Night
I Wanna Be Your Man
Long Tall Sally
Boys
Shout
I'll Be Back (Take 2)
I'll Be Back (Take 3)
You Know What To Do
No Reply (Demo)
Mr Moonlight
Leave My Kitten Alone
No Reply
Eight Days A Week (Sequence)
Eight Days A Week (Complete)
Kansas City/Hey-Hey-Hey-Hey!

Anthology 2

18 March 1996
Apple/Parlophone CDPCSP
728

Real Love
Yes It Is
I'm Down
You've Got To Hide Your Love
Away
If You've Got Trouble
That Means A Lot
Yesterday
It's Only Love
I Feel Fine
Ticket To Ride
Yesterday
Help!

Everybody's Trying To Be My
Baby
Norwegian Wood (This Bird Has
Flown)
I'm Looking Through You
12-Bar Original
Tomorrow Never Knows
Got To Get You Into My Life
And Your Bird Can Sing
Taxman
Eleanor Rigby (Strings Only)
I'm Only Sleeping (Rehearsal)
I'm Only Sleeping (Take 1)
Rock And Roll Music
She's A Woman
Strawberry Fields Forever (Demo
Sequence)
Strawberry Fields Forever (Take
1)
Strawberry Fields Forever (Take
7 & Edit Piece)
Penny Lane
A Day In The Life
Good Morning Good Morning
Only A Northern Song
Being For The Benefit Of Mr Kite!
(Takes 1 and 2)
Being For The Benefit Of Mr Kite!
(Take 7)
Lucy In The Sky With Diamonds
Within You Without You (Instru-
mental)
Sgt Pepper's Lonely Hearts Club
Band (Reprise)
You Know My Name (Look Up
The Number)
I Am The Walrus
The Fool On The Hill (Demo)
Your Mother Should Know
The Fool On The Hill (Take 4)
Hello, Goodbye
Lady Madonna
Across The Universe

Anthology 3

28 October 1996
Apple/Parlophone CDPCSP

A Beginning
Happiness Is A Warm Gun
Helter Skelter
Mean Mr Mustard
Polythene Pam
Glass Onion
Junk
Piggies
Honey Pie
Don't Pass Me By
Ob-La-Di, Ob-La-Da
Good Night
Cry Baby Cry
Blackbird
Sexy Sadie
While My Guitar Gently Weeps
Hey Jude
Not Guilty
Mother Nature's Son
Glass Onion
Rocky Raccoon
What's The New Mary Jane
Step Inside Love
Los Paranoias
I'm So Tired
I Will
Why Don't We Do It In The
Road?
Julia
I've Got A Feeling
She Came In Through The Bath-
room Window
Dig A Pony
Two Of Us
For You Blue
Teddy Boy
Rip It Up/Shake, Rattle And Roll/
Blue Suede Shoes
The Long And Winding Road
Oh! Darling
All Things Must Pass
Mailman, Bring Me No More
Blues
Get Back
Old Brown Shoe
Octopus's Garden
Maxwell's Silver Hammer
Something
Come Together
Come And Get It
Ain't She Sweet
Because
Let It Be
I Me Mine
The End

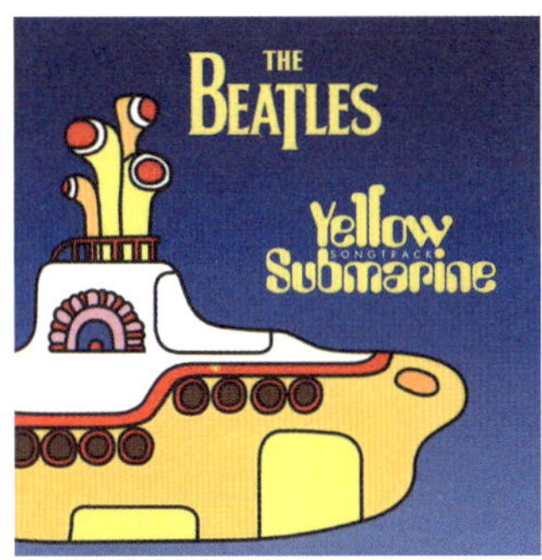

**Yellow Submarine
Songtrack**

*13 September 1999
Apple/Parlophone 521 4812*

Yellow Submarine
Hey Bulldog
Eleanor Rigby
Love You To
All Together Now
Lucy In The Sky With Diamonds
Think For Yourself
Sgt Pepper's Lonely Hearts Club
Band
With A Little Help From My
Friends
Baby You're A Rich Man
Only A Northern Song
All You Need Is Love
When I'm Sixty-Four
Nowhere Man
It's All Too Much

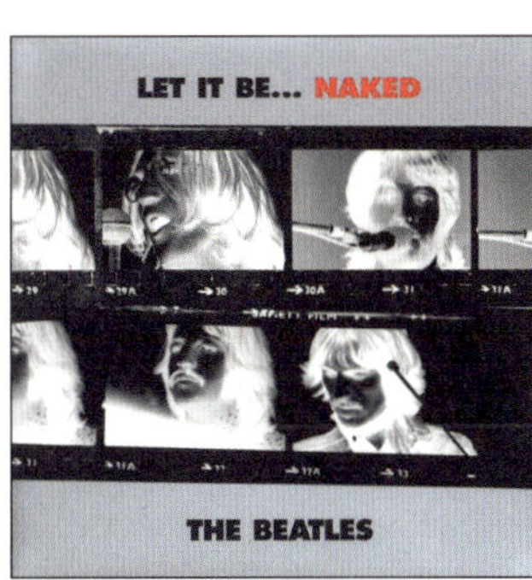

Let It Be... Naked

*17 November 2003
Apple/Parlophone 595 7132*

Get Back
Dig A Pony
For You Blue
The Long And Winding Road
Two Of Us
I've Got A Feeling
One After 909

Don't Let Me Down
I Me Mine
Across The Universe
Let It Be

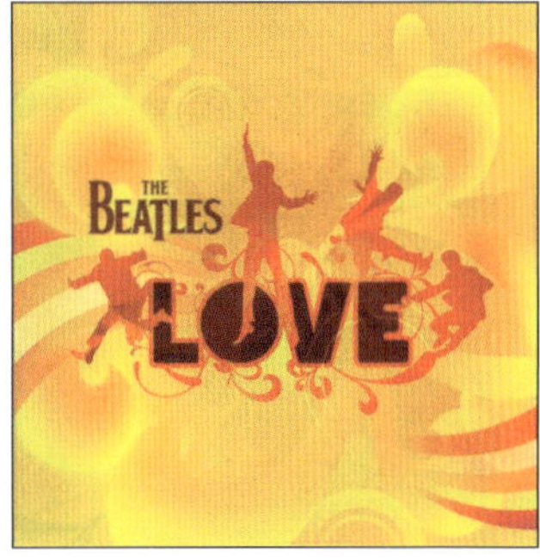

Love

*20 November 2006
Apple/Parlophone 0946 3
79808 2 8 (CD)
Apple/ Parlophone 0946 3
79810 2 3 (CD/DVD-Audio)*

Because
Get Back
Glass Onion
Eleanor Rigby
Julia (Transition)
I Am The Walrus
I Want To Hold Your Hand
Drive My Car/The Word/What
You're Doing
Gnik Nus
Something
Blue Jay Way (Transition)
Being For The Benefit Of Mr
Kite!/I Want You (She's So
Heavy)/Helter Skelter
Help!
Blackbird/Yesterday
Strawberry Fields Forever
Within You Without You
Tomorrow Never Knows
Lucy In The Sky With Diamonds
Octopus's Garden
Lady Madonna
Here Comes The Sun
The Inner Light (Transition)
Come Together/Dear Prudence
Cry Baby Cry (Transition)
Revolution
Back In The USSR
While My Guitar Gently Weeps
A Day In The Life
Hey Jude
Sgt Pepper's Lonely Hearts Club
Band (Reprise)
All You Need Is Love

On Air - Live At The BBC Volume 2

11 November 2013
Apple 602537491698 (CD)

And Here We Are Again (Speech)
Words Of Love
How About It, Gorgeous? (Speech)
Do You Want To Know A Secret
Lucille
Hey, Paul... (Speech)
Anna (Go To Him)
Hello! (Speech)
Please Please Me
Misery
I'm Talking About You
A Real Treat (Speech)
Boys
Absolutely Fab (Speech)
Chains
Ask Me Why
Till There Was You
Lend Me Your Comb
Lower 5E (Speech)
The Hippy Hippy Shake
Roll Over Beethoven
There's A Place
Bumper Bundle (Speech)
PS I Love You
Please Mister Postman
Beautiful Dreamer
Devil In Her Heart
The 49 Weeks (Speech)
Sure To Fall (In Love With You)
Never Mind, Eh? (Speech)
Twist And Shout
Bye, Bye (speech)
John - Pop Profile (Speech)
George - Pop Profile (Speech)
I Saw Her Standing There
Glad All Over
Lift Lid Again (Speech)
I'll Get You
She Loves You
Memphis, Tennessee
Happy Birthday Dear Saturday Club

Now Hush, Hush (Speech)
From Me To You
Money (That's What I Want)
I Want To Hold Your Hand
Brian Bathtubes (Speech)
This Boy
If I Wasn't In America (Speech)
I Got A Woman
Long Tall Sally
If I Fell
A Hard Job Writing Them (Speech)
And I Love Her
Oh, Can't We? Yes We Can (Speech)
You Can't Do That
Honey Don't
I'll Follow The Sun
Green With Black Shutters (Speech)
Kansas City/Hey-Hey-Hey-Hey!
That's What We're Here For (Speech)
I Feel Fine (studio outtake)
Paul - Pop Profile (Speech)
Ringo - Pop Profile (Speech)

(2) 싱글

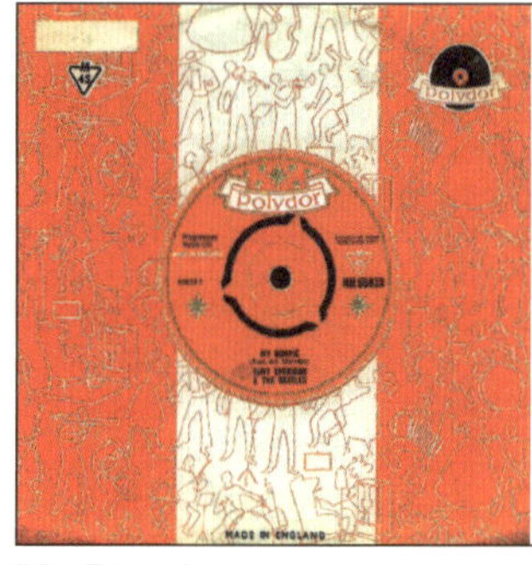

My Bonnie

5 January 1962
Polydor NH 66833

My Bonnie
The Saints

Love Me Do

5 October 1962
Parlophone 45-R 4949

Love Me Do
PS I Love You

Please Please Me

11 January 1963
Parlophone 45-R 4983

Please Please Me
Ask Me Why

From Me To You

11 April 1963
Parlophone R 5015

From Me To You
Thank You Girl

She Loves You

23 August 1963
Parlophone R 5055

She Loves You
I'll Get You

A Hard Day's Night

10 July 1964
Parlophone R 5160

A Hard Day's Night
Things We Said Today

Help!

23 July 1965
Parlophone R 5305

Help!
I'm Down

I Want To Hold Your Hand

29 November 1963
Parlophone R 5084

I Want To Hold Your Hand
This Boy

I Feel Fine

27 November 1964
Parlophone R 5200

I Feel Fine
She's A Woman

Day Tripper/We Can Work It Out

3 December 1965
Parlophone R 5389

We Can Work It Out
Day Tripper

Can't Buy Me Love

20 March 1964
Parlophone R 5114

Can't Buy Me Love
You Can't Do That

Ticket To Ride

9 April 1965
Parlophone R 5265

Ticket To Ride
Yes It Is

Paperback Writer

10 June 1966
Parlophone R 5452

Paperback Writer

Rain

Yellow Submarine/Eleanor Rigby

5 August 1966
Parlophone R 5493

Eleanor Rigby
Yellow Submarine

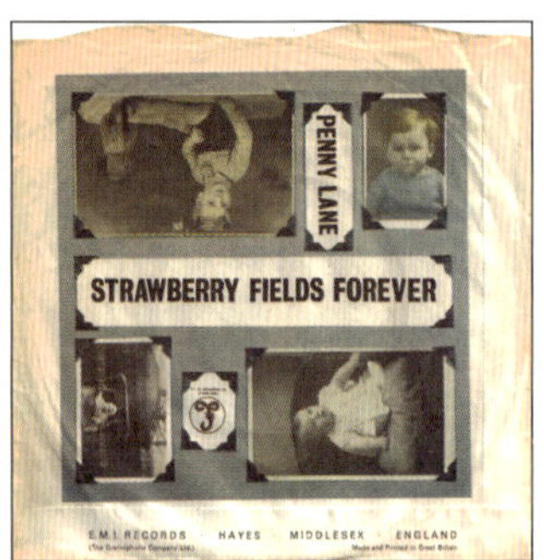

Penny Lane/Strawberry Fields Forever

17 February 1967
Parlophone R 5570

Strawberry Fields Forever
Penny Lane

All You Need Is Love

7 July 1967
Parlophone R 5620

All You Need Is Love
Baby, You're A Rich Man

Hello, Goodbye

24 November 1967
Parlophone R 5655

Hello, Goodbye
I Am The Walrus

Lady Madonna

15 March 1968
Parlophone R 5675

Lady Madonna
The Inner Light

Hey Jude

30 August 1968
Apple R 5722

Hey Jude
Revolution

Get Back

11 April 1969
Apple R 5777

Get Back
Don't Let Me Down

The Ballad Of John And Yoko

30 May 1969
Apple R 5786

The Ballad Of John And Yoko
Old Brown Shoe

Come Together/Something

31 October 1969

Apple R 5814
Something
Come Together

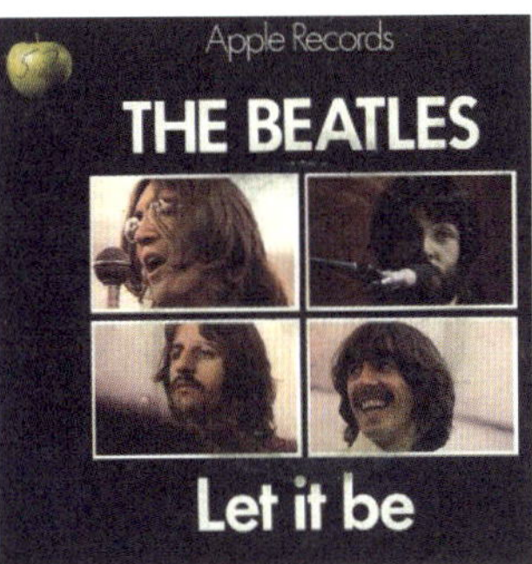

Let It Be

6 March 1970
Apple R 5833

Let It Be
You Know My Name (Look Up
The Number)

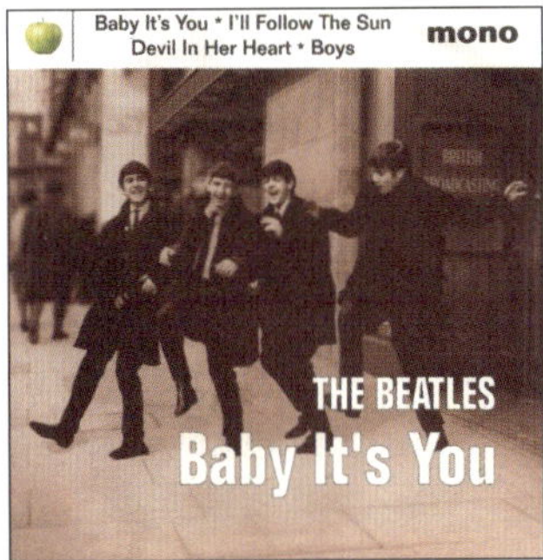

Baby It's You

20 March 1995
Apple R 6406

Baby It's You
I'll Follow The Sun
Devil In Her Heart
Boys

Free As A Bird

12 December 1995
Apple R 6422

Free As A Bird
I Saw Her Standing There
This Boy
Christmas Time (Is Here Again)

Real Love

4 March 1996
Apple R 6425

Real Love
Baby's In Black
Yellow Submarine
Here, There And Everywhere

(3) EPs

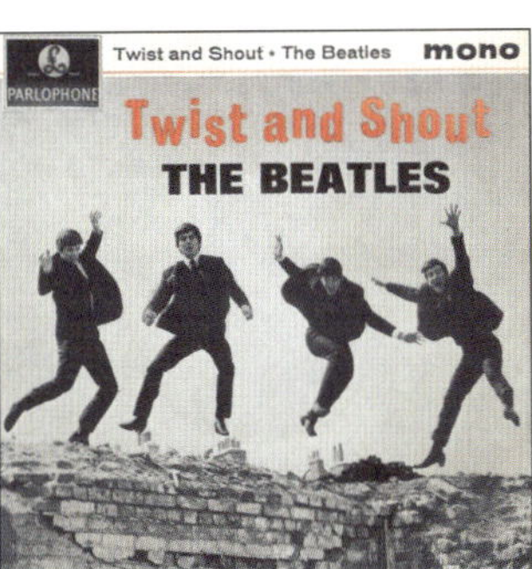

Twist And Shout

12 July 1963
Parlophone GEP 8882

Twist And Shout
A Taste Of Honey
Do You Want To Know A Secret
There's A Place

The Beatles' Hits

6 September 1963
Parlophone GEP 8880

From Me To You
Thank You Girl
Please Please Me
Love Me Do

The Beatles No 1

1 November 1963
Parlophone GEP 8883

I Saw Her Standing There
Misery
Anna (Go To Him)
Chains

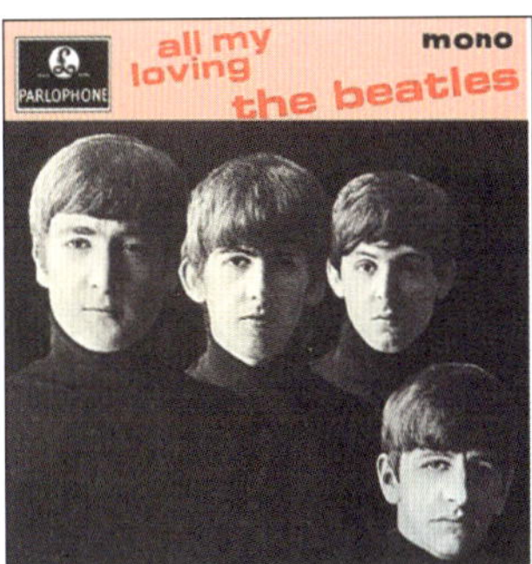

All My Loving

7 February 1964

Parlophone GEP 8891
All My Loving
Ask Me Why
Money (That's What I Want)
PS I Love You

Long Tall Sally

19 June 1964
Parlophone GEP 8913

Long Tall Sally
I Call Your Name
Slow Down
Matchbox

Extracts From The Film A Hard Day's Night

4 November 1964
Parlophone GEP 8920

I Should Have Known Better
If I Fell
Tell Me Why
And I Love Her

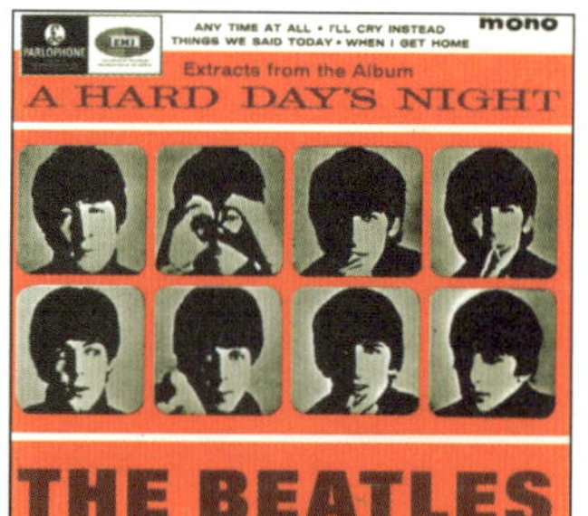

Extracts From The Album A Hard Day's Night

6 November 1964
Parlophone GEP 8924

Any Time At All
I'll Cry Instead
Things We Said Today
When I Get Home

Beatles For Sale

6 April 1965
Parlophone GEP 8931

No Reply
I'm A Loser
Rock And Roll Music
Eight Days A Week

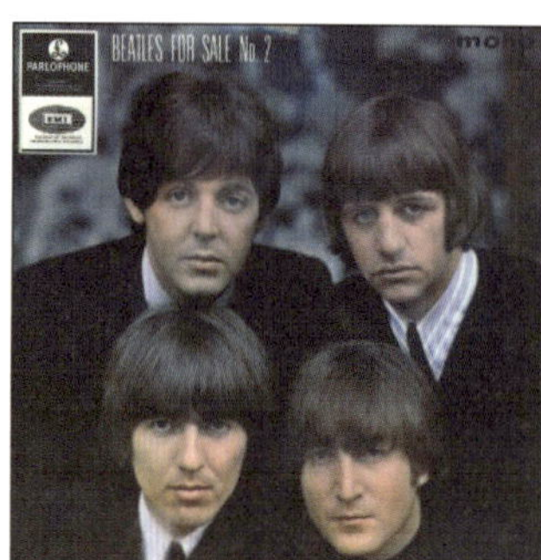

Beatles For Sale No 2

4 June 1965
Parlophone GEP 8938

I'll Follow The Sun
Baby's In Black
Words Of Love
I Don't Want To Spoil The Party

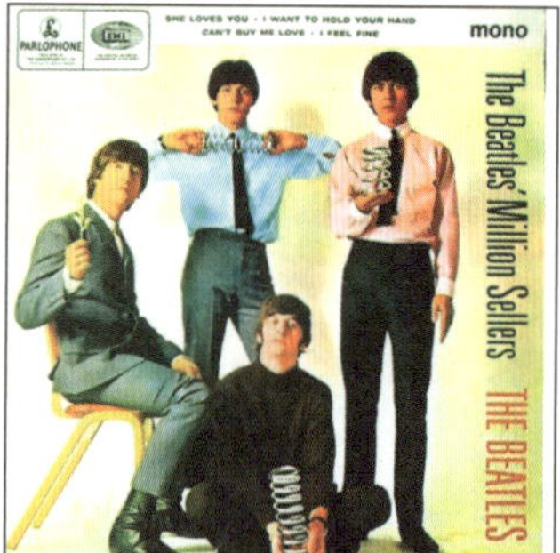

The Beatles' Million Sellers

6 December 1965
Parlophone GEP 8946

She Loves You
I Want To Hold Your Hand
Can't Buy Me Love
I Feel Fine

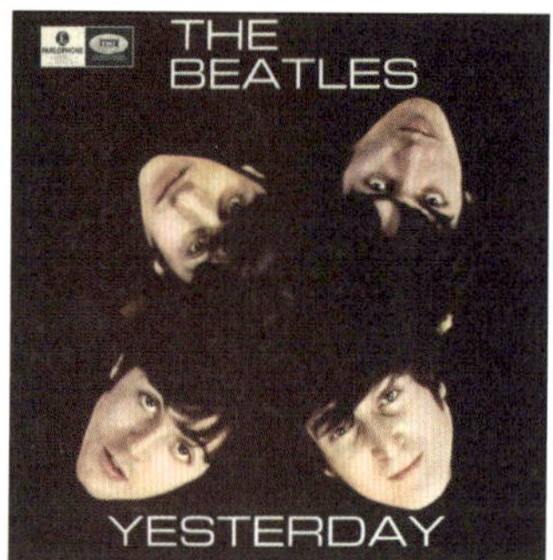

Yesterday

4 March 1966
Parlophone GEP 8948

Yesterday
Act Naturally
You Like Me Too Much
It's Only Love

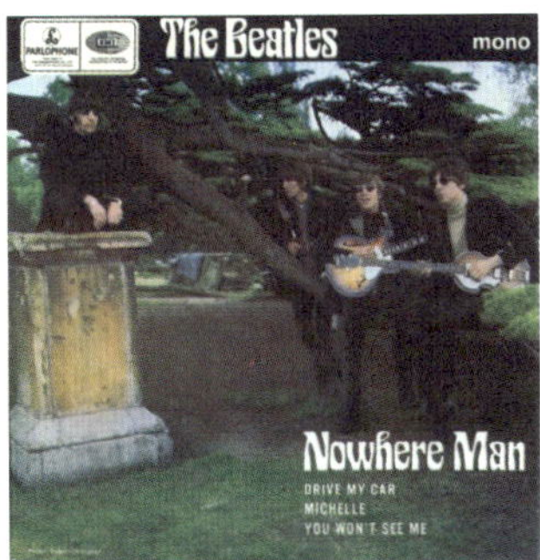

Nowhere Man

8 July 1966
Parlophone GEP 8952

Nowhere Man
Drive My Car
Michelle
You Won't See Me

Magical Mystery Tour

8 December 1967
Parlophone MMT-1 (mono)
Parlophone SMMT-1 (stereo)

Magical Mystery Tour
Your Mother Should Know
I Am The Walrus
The Fool On The Hill
Flying
Blue Jay Way

THE BEATLES
201 • CHORD SONG BOOK

A Day In The Life

Words & Music by
John Lennon & Paul McCartney

Inst. | G Bm | Em Em7 | C | C ||

A1
G   Bm   Em   Em7
I read the news today oh boy

C   C/B   Asus2
About a lucky man who made the grade

G   Bm   Em   Em7
And though the news was rather sad

C   F   Em   Em7
Well I just had to laugh,

C   F   Em   C
I saw the photograph.

A2
G   Bm   Em   Em7
He blew his mind out in a car

C   C/B   Asus2
He didn't notice that the lights had changed

G   Bm   Em   Em7
A crowd of people stood and stared

C   F   Em
They'd seen his face before, Nobody was really sure

Em7   C
If he was from the House of Lords.

A3
G   Bm   Em   Em7
I saw a film today oh boy

C   C/B   Asus2
The English Army had just won the war

G   Bm   Em   Em7
A crowd of people turned away

C   F   Em
but I just had to look

                    Em7   C
Having read the book, I'd love to turn you on

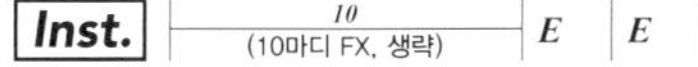

Inst. | *10* (10마디 FX, 생략) | *E* | *E* ‖

B1
E　　　　　　　　　　　　　　　　　　　　　　　*Dsus2*
Woke up, fell out of bed, dragged a comb across my head

　　　　E　　　　　　　*B7sus4*
Found my way downstairs and drank a cup, Ha, ha, ha

　　E　　　*B7sus4*　　　*Em7*
And looking up I noticed I was late.

　　　　　E
Found my coat and grabbed my hat

　　　　　　　Dsus2
Made the bus in seconds flat

　　　E　　　　*B7sus4*
Found my way upstairs and had a smoke,

E　　　　　　　　　　　*B7sus4*
Somebody spoke and I went into a dream

C1
C G ⁄ *D A* *E* ⁄ *C G* ⁄ *D A* | *E* *D* *C* *D* ‖
Ah, ⁄ ah, ⁄ ah, ⁄ ah, ⁄ ah

A4
G　　　*Bm*　　　　　*Em*　*Em7*
I read the news today oh boy

C　　　　　*C/B*　　　　　*Asus2*
Four thousands holes in Blackburn, Lancashire

G　　　*Bm*　　　　*Em*　*Em7*
And though the holes were rather small

C　　　*F*
They had to count them all

Em　　　　　　　　*Em7*　　　　　*C*
Now they know how many holes it takes to fill the Albert Hall.

I'd love to turn you on

Inst. | *10* | *E* ‖

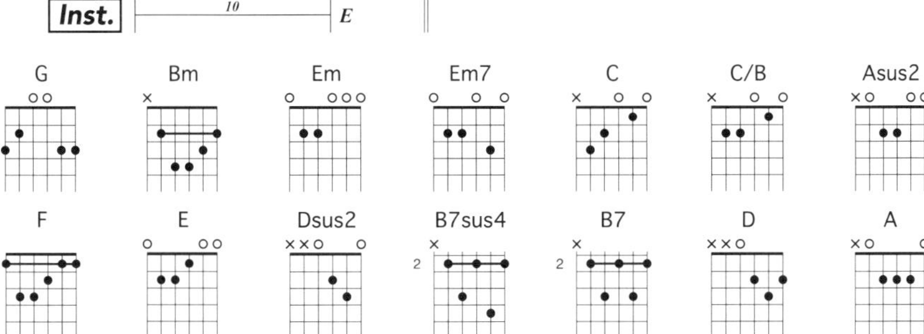

A Hard Day's Night

Words & Music by
John Lennon & Paul McCartney

A1
G7sus4   *G*   *C*   *G*   *F*   *G*
It's been a hard day's night, and I been working like a dog

                C   *G*   *F*   *G*
It's been a hard day's night, I should be sleeping like a log

         G   *D*
But when I get home to you I'll find the things that you do

         G   *C7*   *G*
Will make me feel alright

A2
         G   *C*   *G*   *F*   *G*
You know I work all day to get you money to buy you things

      G   *C*   *G*   *F*   *G*
And it's worth it just to hear you say you're going to give me everything

         C   *D*
So why on earth should I moan, 'cause when I get you alone

         G   *C7*   *G*
You Know I feel o - k

B1
         Bm   *Em*   *Bm*
When I'm home everything seems to be right

         G   *Em*   *C7*   *D7*
When I'm home feeling you holding me tight, tight, Owww!

A3
         G   *C*   *G*   *F*   *G*
It's been a hard day's night, and I been working like a dog

         G   *C*   *G*   *F*   *G*
It's been a hard day's night, I should be sleeping like a log

         C   *D*
But when I get home to you I'll find the things that you do

         G   *C7*   *G*
Will make me feel alright

Inst. ‖: *G*   *C* | *G* | *F* | *G*   :‖

      C   *D*
So why on earth should I moan, 'cause when I get you alone

      G   *C7* *G*
You Know I feel o - k

       Bm   *Em*   *Bm*
B2 When I'm home everything seems to be right

      G   *Em*   *C7* *D7*
When I'm home feeling you holding me tight, tight, yeah

       G   *C*   *G*   *F*   *G*
A4 It's been a hard day's night, and I been working like a dog

       G   *C*   *G*   *F*   *G*
It's been a hard day's night, I should be sleeping like a log

      C   *D*
But when I get home to you I'll find the things that you do

      G *C7* *G*
Will make me feel alright

 C7   *G* *C7* *G*
OUTRO You know I feel alright

 C7   *G* *Cadd9* *Fadd9* *F*
You know I feel alright…

‖: *Fadd9* (F) | *Fadd9* (F) :‖ … *fade out*

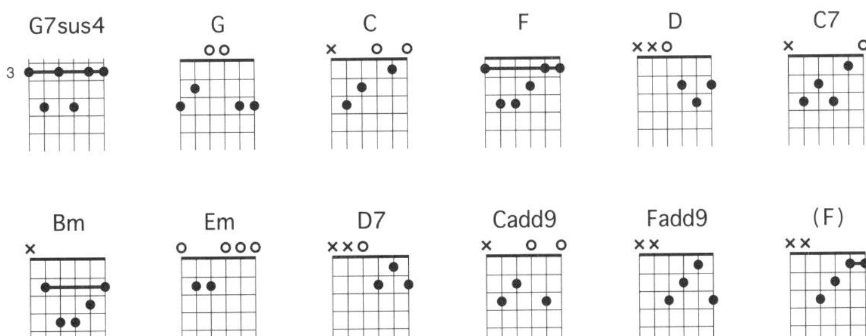

Across The Universe

* 반음 낮추어 튜닝합니다.

Words & Music by
John Lennon & Paul McCartney

Inst. | D | F#m | A ||

A1
                    D   Bm   F#m
Words are flowing out like endless rain into a paper cup,

            Em7   A7
They slither while they pass, they slip away across the universe

        D   Bm   F#m
Pools of sorrow, waves of joy are drifting through my open mind,

Em7   Gm
Possessing and caressing me.

B1
        D   A7
Jai guru de va om

        A
Nothing's gonna change my world,

G   D
Nothing's gonna change my world.

A
Nothing's gonna change my world,

G   D
Nothing's gonna change my world.

A2
        D   Bm   F#m   Em7
Images of broken light which dance before me like a million eyes,

                        A7
That call me on and on across the universe,

        D   Bm   F#m
Thoughts meander like a restless wind inside a letter box they

Em7
Tumble blindly as they make their

A7
Way across the universe

|B2|
```
  D              A7
Jai guru de va om

    A
Nothing's gonna change my world,

    G                         D
Nothing's gonna change my world.

    A
Nothing's gonna change my world,

    G                         D
Nothing's gonna change my world.
```

|A3|
```
  D                    Bm              F#m
Sounds of laughter shades of earth are ringing

                        Em7          Gm
Through my open ears inciting and inviting me

  D           Bm              F#m
Limitless undying love which shines around me like a

          Em7
Million suns, it calls me on and on

  A7
Across the universe
```

|B3|
```
  D              A7
Jai guru de va om

    A
Nothing's gonna change my world,

    G                         D
Nothing's gonna change my world.

    A
Nothing's gonna change my world,

    G                         D
Nothing's gonna change my world.
```

```
    D
‖: Jai guru de va…  :‖      … fade out
```

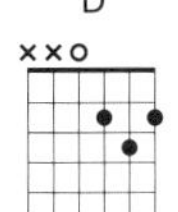 D   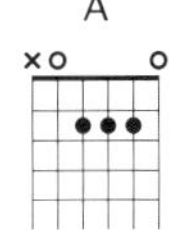 F#m   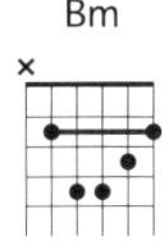 A   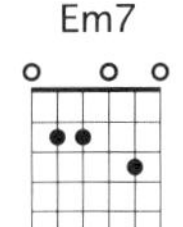 Bm   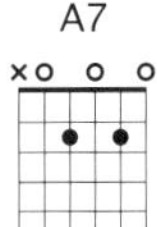 Em7    A7   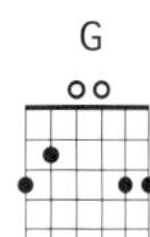 Gm   G

All I've Got To Do

Words & Music by
John Lennon & Paul McCartney

Inst. | *E11(#5)* |

        C#m   *E*
A1 Whenever I want you around, yeah.

           C#m
All I gotta do — is

F#m
Call you on the phone, and you'll come running home,

     Am   *E*
Yeah, that's all I gotta do.

   E   *C#m*   *E*
A2 And when I, I wanna kiss you, yeah.

           C#m
All I gotta do — is

F#m
Whisper in your ear, the words you long to hear,

     Am   *E*
And I'll be kissing you.

   E   *A*
B1 And the same goes for me,

Whenever you want me at all.

      C#m
I'll be here, yes I will, whenever you call.

    A   *E*   *C#m*
You just gotta call on me,   yeah,

    A   *E*
You just gotta call on me.

<pre>
      E   C#m   E
A3 And when I, I want to kiss you, yeah.

              C#m
    All I gotta do — is

    F#m
    Call you on the phone, and you'll come running home,

         Am   E
    Yeah, that's all I gotta do.

      E   A
B2 And the same goes for me,

    Whenever you want me at all.

        C#m
    I'll be here, yes I will, whenever you call.

        A   E   C#m
    You just gotta call on me,   yeah,

        A   E
    You just gotta call on me.

        A   E
    You just gotta call on me.

    E   C#m   E   C#m
    Mmm.
                            ... fade out
</pre>

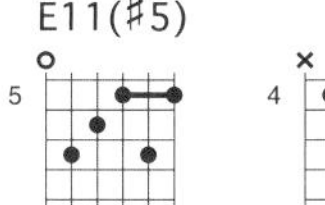

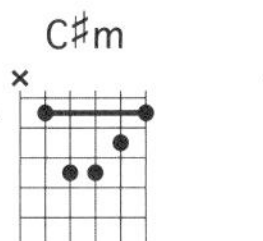

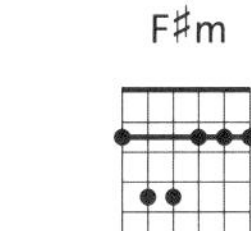

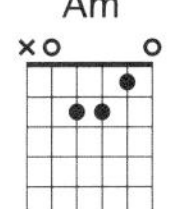

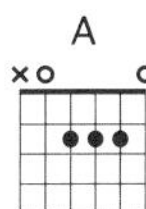

All My Loving

Words & Music by
John Lennon & Paul McCartney

|A1|
```
        F#m           B
Close your eyes and I'll kiss you,

     E          C#m
Tomorrow I'll miss you,

   A          F#m         D   B7
Remember I'll always be true.

      F#m          B
And then while I'm away,

          E          C#m
I'll write home every day,

         A           B         E
And I'll send all my loving to you.
```

|A2|
```
         F#m          B
I'll pretend That I'm kissing

     E          C#m
the lips I am missing

     A          F#m               D   B7
And hope that my dreams will come true.

       F#m          B
And then while I'm away,

        E          C#m
I'll write home every day,

         A           B         E
And I'll send all my loving to you.
```

|B1|
```
      C#m     Caug        E
All my loving I will send to you.

      C#m     Caug        E
All my loving, darling I'll be true.
```


Inst. | *A7* | *A7* | *E* | *E* |
| *B7* | *B7* | *E* | *E* ||

[A3]

        F#m   *B*
Close your eyes and I'll kiss you,

   E   *C#m*
Tomorrow I'll miss you,

 A   *F#m*   *D* *B7*
Remember I'll always be true.

     F#m   *B*
And then while I'm away,

     E   *C#m*
I'll write home every day,

     A   *B*   *E*
And I'll send all my loving to you.

[B2]

    C#m *Caug*   *E*
All my loving I will send to you.

    C#m *Caug*   *E*
All my loving, darling I'll be true.

    C#m
All my loving,

    E
All my loving oh,

    C#m
All my loving

    E
I will send to you.

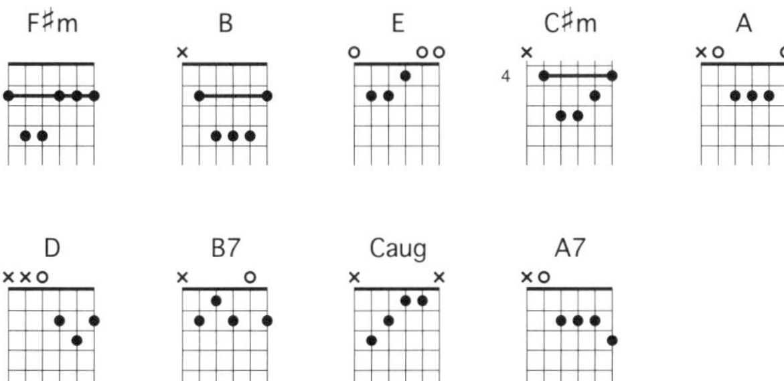

All Together Now

Words & Music by
John Lennon & Paul McCartney

Inst.　*F#*　‖: *G*　| *G*　| *G*　| *G*　:‖

A1
G　　　　　　　　　*D7*
One, two, three, four, can I have a little more?

G　　　　　　　　　　　*D7*　　*G*
five, six, seven eight nine ten I love you.

A2
G　　　　　*D7*
A, B, C, D, can I bring my friend to tea?

G　　　　*D7*　　*G*
E, F, G, H, I, J, I love you. (Boom boom boom)

B1
C6
(Boom boom boom.) Sail the ship,

G
(Boom boom boom.) Jump the tree

C6
(Boom boom boom.) Skip the rope,

D7　　　　　　　　*D7*
(Boom boom boom.) Look at me!

(All together now.)

C1
G
All together now, (all together now.)

All together now, (all together now.)

D7
All together now, (all together now.)

G
All together now, (all together now.)

                       G   *D7*
[A3] Black, white, green, red, can I take my friend to bed?

                       G   *D7*   *G*
Pink, brown, yellow orange blue I love you

(All together now.)

            G
[C2] ‖:All together now, (all together now.)

All together now, (all together now.)

     D7
All together now, (all together now.)

     G
All together now, (all together now.) :‖ (2번 반복)

     C6
[B2] (Boom boom boom.) Sail the ship,

     G
(Boom boom boom.) Jump the tree

     C6
(Boom boom boom.) Skip the rope,

     D6   *D7*
(Boom boom boom.) Look at me!

(All together now.)

     G
[C3] ‖:All together now, (all together now.)

All together now, (all together now.)

     D7
All together now, (all together now.)

     G
All together now, (all together now.) :‖

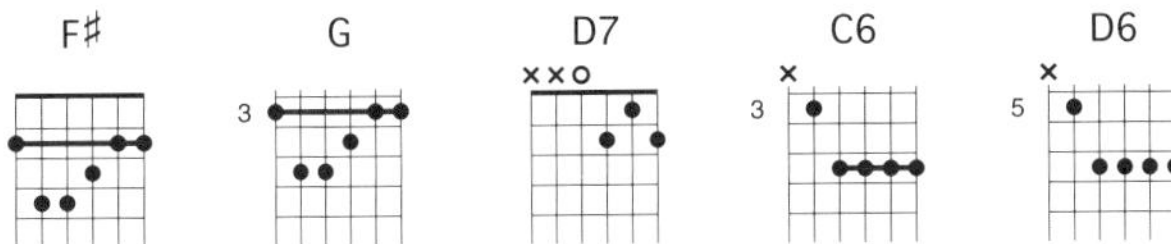

All You Need Is Love

Words & Music by
John Lennon & Paul McCartney

Inst. | G D | G | C | D7 ||

| G   D   Em7   G   D   Em7   G7/A   G   D7/F#   D7/E
INTRO Love, Love, Love. Love, Love, Love. Love, Love, Love.

| D D/C | D7 ||

A1
G   D/F#   Em7
There's nothing you can do that can't be done.

G   D/F#   Em7
Nothing you can sing that can't be sung.

D7/A   G   D/F#   D7/E
Nothing you can say but you can learn how to play the game.

        D   D/C   D
It's easy.

A2
G   D/F#   Em7
Nothing you can make that can't be made.

G   D/F#   Em7
No one you can save that can't be saved.

D7/A   G   D/F#   D7/E
Nothing you can do but you can learn how to be you in time.

        D   D/C   D
It's easy.

B1
G   A7   D   D7
All you need is love.

G   A7   D   D7
All you need is love.

G   B7   Em   Em7
All you need is love, love.

Cmaj7   D7   G
Love is all you need.

Inst. | G D | Em7 | G D | Em7 | D7/A G | D7/A F# | D7/E | D D/C | D ||

[B1] 을 반복.

[A3]
G   D/F#   Em7
Nothing you can know that isn't known.

G   D/F#   Em7
Nothing you can see that isn't shown.

D7/A   G   D/F#   D7/E
Nowhere you can be that isn't where you're meant to be.

*   D   D/C   D*
It's easy.

[B3]
G   A7   D   D7
All you need is love.

G   A7   D   D7
All you need is love.

G   B7   Em   Em7
All you need is love, love.

Cmaj7   D7   G
Love is all you need.

[B4]
G   A7   D   D7
All you need is love (All together, now!)

G   A7   D   D7
All you need is love. (Everybody!)

G   B7   Em   Em7
All you need is love, love.

Cmaj7   D7   G
Love is all you need (love is all you need).

G
Yee-hai!

Oh yeah!

She loves you, yeah yeah yeah.

She loves you, yeah yeah yeah.

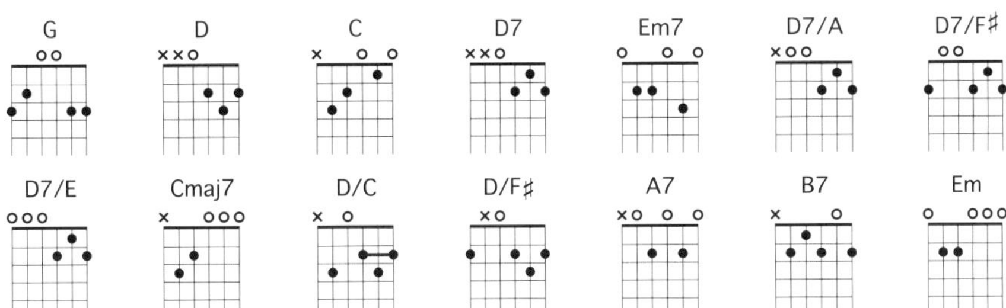

And I Love Her

Words & Music by
John Lennon & Paul McCartney

Inst. | *F#m* | *F#m* | *E6* | *E6* ‖

A1
F#m   *C#m*
I give her all my love

F#m   *C#m*
That's all I do

F#m   *C#m*
And if you saw my love

A   *B*
You'd love her too

E
I love her

A2
F#m   *C#m*
She gives me everything

F#m   *C#m*
And tenderly

F#m   *C#m*
The kiss my lover brings

A   *B*
She brings to me

   E
And I love her

B1
C#m   *B*
A love like ours

C#m   *G#m*
Could never die

C#m   *G#m*
As long as I

   B   *B7*
Have you near me

A3
F#m   *C#m*
Bright are the stars that shine

F#m   *C#m*
Dark is the sky

F#m   *C#m*
I know this love of mine

A   *B*
Will never die

       E
And I love her

Inst. | *Gm* | *Dm* | *Gm* | *Dm* | *Gm* |
| *Dm* | *Bb* | *C* | *F* | *F* ||

A4
Gm   *Dm*
Bright are the stars that shine

Gm   *Dm*
Dark is the sky

Gm   *Dm*
I know this love of mine

Bb   *C*
Will never die

       F
And I love her

Inst. | *Gm* | *Gm* | *F* | *F* |
| *Gm* | *Gm* | *D* ||

F#m

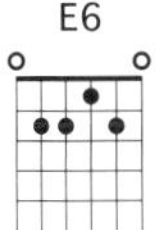

E6

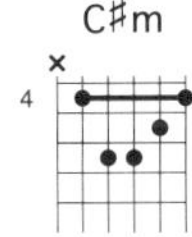

C#m

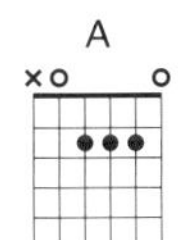

A

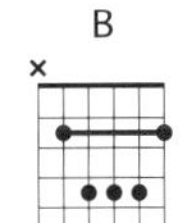

B

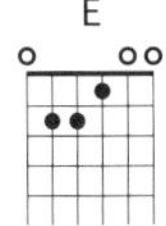

E

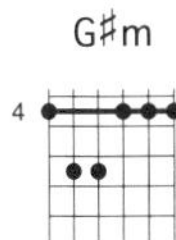

G#m

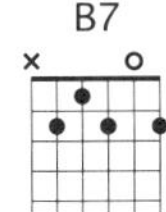

B7

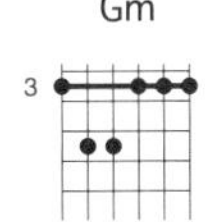

Gm

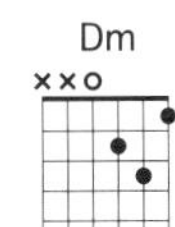

Dm

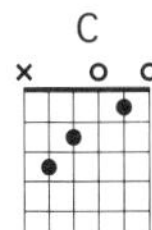

Bb

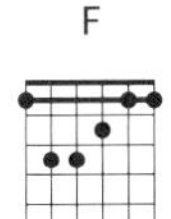

C

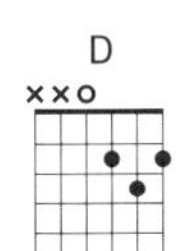

F

D

And Your Bird Can Sing

** CAPO : 2 FRET.*

Words & Music by
John Lennon & Paul McCartney

Inst. | D | D | D | D ‖

A1
    D
You tell me that you've got everything you want

And your bird can sing

          Em
But you don't get me,

G   *D*
You don't get me

A2
   D
You say you've seen seven wonders,

And your bird is green

          Em
But you can't see me,

G   *D*
You can't see me

B1
F#m   *F#m(maj7)*
When your prized possessions

F#m7   *B7*
Start to wear you down

D   *Em*
Look in my direction,

                 A
I'll be round, I'll be round

Inst. | D | D | D | D |
| Em | G | D | D ||

F#m   *F#m(maj7)*
B2 When your bird is broken

F#m7   *B7*
Will it bring you down?

D   *Em*
You may be awoken,

                              A
I'll be round, I'll be round

                D
A3 You tell me that you've heard every sound there is,

And your bird can swim

                    Em
But you can't hear me,

G   *D*
You can't hear me

Inst. | D | D | D | D |
| Em | G | D | D ||
| D | D | D | G/D ||

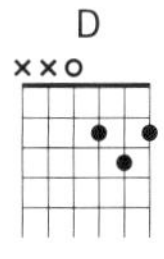
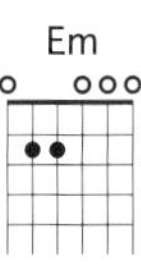
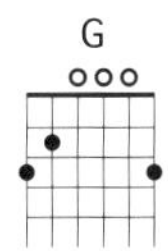
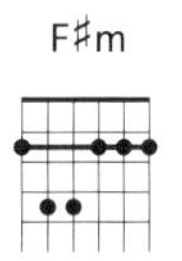
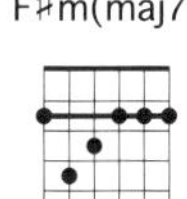

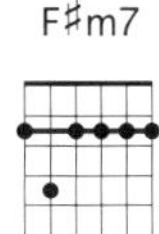
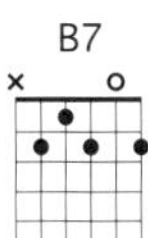
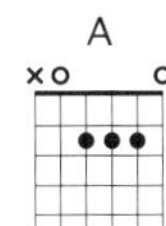
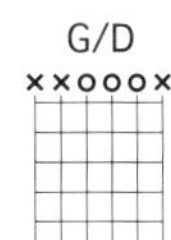

Another Girl

Words & Music by
John Lennon & Paul McCartney

|INTRO|
          A7   *D7*   *A7*   *D7*   *A*
For I have got another girl, another girl.

|A1|
A   *G*   *A*   *D*
You're making me say that I've got nobody but you,

          G   *A*   *D*
But as from today, well, I've got somebody that's new.

D7   *E7*
I ain't no fool and I don't take what I don't want,

         A7 *D7*   *A7* *D7*   *A*
For I have got another girl, another girl.

|A2|
A   *G*   *A*   *D*
She's sweeter than all the girls and I met quite a few.

A   *G*   *A*   *D*
Nobody in all the world can do what she can do.

D7   *E7*
And so I'm telling you, this time you'd better stop.

         A7 *D7*   *A7* *D7*
For I have got another girl.

|B1|
            C   *G7*   *C*
Another girl who will love me till the end.

G7   *C*
Through thick and thin

      E7   *A*   *E7*
She will always be my friend.

A3

  A   *G*   *A*   *D*
I don't want to say that I've been unhappy with you,

  A   *G*   *A*   *D*
But, as from today, well, I've seen somebody that's new.

  D7   *E7*
I ain't no fool and I don't take what I don't want,

        A7 *D7*   *A7* *D7*
For I have got another girl.

B2

        C   *G7*   *C*
Another girl who will love me till the end.

  G7   *C*
Through thick and thin

      E7   *A*   *E7*
She will always be my friend.

A4

  A   *G*   *A*   *D*
I don't want to say that I've been unhappy with you,

  A   *G*   *A*   *D*
But, as from today, well, I've seen somebody that's new.

  D7   *E7*
I ain't no fool and I don't take what I don't want,

        A7 *D7*   *A7*
For I have got another girl.

  D7   *A7*
Another girl.

  D7   *A*
Another girl.

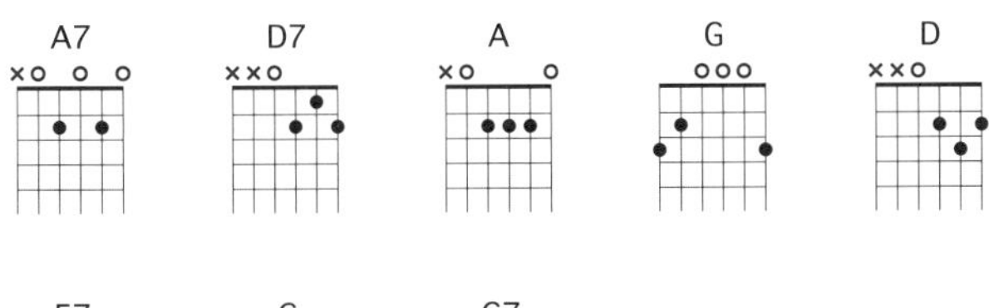

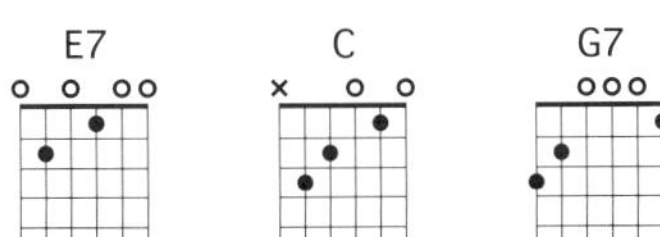

Any Time at All

Words & Music by
John Lennon & Paul McCartney

A1
         Bm *D*
Any time at all,

        A   *Bm*
Any time at all, any time at all,

            G   *A*   *Dsus4* *D* *Dsus2* *D*
All you've gotta do is call and I'll be there.

B1
D   *F#m*   *Bm*   *Gm*
If you need somebody to love, just look into my eyes,

D/A   *A*   *D*
I'll be there to make you feel right.

B2
D   *F#m*   *Bm*   *Gm*
If you're feeling sorry and sad, I'd really sympathize.

D/A   *A*   *Dsus4* *D* *Dsus2* *D*
Don't you be sad, just call me tonight.

A2
         Bm *D*
Any time at all,

        A   *Bm*
Any time at all, any time at all,

            G   *A*   *Dsus4* *D* *Dsus2* *D*
All you've gotta do is call and I'll be there.

B3
D   *F#m*   *Bm*   *Gm*
If the sun has faded away, I'll try to make it shine,

D/A   *A*   *D*
There is nothing I won't do

B4
| D | F#m | Bm | Gm |
When you need a shoulder to cry on, I hope it will be mine.

| D/A | A | Dsus4 | D | Dsus2 | D |
Call me tonight, and I'll come to you.

A3
| | Bm | D |
Any time at all,

| | A | Bm |
Any time at all, any time at all,

| | G | A | Dsus4 | D | Dsus2 | D |
All you've gotta do is call and I'll be there.

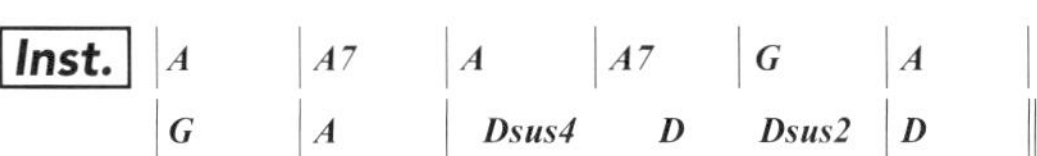

Inst. | A | A7 | A | A7 | G | A | |
| G | A | Dsus4 | D | Dsus2 | D | ||

A4
| | Bm | D |
Any time at all,

| | A | Bm |
Any time at all, any time at all,

| | G | A | Dsus4 | D | Dsus2 | D |
All you've got do is call and I'll be there.

| | G | A | Dsus4 | D | Dsus2 | D |
Any time at all, all you've got do is call and I'll be there.

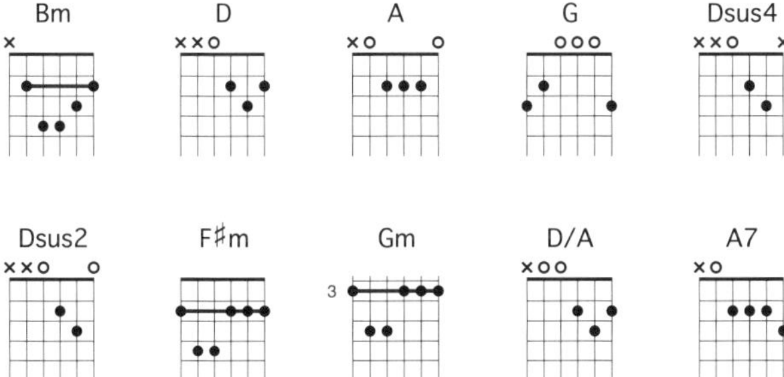

Ask Me Why

Words & Music by
John Lennon & Paul McCartney

| Inst. | | E || |

A1
```
E   F#m7  G#m7
```
I love   you ——

```
F#m7                        E
```
'Cause you tell me things I want to know.

```
E       F#m7  G#m7
```
And it's   true ——

```
F#m7                    E
```
That it really only goes to show,

```
G#7              C#7            Am                      F#7        B
```
That I know, that I, I, I, I should never, never, never be blue. ——

A2
```
E       F#m7    G#m7
```
Now you're mine,

```
F#m7                      E
```
My happiness still makes me cry.

```
E       F#m7  G#m7
```
And in   time ——

```
F#m7                        E
```
You'll understand the reason why,

```
G#7
```
If I cry,

```
      C#7
```
It's not because I'm sad,

```
              Am                    E    Eaug
```
But you're the only love that I've ever had.

B1
```
              A    B                    E   Eaug
```
I can't believe it's happened to me

```
              A    B              E        B
```
I can't conceive of any more misery.

E   *F#m7 G#m7*   *A*
[C1] Ask   me   why, I'll say love you,

                G#m7   *A*   *E*
And I'm always thinking of you.

E   *F#m7   G#m7*
[A3] I   love   you ——

F#m7   *E*
'Cause you tell me things I want to know.

E   *F#m7   G#m7*
And   it's   true ——

F#m7   *E*
That it really only goes to show,

G#7   *C#m*   *Am*   *F#7*   *B*
That I know, that I, I, I, I should never, never, never be blue.

E   *F#m7   G#m7*   *A*
[C2] Ask   me   why, I'll say love you,

                G#m7   *A*   *E*   *Eaug*
And I'm always thinking of you.

                A   *B*   *E*   *Eaug*
[B2] I can't believe it's happened to me.

                A   *B*   *E*   *B*
I can't conceive of any more misery.

E   *F#m7   G#m7*   *A*
[C3] Ask   me   why, I'll say love you,

                G#m7   *A*   *E*
And I'm always thinking of you.

A   *E*
You

A   *G#m7*
You.

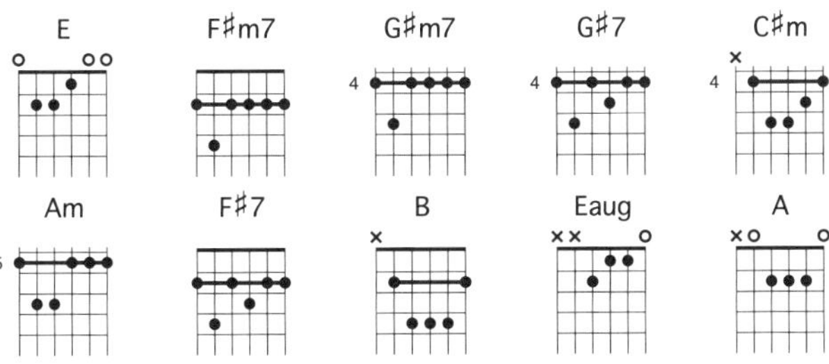

Baby You're A Rich Man

Words & Music by
John Lennon & Paul McCartney

Inst. | *G* | *C/G* | *G* | *C/G* | *G7* | *C/G* | *G7* | *C/G* ‖

G   *C/G*   *G7*
A1 How does it feel to be one of the beautiful people?

G   *F/G*
Now that you know who you are

F   *G*   *C*
What do you want to be?

G   *F/G*
And have you travelled very far?

F   *G*   *C*
Far as the eye can see.

G   *C/G*   *G7*
A2 How does it feel to be one of the beautiful people?

G   *F/G*
How often have you been there?

F   *G*   *C*
Often enough to know.

G   *F/G*
What did you see, when you were there?

F   *G*   *C*
Nothing that doesn't show.

G
B1 Baby you're a rich man,

C
Baby you're a rich man,

G   *C*
Baby you're a rich man too.

  Bb6   *G7/B* *C*   *G7*
You keep all your money in a big brown bag inside a zoo.

      C
What a thing to do.

G
Baby you're a rich man,

C
Baby you're a rich man,

G   *C*
Baby you're a rich man too.

|A3|
G   *C/G*   *G7*
How does it feel to be one of the beautiful people?

G   *F/G*
Tuned to A natural E

F   *G*   *C*
Happy to be that way.

G   *F/G*
Now that you've found another key

F   *G*   *C*
What are you going to play?

|B2|
G
Baby you're a rich man,

C
Baby you're a rich man,

G   *C*
Baby you're a rich man too.

   Bb6   *G7/B*   *C*   *G7*
You keep all your money in a big brown bag inside a zoo.

              C
What a thing to do.

|OUTRO| ‖:
G
Baby you're a rich man,

C
Baby you're a rich man,

G   *C*
Baby you're a rich man too. :‖   *... fade out*

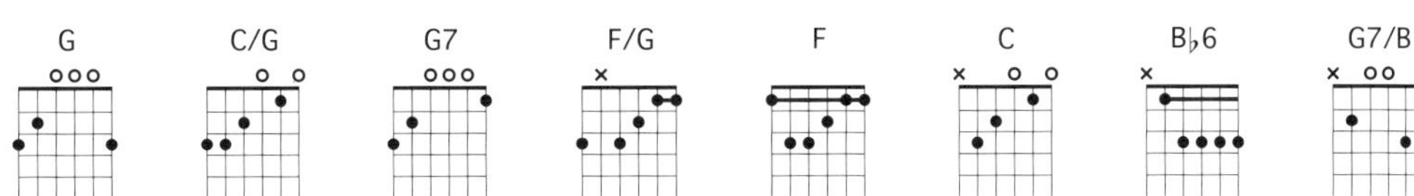

Baby's In Black

Words & Music by
John Lennon & Paul McCartney

Inst. | A | A |

A1
A   E7
Oh dear, what can I do?

D7   E
Baby's in black and I'm feeling blue,

   A D A
Tell me, oh what can I do?

A   A7   D
She thinks of him and so she dresses in black,

        A E   A
And though he'll never come back, she's dressed in black.

A2
A   E7
Oh dear, what can I do?

D7   E
Baby's in black and I'm feeling blue,

   A D A
Tell me, oh what can I do?

A   A7   D
I think of her, but she thinks only of him,

       A E   A
And though it's only a whim, she thinks of him.

B1
F#m   B7
Oh how long will it take,

D   E   E7   A
Till she sees the mistake she has made?

   E7
Dear what can I do?

D7   E
Baby's in black and I'm feeling blue,

   A D A
Tell me, oh what can I do?

Inst. | A | E | D | E | A D | A ‖

F#m   *B7*

B2 Oh how long will it take,

D   *E*   *E7*   *A*

Till she sees the mistake she has made?

        E7

Dear what can I do?

D7   *E*

Baby's in black and I'm feeling blue,

        A   *D*   *A*

Tell me, oh what can I do?

A   *A7*   *D*

A3 She thinks of him and so she dresses in black,

        A   *E*   *A*

And though he'll never come back, she's dressed in black.

A   *E7*

Oh dear, what can I do?

D7   *E*

Baby's in black and I'm feeling blue,

        A   *D*   *A*

Tell me, oh what can I do?

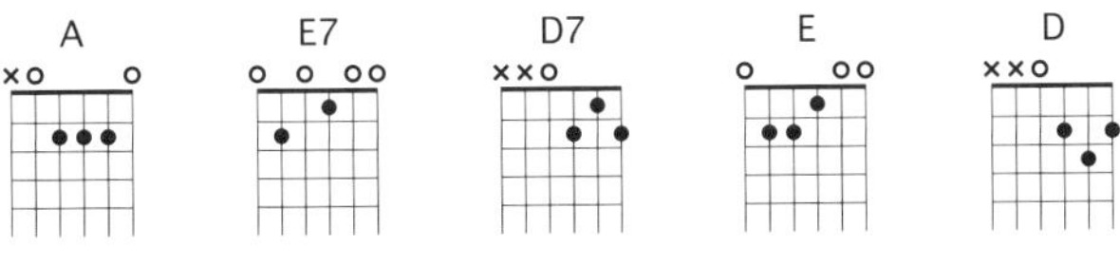

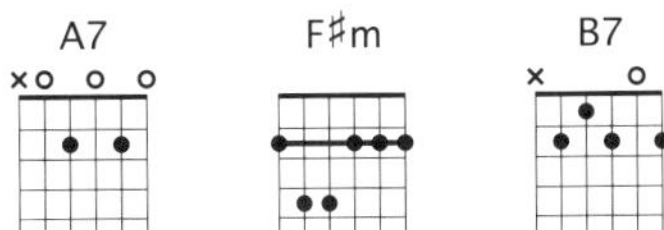

Back In The USSR

Words & Music by
John Lennon & Paul McCartney

Inst. | E7 | E7 | E7 | E7 ‖

A1 Flew in from Miami Beach BOAC

Didn't get to bed last night

On the way the paper bag was on my knee

Man I had a dreadful flight

B1 I'm back in the U.S.S.R.

You don't know how lucky you are boy

Back in the U.S.S.R.

A2 Been away so long I hardly knew the place

Gee it's good to be back home

Leave it till tomorrow to unpack my case

Honey disconnect the phone

B2 I'm back in the U.S.S.R.

You don't know how lucky you are boy

Back in the U.S Back in the U.S. Back in the U.S.S.R.

C1
       D
Well the Ukraine girls really knock me out

       A
They leave the West behind

      D   *Db*   *C*   *B*
And Moscow girls make me sing and shout

       E7   *D7*   *A* *E7*
That Georgia's always on my my-my-my-my-my-my-my mind.

Inst. | *A* | *D* | *C* | *D* |
       | *A* | *D* | *C* | *D* ‖

B3 I'm back in the U.S.S.R. *A*

C   *D*
You don't know how lucky you are boys

D   *A*
Back in the U.S.S.R.

* C 반복

A
A3 Show me round your snow peaked mountains way down south   *D*

C   *D*
Take me to your daddy's farm

A   *D*
Let me hear your balalaika's ringing out

C   *D*
Come and keep your comrade warm.

B4 I'm back in the U.S.S.R. *A*

C   *D*
You don't know how lucky you are boys

D   *A*
Back in the U.S.S.R.

      E7   *A*
Oh, let me tell you honey

Inst. | *A* | *A* | *A* | *A* | *A* ‖

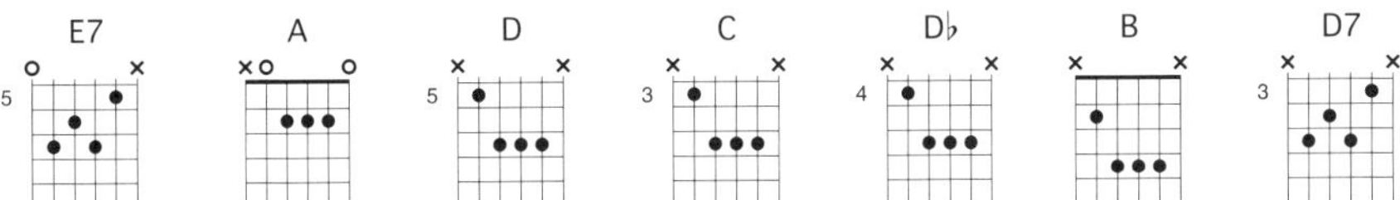

Because

Words & Music by
John Lennon & Paul McCartney

Inst. | C#m | C#m | D#m7b5 | G#7 |
| A | C#m | A7 | A7add13 |

D   D(b5)   Ddim
(Ah.) —

C#m   D#m7b5   G#7
A1 Because the world is round it turns me on

*   A   C#m   A7   A7add13*
Because the world is round…

D   D(b5)   Ddim
(Ah.) —

C#m   D#m7b5   G#7
A2 Because the wind is high it blows my mind —

*   A   C#m   A7   A7add13*
Because the wind is high……

D   D(b5)   Ddim
(Ah.) —

Ddim   F#
B1 Love is all, love is new

*   G#7*
Love is all, love is you

C#m   D#m7b5   G#7
A3 Because the sky is blue, it makes me cry

*   A   C#m   A7   A7add13*
Because the sky is blue…….

D   D(b5)   Ddim
(Ah.) —

Inst. *C#m*
(Ah.) —

  D#m7b5 *G#7*
(Ah.) —

  A   *C#m*
(Ah.) —

  A7   *A7add13*
(Ah.) —

  D   *D(b5)* *Ddim*
(Ah.) —

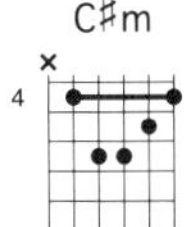
C♯m

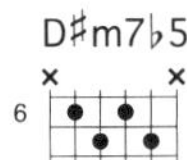
D♯m7♭5

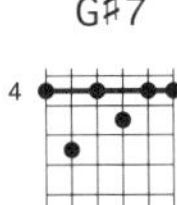
G♯7

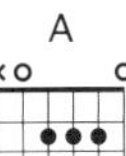
A

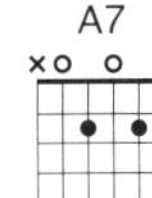
A7

A7add13

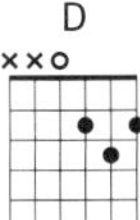
D

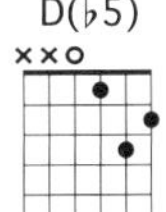
D(♭5)

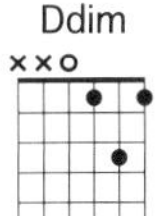
Ddim

F♯

Being For The Benefit of Mr.Kite

Words & Music by
John Lennon & Paul McCartney

Inst. | Bb | A | Dm G ‖

A1
           Cm   *Gaug*
For the benefit of Mr. Kite

Bb   *Dm*   *G*   *Gaug*
There will be a show tonight on trampoline

Cm   *Gaug*
The Hendersons will all be there

Bb   *Dm*   *A*
Late of Pablo Fanque's fair, what a scene

Dm   *Dm7*
Over men and horses, hoops and garters

Bb   *A*   *Dm*
Lastly through a hogshead of real fire!

Gm   *A*   *Dm*
In this way Mr. K. will challenge the world!

Inst. | Gm A | Dm G ‖

A2
           Cm   *Gaug*
The celebrated Mr. K.

Bb   *Dm*   *G*   *Gaug*
Performs his feat on Saturday at Bishopsgate

Cm   *Gaug*
The Hendersons will dance and sing

Bb   *Dm*   *A*
As Mr. Kite flies through the ring don't be late

Dm   *Dm7*
Messrs. K and H. assure the public

Bb   *A*   *Dm*
Their production will be second to none

Gm   *A*
And of course, Henry The Horse dances the waltz!

Inst.	Dm Dm(maj7)	Dm7 Dm6	A		A		
	Dm Dm(maj7)	Dm7 Dm6	B		Em	Em7	
	C B	Em Em7	C B	Em		G	

       Cm   **Gaug**

A3 The band begins at ten to six

      Bb   **Dm**   **G**   **Gaug**

When Mr. K. performs his tricks without a sound

      Cm   **Gaug**

And Mr. H. will demonstrate

     Bb   **Dm**   **A**

Ten summersets he'll undertake on solid ground

       Dm   **Dm7**

Having been some days in preparation

     Bb   **A**   **Dm**

A splendid time is guaranteed for all

      Gm   **A**   **Dm Gm A**

And tonight Mr. Kite is topping the bill.

Inst.	Dm Dm(maj7)	Dm7 Dm6	A		A		
	Dm Dm(maj7)	Dm7 Dm6	B				
	Em Em7	C B	Em Em7	C B			
	Em Em7	C B	Em Em7	C B			
	Em						

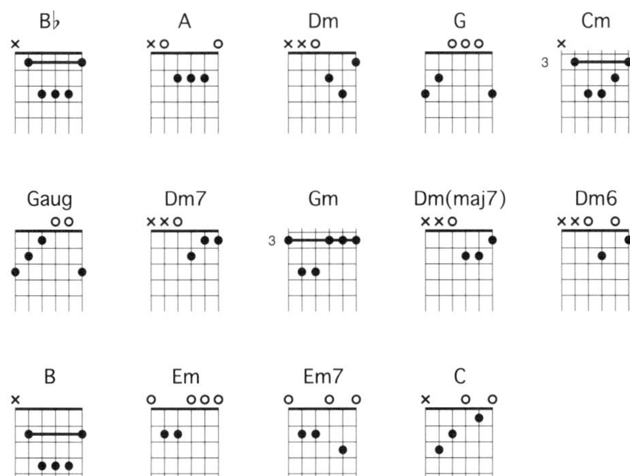

Birthday

Words & Music by
John Lennon & Paul McCartney

Inst. | A7 | A7 | A7 | A7 | D7 | D7 |
| A7 | A7 | E7 | E7 | A7 | A7 ‖

A1
A7
You say it's your birthday

A7
It's my birthday too--yeah

D7
They say it's your birthday

A7
We're gonna have a good time

E7
I'm glad it's your birthday

A7
Happy birthday to you.

Inst. 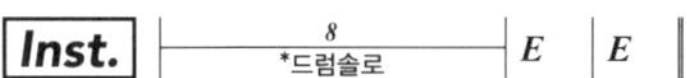

| E | E |

B1
E
Yes we're going to a party party

Yes we're going to a party party

Yes we're going to a party party.

C1
C   *G*   *C*
I would like you to dance--Birthday

G   *C*
Take a cha-cha-cha-chance-Birthday

G   *C*
I would like you to dance--Birthday

G   *E*
Dance

Inst.		A7		A7		A7		A7		D7		D7		
		A7		A7		E7		E7		A7		A7		
		A		A	G	A		A	G					

C2
C   **G**   **C**
I would like you to dance--Birthday

            G   **C**
Take a cha-cha-cha-chance-Birthday

            G   **C**
I would like you to dance--Birthday

G   **E**
Dance

A2
A7
You say it's your birthday

Well it's my birthday too--yeah

D7
You say it's your birthday

 A7
We're gonna have a good time

E7
I'm glad it's your birthday

 A7
Happy birthday to you.

Inst.		A		A		

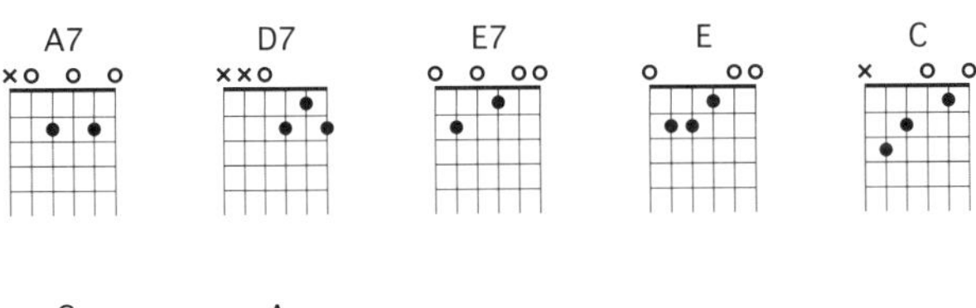

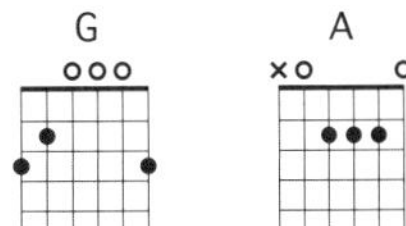

Blackbird

Words & Music by
John Lennon & Paul McCartney


```
        G              Am7          G/B       (G)
A1  Blackbird singing in the dead of night

        C           C#dim         D         D#dim    Em     Em(maj7)/Eb
    Take these broken wings and learn to fly

        D    C#dim   C    Cm
    All  your  life

        G/B                  A7              D7              G
    You were only waiting for this moment to arise.
```



```
        G              Am7          G/B       (G)
A2  Blackbird singing in the dead of night

        C           C#dim         D         D#dim    Em     Em(maj7)/Eb
    Take these sunken eyes and learn to see

        D    C#dim   C    Cm
    All your life

        G/B                  A7              D7              G
    You were only waiting for this moment to be free.
```

```
        F    C/E    Dm   C       Bb6  C
B1  Black - bird,  fly.

        F    C/E    Dm   C       Bb6  A7
    Black - bird,  fly.

                    D7sus4                   G
    Into the light of the dark black night.
```


Inst. | G Am7 G/B (G) | C C#dim D D#dim | Em Em(maj7)/Eb |
D C#dim | C Cm | G/B A7 | D7sus4 G |

B2

F C/E Dm C Bb6 C
Black - bird, fly.

F C/E Dm C Bb6 A7
Black - bird, fly.

D7sus4   G
Into the light of the dark black night.

Inst. | G Am7 G/B | (G) | G | G |
G Am7 G/B | C G/B A7 | D7sus4 ‖

A3

G   Am7   G/B   (G)
Blackbird singing in the dead of night

C   C#dim   D   D#dim   Em   Em(maj7)/Eb
Take these broken wings and learn to fly

D   C#dim   C   Cm
All your life

G/B   A7   D7sus4   G
You were only waiting for this moment to arise

C   G/B   A7   D7sus4   G
You were only waiting for this moment to arise

C   G/B   A7   D7sus4   G
You were only waiting for this moment to arise.

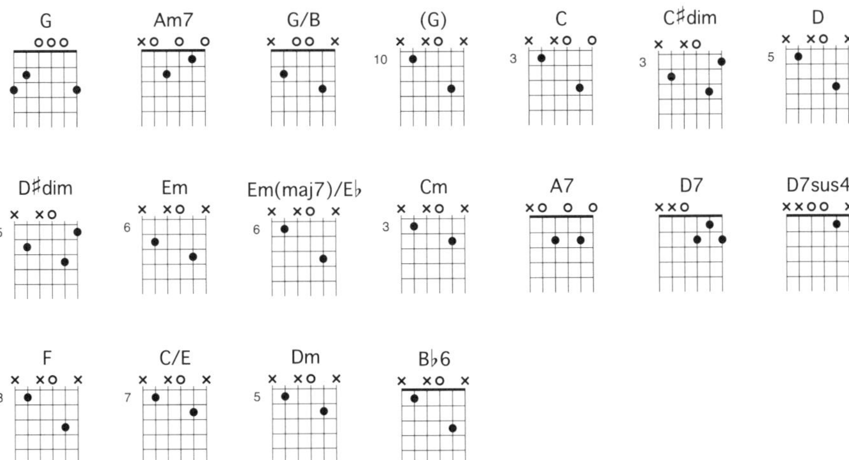

Blue Jay Way

Words & Music by
George Harrison

Inst. | *C* | *C* | *C6 Cmaj7* | *C5 Cmaj7* |
| *Cmaj7 C6 Cmaj7 Cadd9* | *C Cmaj7* | *C* ||

                             C
A1 There's a fog upon L.A.

Cdim   *C*
And my friends have lost their way

Cdim   *C(b5)*
We'll be over soon they said

Cdim   *C*
Now they've lost themselves instead.

C6   *Cmaj7 C5 Cmaj7 C6*   *Cmaj7*   *C5*   *Cmaj7*
B1 Please don't be long please don't you be very long

C6   *Cmaj7*   *C5 Cmaj7 C6 C5 Cmaj7 C6 C5*   *C*
Please don't be long or I may be a - sleep

                             C
A2 Well it only goes to show

Cdim   *C*
And I told them where to go

Cdim   *C(b5)*
Ask a policeman on the street

Cdim   *C*
There's so many there to meet

C6   *Cmaj7 C5 Cmaj7 C6*   *Cmaj7*   *C5*   *Cmaj7*
B2 Please don't be long please don't you be very long

C6   *Cmaj7*   *C5 Cmaj7 C6 C5 Cmaj7 C6 C5*   *C*
Please don't be long or I may be a - sleep

|A3| *C*
Now it's past my bed I know

Cdim   *C*
And I'd really like to go

Cdim   *C(b5)*
Soon will be the break of day

Cdim   *C*
Sitting here in Blue Jay Way

C6   Cmaj7   C5 Cmaj7   C6   Cmaj7   C5   Cmaj7
|B3| Please don't be long please don't you be very long

C6   Cmaj7   C5 Cmaj7   C6 C5 Cmaj7 C6 C5   C
Please don't be long or I may be a - sleep

C6   Cmaj7   C5 Cmaj7   C6   Cmaj7   C5   Cmaj7
|B4| Please don't be long please don't you be very long

C6   Cmaj7   C5 Cmaj7   C5
Please don't be long

C6   Cmaj7   C5 Cmaj7   C6   Cmaj7   C5   Cmaj7
|B5| Please don't be long please don't you be very long

C6   Cmaj7   C5 Cmaj7   C5
Please don't be long

C6   Cmaj7   C5 Cmaj7   C6   Cmaj7   C5   Cmaj7
|B6| Please don't be long please don't you be very long

C6   Cmaj7   C5 Cmaj7
Please don't be long

      C
|OUTRO| Don't be long -don't be long - don't be long

Don't be long - don't be long - be long.

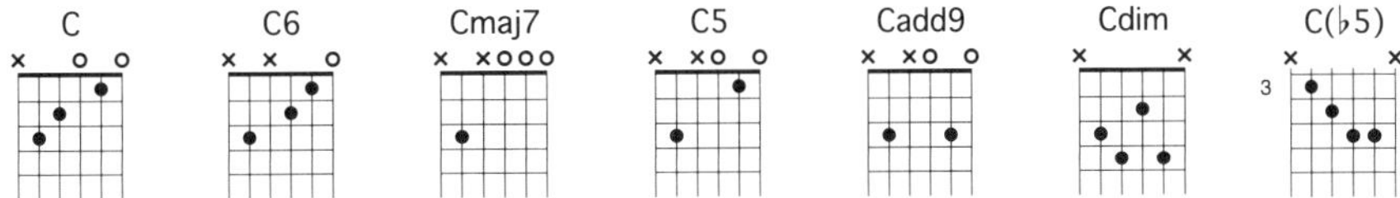

Can't Buy Me Love

Words & Music by
John Lennon & Paul McCartney

A1   *Em   Am   Em   Am*
Can't buy me love,   love

                                Dm   G7
Can't buy me love

B1   *C7*
I'll buy you a diamond ring my friend if it makes you feel alright

        F7   *C7*
I'll get you anything my friend if it makes you feel alright

        G7   *F7*   *C7*
'Cause I don't care too much for money, money can't buy me love

B2   *C7*
I'll give you all I got to give if you say you love me too

        F7   *C7*
I may not have a lot to give but what I got I'll give to you

     G7   *F7*   *C7*
I don't care too much for money, money can't buy me love

C1   *Em   Am*
Can't buy me love,

        C7
Everybody tells me so.

                          Em   Am
Can't buy me love,

Dm   *G7*
No, no, no, no.

B3
C7
Say you don't need no diamond ring and I'll be satisfied

F7 *C7*
Tell me that you want the kind of thing that money just can't buy

G7 *F7* *C7*
I don't care too much for money, money can't buy me love

Inst. | *C7* | *C7* | *C7* | *C7* |
| *F7* | *F7* | *C7* | *C7* |
| *G7* | *F7* | *C7* | *C7* ||

C2
Em *Am*
Can't buy me love,

C7
Everybody tells me so

Em *Am*
Can't buy me love,

Dm *G7*
No, no, no, no.

B4
C7
Say you don't need no diamond ring and I'll be satisfied

F7 *C7*
Tell me that you want the kind of thing that money just can't buy

G7 *F7* *C7*
I don't care too much for money, money can't buy me love

A2
Em *Am* *Em* *Am*
Can't buy me love,   love

Dm *G7*
Can't buy me love,

C7
Oh

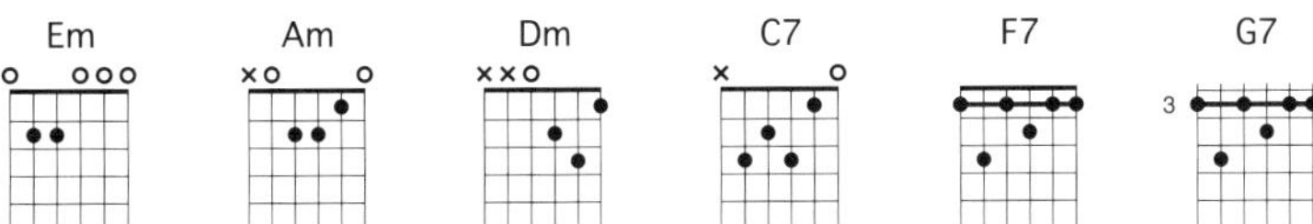

Carry That Weight

Words & Music by
John Lennon & Paul McCartney

```
        C                    G
[A1] Boy, you're gonna carry that weight,

                         C
     Carry that weight a long time.

      C              G
     Boy, you gotta carry that weight,

                           C        G/B
     Carry that weight a long time.
```

```
[Inst.] | Am7      | Am7/D   Dm7  | G7        | Csus4  C  Cmaj7 |
        | Fmaj7    | Bm7b5   E7   | Am        |                 |
```

```
     Am7               Am7/D      Dm7
[B1] I never give you my pil  -  low

     G7            Csus4  C    Cmaj7
     I only send you my in - vi - tation

     Fmaj7                    Bm7b5     E7
     And in the middle of the celebrations

     Am7          G    C
     I break down.
```

```
        C                    G
[A2] Boy, you're gonna carry that weight

                         C
     Carry that weight a long time

      C              G
     Boy, you gotta carry that weight

                           C        G/B   A
     Carry that weight a long time
```

```
        | C      G/B  | A        ||
```


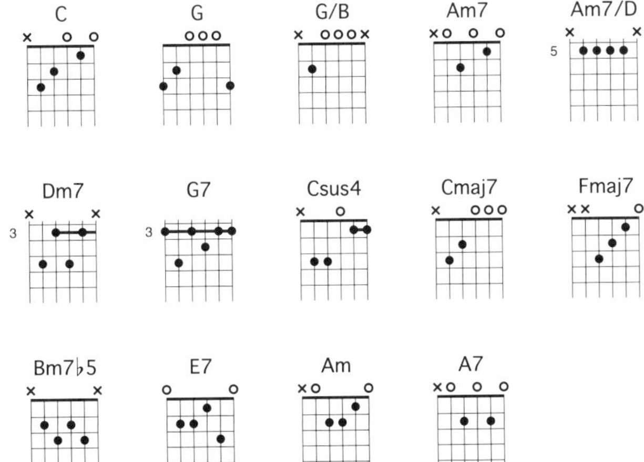
C
G
G/B
Am7
Am7/D
Dm7
G7
Csus4
Cmaj7
Fmaj7
Bm7♭5
E7
Am
A7

Come Together

Words & Music by
John Lennon & Paul McCartney

Inst. | D7#9 | D7#9 | D7#9 | D7#9 ‖

D7#9
A1 Here come old flat top he come grooving up slowly,

He got joo-joo eyeball he one holy roller,

      A
He got hair down to his knees,

G7
Got to be a joker he just do what he please.

Inst. | D7#9 | D7#9 | D7#9 | D7#9 ‖

D7#9
A2 He wear no shoeshine he got toe-jam football,

He got monkey finger he shoot coca-cola,

      A
He say "I know you, you know me.

G7
One thing I can tell you is you got to be free."

      Bm Bm/A G A
B1 Come together, right now,

Over me.

Inst. | D7#9 | D7#9 | D7#9 | D7#9 ‖

D7#9
A3 He bag production he got walrus gumboot,

He got Ono sideboard he one spinal cracker,

      A
He got feet down below his knee,

G7
Hold you in his armchair you can feel his disease.

Bm   Bm/A   G   A

B2 Come together, right now,

Over me.

Inst. | *D7#9* | *D7#9* | *D7#9* | *D7#9* | *D7#9* | *D7#9* |
| *A* | *A* | *A* | *A* | *D7#9* | *D7#9* ‖

D7#9

A4 He roller-coaster he got early warning,

He got muddy water he one mojo filter,

    A
He say "One and one and one is three."

G7
Got to be good-looking 'cause he's so hard to see.

Bm   Bm/A   G   A

B3 Come together, right now,

Over me.

Inst. | *D7#9* | *D7#9* | *D7#9* | *D7#9* |
| *D7#9* | *D7#9* ‖

D7#9

OUTRO ‖: Come together, yeah :‖   *... fade out*

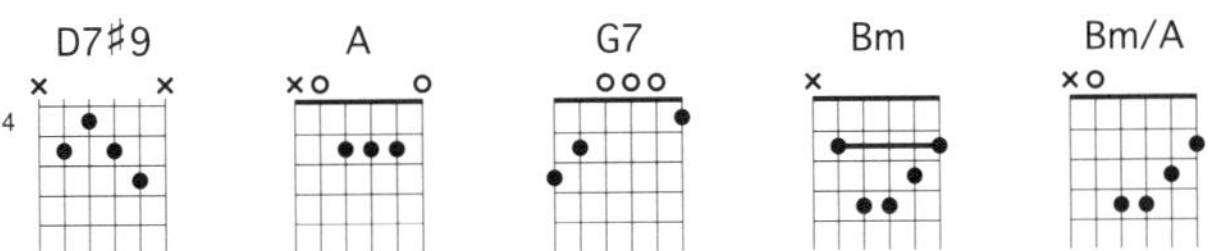

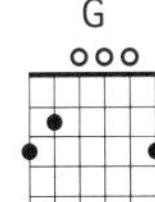

Cry Baby Cry

Words & Music by
John Lennon & Paul McCartney


```
        Em              Em(maj7)        Em7
B3  The Duchess of Kircaldy always smiling

          Em6                  C7   G
    And arriving late for tea

          Em                      Em(maj7)
    The duke was having problems

            Em7             Em6             C7
    With a message at the local bird and bee.


        G         Am    F                 G
A4  Cry baby cry,    make your mother sigh

          Em                  A7      F         G
    She's old enough to know better, so cry baby cry.


        Em              Em(maj7)        Em7
B4  At twelve o'clock a meeting round the table

          Em6                  C7   G
    For a seance in the dark

          Em                  Em(maj7)
    With voices out of nowhere

            Em7             Em6             C7
    Put on specially by the children for a lark.


        G         Am    F                 G
A5  Cry baby cry,    make your mother sigh

          Em                  A7      F       G       Am        F
    She's old enough to know better, so cry baby cry cry cry cry baby

                    G
    Make your mother sigh.

          Em                  A7
    She's old enough to know better

    F        G         Am
    Cry baby cry, cry, cry, cry,

    F                  G
    Make your mother sigh

          Em                  A7      F         Em
    She's old enough to know better, so cry baby cry.
```

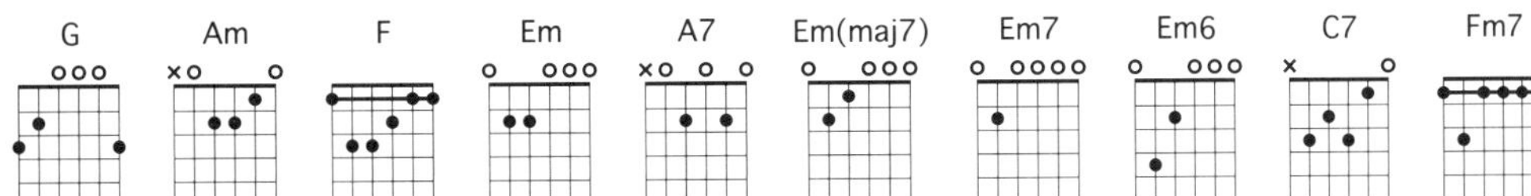

Day Tripper

Words & Music by
John Lennon & Paul McCartney

Inst. | E7 | E7 |
| E7 | E7 | E7 | E7 |
| E7 | E7 | E7 | E7 ‖

E7
A1 Got a good reason for taking the easy way out

A7   *E7*
Got a good reason for taking the easy way out now

F#7
B1 She was a day tripper, a one way ticket yea

              A7   *G#7*   *C#7*   *B7*
It took me so   long to find out, and I found out

Inst. | E7 | E7 | E7 | E7 ‖

E7
A2 She's a big teaser, she took me half the way there

A7   *E7*
She's a big teaser, she took me half the way there now

F#7
B2 She was a day tripper, a one way ticket yea

              A7   *G#7*   *C#7*   *B7*
It took me so   long to find out, and I found out

Inst. | B7 | B7 | B7 | B7 |
| B7 | B7 | B7 | B7 |
| B7 | B7 | B7 | B7 |
| E7 | E7 | E7 | E7 ‖

A3 Tried to please her, she only played one night stands

A7　　　　　　　　　　*E7*
Tried to please her, she only played one night stands now

　　　　　　　　F#7
B3 She was a day tripper, a Sunday driver yea

　　　　　　(A7)　*G#7*　　　　*C#7*　　　　　　　　*B7*
Took me so　long to find out, and I found out

Inst. | *E7* | *E7* | *E7* | *E7* |
　　　　 | *E7* | *E7* | *E7* | *E7* ‖

E7
OUTRO Day tripper, day tripper yeah.

Day tripper, day tripper yeah.　　　　　*...fade out*

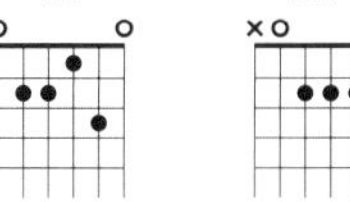
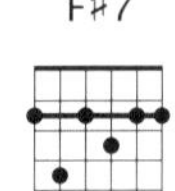
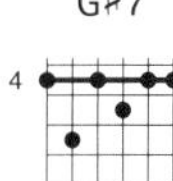

Dear Prudence

*6번현을 D로 튜닝합니다.(DROP D)

Words & Music by
John Lennon & Paul McCartney

Inst. | *Dadd9 (D)* | *(C/D) (G/D)* | *A/D   C/D* | $\frac{2}{4}$ *C/D* |
| *D   D/C* | *Gmaj7/B   Gm/Bb* |

|A1|
    D   *D/C*   *Gmaj7/B*   *Gm/Bb*
Dear Prudence,

              D   *D/C*   *Gmaj7/B*   *Gm/Bb*
won't you come out to play

    D   *D/C*   *Gmaj7/B*   *Gm/Bb*
Dear Prudence,

           D   *D/C*   *Gmaj7/B*   *Gm/Bb*
greet the brand new day

|B1|
    D   *D/C*
The sun is up, the sky is blue

    Gmaj7/B   *Gm/Bb*   *D*   *D/C*
It's beautiful and so are you, dear Prudence

    C   *G*
Won't you come out and play

Inst. | *D   D/C* | *Gmaj7/B   Gm/Bb* |

|A2|
    D   *D/C*   *Gmaj7/B*   *Gm/Bb*
Dear Prudence,

       D   *D/C*   *Gmaj7/B*   *Gm/Bb*
Open up your eyes

    D   *D/C*   *Gmaj7/B*   *Gm/Bb*
Dear Prudence,

       D   *D/C*   *Gmaj7/B*   *Gm/Bb*
See the sunny skies

|B2|
    D   *D/C*
The wind is low the birds will sing

    Gmaj7/B   *Gm/Bb*   *D*   *D/C*
That you are part of everything, Dear Prudence,

    C   *G*
Won't you open up your eyes?

Inst. | *D   G/D* | *A/D   G/D* |

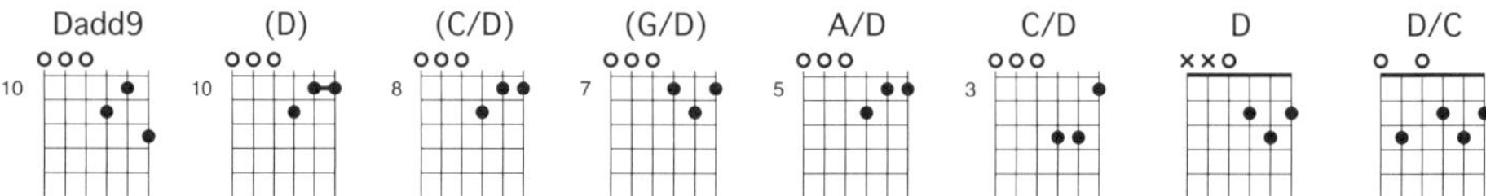

|C1|
     D   *G/D*   *A/D*   *G/D*

C1 Look around round, (round round round round round round round round)

     D   *G/D*   *A/D*   *G/D*

Look around round round (round round round round round round round)

     F   *Ab*   *G*

Look around, ah

Inst. | D   D/C | Gmaj7/B   Gm/Bb |

    D   *D/C*   *Gmaj7/B*   *Gm/Bb*

A3 Dear Prudence,

        D   *D/C*   *Gmaj7/B*   *Gm/Bb*

Let me see you smile

    D   *D/C*   *Gmaj7/B*   *Gm/Bb*

Dear Prudence,

      D *D/C*   *Gmaj7/B*   *Gm/Bb*

Like a little child.

    D   *D/C*

B3 The clouds will be a daisy chain

    Gmaj7/B   *Gm/Bb*   *D*   *D/C*

So let me see you smile again, dear Prudence,

    C   *G*

Won't you let me see you smile?

Inst. | D   D/C | Gmaj7/B   Gm/Bb |

    D   *D/C*   *Gmaj7/B*   *Gm/Bb*

A4 Dear Prudence,

        D *D/C*   *Gmaj7/B*   *Gm/Bb*

Won't you come out to play

    D   *D/C*   *Gmaj7/B*   *Gm/Bb*

Dear Prudence,

        D *D/C*   *Gmaj7/B*   *Gm/Bb*

Greet the brand new day

    D   *D/C*

B4 The sun is up, the sky is blue

    Gmaj7/B   *Gm/Bb*   *D*   *D/C*

It's beautiful and so are you, dear Prudence,

    C   *G*   *D*

Won't you come out and play

Inst. | D6   Dadd9 | D (C/D) | (G/D) A/D | C/D | ... *fade out*

Gmaj7/B   Gm/B♭   C   G   G/D   F   A♭   D6

Dig A Pony

Words & Music by
John Lennon & Paul McCartney

Inst. ‖: *G* | *D* | *A* | *A* :‖

A1
A D6/A A D6/A A D6/A A
|, |, |, |, |

       F#m
Dig a pony

           Bm   *G7*
Well you can celebrate anything you want

      Bm   *G7*   *E*
Well you can celebrate anything you want, Oh.

A2
A D6/A A D6/A A D6/A A
|, |, |, |, |

       F#m
Do a road hog.

           Bm   *G7*
Well you can penetrate any place you go.

     Bm   *G7*   *E*
Yes you can penetrate any place you go. I told you so,

B1
G   *D*   *A*
All I want is you.

G   *D*   *A*
Everything has got to be just like you want it to, because

A3
A D6/A A D6/A A D6/A A
|, |, |, |, |

       F#m
Pick a moon dog

          Bm   *G7*
Well you can radiate everything you are

     Bm   *G7*   *E*
Yes you can radiate everything you are, Oh.

A4

```
A  D6/A  A  D6/A  A  D6/A  A
|,   |,   |,   |,   |
```

F#m
Roll a stoney.

Bm   *G7*
Well you can imitate everyone you know.

Bm   *G7*   *E*
Yes you can imitate everyone you know, I told you so,

B2

G   *D*   *A*
All I want is you.

G   *D*   *A*
Everything has got to be just like you want it to, because

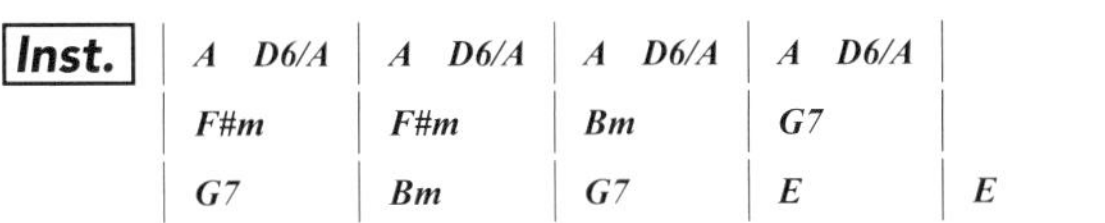

Inst.

```
| A   D6/A | A   D6/A | A   D6/A | A   D6/A |
| F#m      | F#m      | Bm       | G7       |
| G7       | Bm       | G7       | E    | E      ||
```

A5

```
A  D6/A  A  D6/A  A  D6/A  A
|,   |,   |,   |,   |
```

F#m
Feel the wind blow.

Bm   *G7*
Well you can indicate everything you see.

Bm   *G7*   *E*
Yes you can indicate everything you see, Oh.

A6

```
A  D6/A  A  D6/A  A  D6/A  A
|,   |,   |,   |,   |
```

F#m
Cold and lonely.

Bm   *G7*
Well you can syndicate any boat you row.

Bm   *G7*   *E*
Yes you can syndicate any boat you row, I told you so,

B3

G   *D*   *A*
All I want is you.

G   *D*   *A*
Everything has got to be just like you want it to, because

Inst.

```
||: G | D | A | A :| A |
```

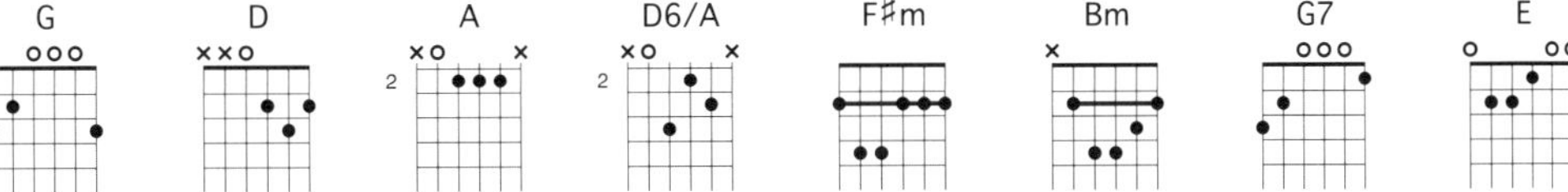

Dig It

Words & Music by
John Lennon, Paul McCartney, George Harrison & Ringo Starr

A1
    Bb   *F*   *Bb*   *C*
Like a rolling stone

      Bb   *F*   *Bb*   *C*
A like a rolling stone

    Bb *F* *Bb*   *C*
Like the F.B.I.

    Bb *F* *Bb*   *C*
And the C.I.A.

    Bb *F* *Bb*   *C*
And the B.B.C.

Bb   *F* *Bb*   *C*
B.B. King,

     Bb *F* *Bb*   *C*
And Doris Day,

   Bb
Matt Busby,

B1
F   *Bb*   *C*
Dig it, dig it, dig it

Bb   *F*   *Bb*
Dig it, dig it, dig it

C   *Bb*
Dig it, dig it…   *… fade out*

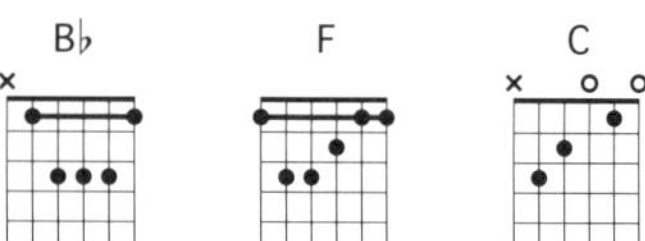

Do You Want To Know A Secret

Words & Music by
John Lennon & Paul McCartney

`INTRO`
Em ... *Am* *Em*
You'll never know how much I really love you.

G ... *F* *B7*
You'll never know how much I really care.

`A1`
E *G#m7* *Gm7* *F#m7*
Listen,

B7 *E* *G#m7* *Gm7* *F#m7*
Do you want to know a secret,

B7 *E* *G#m7* *Gm7* *F#m7* *Am7*
Do you promise not to tell? whoa oh, oh.

E *G#m7* *Gm7* *F#m7*
Closer,

B7 *E* *G#m7* *Gm7* *F#m7*
Let me whisper in your ear,

B7 *A*
Say the words you long to hear,

B7 *C#m/G#* *F#m7* *B7*
I'm in love with you. woo - oo - oo - ooh.

`A2`
E *G#m7* *Gm7* *F#m7*
Listen,

B7 *E* *G#m7* *Gm7* *F#m7*
Do you want to know a secret,

B7 *E* *G#m7* *Gm7* *F#m7* *Am7*
Do you promise not to tell, whoa oh, oh.

E *G#m7* *Gm7* *F#m7*
Closer,

B7 *E* *G#m7* *Gm7* *F#m7*
Let me whisper in your ear,

B7 *A*
Say the words you long to hear,

B7 *C#m/G#* *F#m7* *B7*
I'm in love with you. woo - oo - oo - ooh.

|B1|
A   *F#m*   *C#m*   *Bm*
I've known the secret for a week or two,

A   *F#m*
Nobody knows,

C#m7   *Bm* *F#m* *B7*
Just we two.

|A3|
E   *G#m7*   *Gm7*   *F#m7*
Listen,

     B7   *E*   *G#m7*   *Gm7*   *F#m7*
Do you want to know a secret,

     B7   *E G#m7 Gm7 F#m7 Am7*
Do you promise not to tell,   whoa oh, oh.

E   *G#m7*   *Gm7*   *F#m7*
Closer,

     B7   *E*   *G#m7*   *Gm7*   *F#m7*
Let me whisper in your ear,

     B7   *A*
Say the words you long to hear,

B7   *C#m/G#*   *F#m7* *B7*
I'm in love with you. woo - oo - oo - ooh.

|OUTRO|
C#m/G#   *F#m7* *B7*
 woo - oo - oo - ooh.

C#m/G#   *F#m7* *B7*
 woo - oo - oo - ooh.   *... fade out*

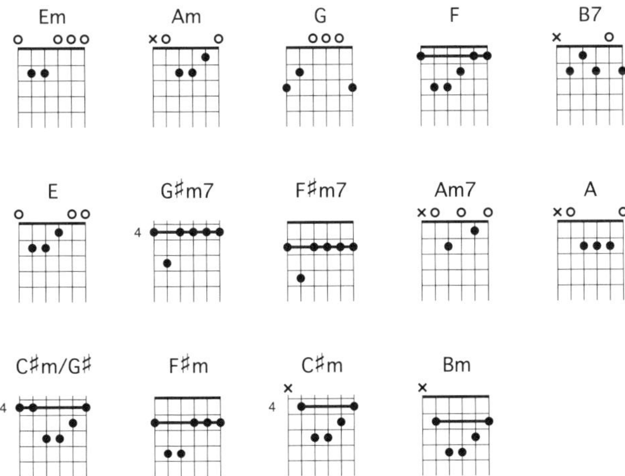

Doctor Robert

Words & Music by
John Lennon & Paul McCartney

Inst. | *A7 Asus4* | *A7 Asus4* | *A7 Asus4* | *A7 Asus4* ||

A1
   A7
Ring my friend, I said you call Doctor Robert

Day or night he'll be there any time at all, Doctor Robert

      F#7
Doctor Robert, you're a new and better man,

He helps you to understand

      E7   *F#7*   *B*
He does everything he can, Doctor Robert

A2
   A7
If you're down he'll pick you up, Doctor Robert

Take a drink from his special cup, Doctor Robert

     F#7
Doctor Robert, he's a man you must believe,

Helping everyone in need

E7   *F#7*   *B*
No one can succeed like Doctor Robert

B1
B   *E/B* *B*
Well, well, well, you're feeling fine

             E/B
Well, well, well, he'll make you ...

     A7
Doctor Robert.

A7
A3 My friend works for the national health, Doctor Robert

Don't pay money just to see yourself with Doctor Robert

F#7
Doctor Robert, you're a new and better man,

He helps you to understand

E7   *F#7*   *B*
He does everything he can, Doctor Robert

B   *E/B*   *B*
B2 Well, well, well, you're feeling fine

E/B
Well, well, well, he'll make you ...

A7
Doctor Robert.

A7
OUTRO Ring my friend, I said you'd call Doctor Robert

Ring my friend, I said you'd call Doctor Robert

F#7
Doctor Robert.

... fade out

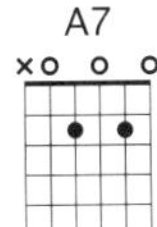
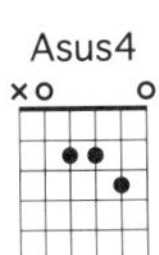
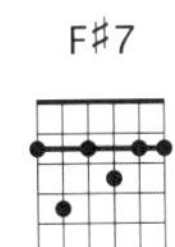
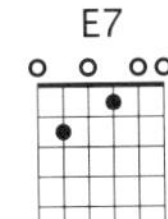
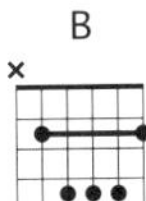

Don't Bother Me

Words & Music by
John Lennon & Paul McCartney

Inst. | D | D | Em |

A1
Em   B7   A7   G   Em
Since she's been gone I want no one to talk to me.

B7   A7   G
It's not the same but I'm to blame, it's plain to see.

B1
Em   A   Em
So go away, leave me alone, don't bother me.

A2
B7   A7   G   Em
I can't believe that she would leave me on my own.

B7   A7   G
It's just not right when every night I'm all alone.

B2
Em   A   Em
I've got no time for you right now, don't bother me.

C1
D   Em   D   Em
I know I'll never be the same if I don't get her back again.

Bm   Am   C   Em
Because I know she'll always be the only girl for me.

A3
B7   A7   G   Em
But 'till she's here please don't come near, just stay away.

B7   A7   G
I'll let you know when she's come home. Until that day,

B3
Em   A   Em
Don't come around, leave me alone, don't bother me.

Inst. | *B7* | *A7* | *G* | *Em* |
| *B7* | *A7* | *G* | *G* ||

    Em   *A*   *Em*

B4 I've got no time for you right now, don't bother me.

    D   *Em*   *D*   *Em*

C2 I know I'll never be the same if I don't get her back again.

    Bm   *Am*   *C*   *Em*

Because I know she'll always be the only girl for me.

    B7   *A7*   *G* *Em*

A4 But 'till she's here please don't come near, just stay away.

    B7   *A7*   *G*

I'll let you know when she's come home. Until that day,

    Em   *A*   *Em*

B5 Don't come around, leave me alone, don't bother me.

    A   *Em*

OUTRO Don't bother me.

    A   *Em*

Don't bother me.

    A   *Em*

Don't bother me.

    A   *Em*

Don't bother me.   *... fade out*

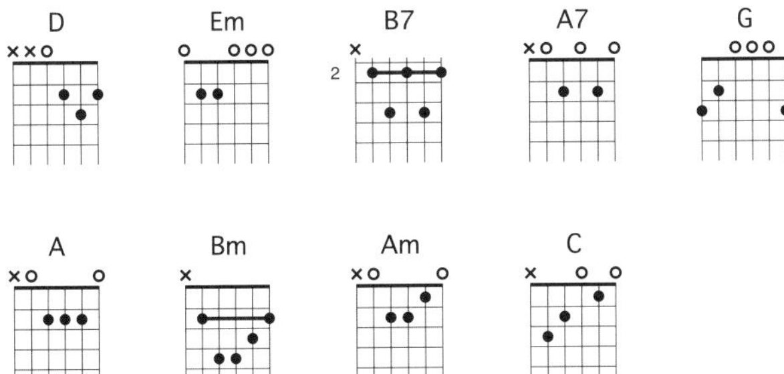

Don't Let Me Down

Words & Music by
John Lennon & Paul McCartney

Inst. | E Esus4 | E ‖

A1
         F#m   **E**   **Esus4** **E**
Don't let me down, don't let me down.

         F#m   **E**   **Esus4** **E**
Don't let me down, don't let me down.

B1
                             F#m
Nobody ever loved me like she does,

            E   **Esus4**   **E**
Oh, she does, yes, she does.

                            F#m7
And if somebody loved me like she do me,

             E   **Esus4**   **E**
Oh, she do me, yes, she does.

A2
         F#m   **E**   **Esus4** **E**
Don't let me down, don't let me down.

         F#m   **E**   **Esus4** **E**
Don't let me down, don't let me down.

B2
                  E
I'm in love for the first time.

                   B7
Don't you know it's gonna last.

It's a love that lasts forever,

            E   **Esus4**   **E**
It's a love that had no past.

|A3| *F#m*   *E*   *Esus4*   *E*

Don't let me down, don't let me down.

               F#m   *E*   *Esus4*   *E*

Don't let me down, don't let me down.

|B3| *F#m7*

And from the first time that she really done me,

                             E   *Esus4*   *E*

Oh, she done me, she done me good.

                      F#m7

I guess nobody ever really done me,

                             E   *Esus4*   *E*

Oh, she done me, she done me good.

|A4| *F#m*   *E*   *Esus4*   *E*

Don't let me down, don't let me down.

               F#m   *E*   *Esus4*   *E*

Don't let me down, don't let me down.

|OUTRO| *F#m*   *E*   *Esus4*   *E*

Don't let me down,

             F#m

Don't let me down.

Can you dig it?

             E   *Esus4*   *E*

Don't let me down.

E   Esus4   F♯m   F♯m7   B7

Don't Pass Me By

Words & Music by
Ringo Starr

Inst. | C | C ||

A1
C
I listen for your footsteps coming up the drive,

F
Listen for your footsteps but they don't arrive

G
Waiting for your knock dear on my old front door

    F
I don't hear it

                    C
Does it mean you don't love me anymore?

A2
C
I hear the clock a-ticking on the mantel shelf

F
See the hands a-moving but I'm by myself

  G
I wonder where you are tonight and why I'm by myself

    F
I don't see you

                    C
Does it mean you don't love me anymore?

B1
          C
Don't pass me by don't make me cry don't make me blue

           F
'Cause you know darling I love only you

        C
You'll never know it hurt me so I hate to see you go,

          G   *F*
Don't pass me by, don't make me cry.

Inst. | *C* | *C* | ‖

C
A3 I'm sorry that I doubted you, I was so unfair,

F
You were in a car crash and you lost your hair.

G
You said you would be late about an hour or two

F
I said that's alright I'm waiting here,

C
Just waiting to hear from you.

C
B2 Don't pass me by don't make me cry don't make me blue

F
'Cause you know darling I love only you

C
You'll never know it hurt me so I hate to see you go,

G   *F*
Don't pass me by, don't make me cry.

Inst. | *C* | *C* | ⌐ *2* DRUMS ¬ | *C* | *C* | ‖

C
B3 Don't pass me by don't make me cry don't make me blue

F
'Cause you know darling I love only you

C
You'll never know it hurt me so I hate to see you go,

G   *F*
Don't pass me by, don't make me cry.

Inst. | *C* | *C* | *F* | *G* | *Dm7* *C* ‖   *... fade out*

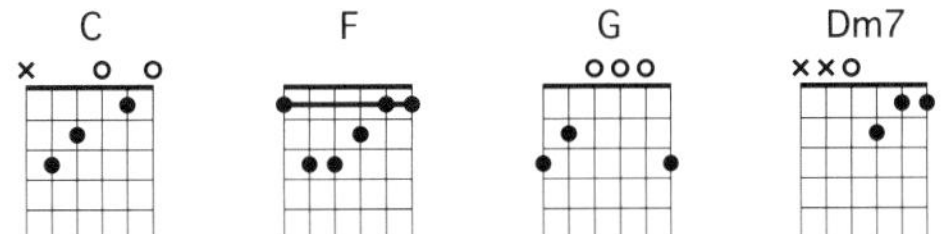

Drive My Car

Words & Music by
John Lennon & Paul McCartney

Inst. | D7 | D7 |

A1
D7   G7
Asked a girl what she wanted to be

D7   G7
She said baby, can't you see

D7   G7
I wanna be famous, a star on the screen

         A7aug
But you can do something in between

B1
Bm   G7 Bm   G7
Baby you can drive my car, yes I'm gonna be a star

Bm   E   A   D   G A
Baby you can drive my car, and maybe I'll love you

A2
D7   G7
I told a girl that my prospects were good

D7   G7
And she said baby, it's understood

D7   G7
Working for peanuts is all very fine

         A7aug
But I can show you a better time

B2
Bm   G7 Bm   G7
Baby you can drive my car, yes I'm gonna be a star

Bm   E   A   D   G
Baby you can drive my car, and maybe I'll love you

A
Beep beep'm beep beep, yeah.

Inst. | *D7* | *G7* | *D7* | *G7* |
| *D7* | *G7* | *A* | *A* ||

Bm   *G7* *Bm*   *G7*
B3 Baby you can drive my car, yes I'm gonna be a star

Bm   *E*   *A*   *D*   *G* *A*
Baby you can drive my car, and maybe I'll love you

D7   *G7*
A3 I told a girl I can start right away

D7   *G7*
And she said listen babe I got something to say

D7   *G7*
I got no car and it's breaking my heart

        A7aug
But I've found a driver and that's a start

Bm   *G7* *Bm*   *G7*
B4 Baby you can drive my car, yes I'm gonna be a star

Bm   *E*   *A*   *D*   *G*
Baby you can drive my car, and maybe I'll love you

A   *D* *G*
Beep beep'm beep beep yeah

A   *D* *G*
‖: Beep beep'm beep beep yeah   :‖   *... fade out*

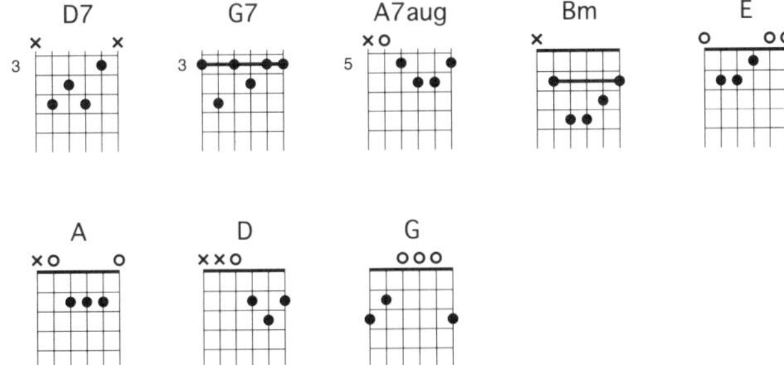

Eight Days A Week

Words & Music by
John Lennon & Paul McCartney

Inst. | Dadd9 | E/D | G6/D | Dadd9 ||

D   E7   G   D
A1 Ooh I need your love babe, guess you know it's true.

D   E7 G   D
Hope you need my love babe, just like I need you.

Bm   G   Bm   E
B1 Hold me, love me, hold me, love me.

D   E7   G   D
Ain't got nothing but love babe, eight days a week.

D   E7   G   D
A2 Love you every day girl, always on my mind.

D   E7 G   D
One thing I can say girl, love you all the time.

Bm   G   Bm   E
B2 Hold me, love me, hold me, love me.

D   E7   G   D
Ain't got nothing but love babe, eight days a week.

A
C1 Eight days a week

Bm
I love you.

E
Eight days a week

G   A
Is not enough to show I care.

A3
D   *E7*   *G*   *D*
Ooh I need your love babe, guess you know it's true.

D   *E7*   *G*   *D*
Hope you need my love babe, just like I need you.

B3
Bm   *G*   *Bm*   *E*
Hold me, love me, hold me, love me.

D   *E7*   *G*   *D*
Ain't got nothing but love babe, eight days a week.

C2
A
Eight days a week

Bm
I love you.

E
Eight days a week

G   *A*
Is not enough to show I care.

A4
D   *E7*   *G*   *D*
Love you every day girl, always on my mind.

D   *E7*   *G*   *D*
One thing I can say girl, love you all the time.

B4
Bm   *G*   *Bm*   *E*
Hold me, love me, hold me, love me.

D   *E7*   *G*   *D*
Ain't got nothing but love babe,

G   *D*   *G*   *D*   *G*   *D*
Eight days a week, eight days a week, eight days a week.

Inst. ‖ *Dadd9* | *E/D* | *G6/D* | *Dadd9* ‖

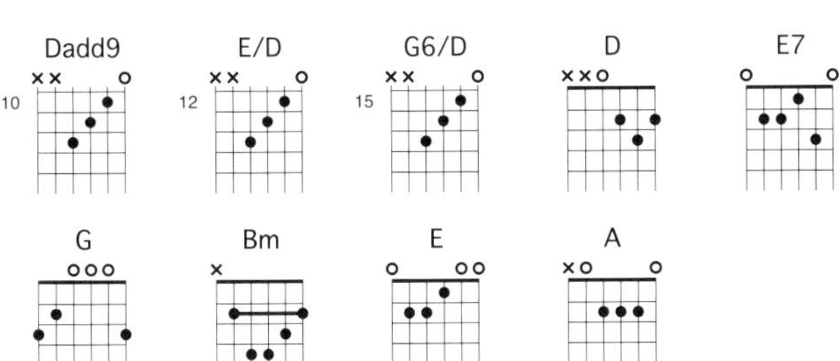

Eleanor Rigby

Words & Music by
John Lennon & Paul McCartney

<pre>
     C   Em
A1 Ah, look at all the lonely people

     C   Em
    Ah, look at all the lonely people

     Em   C
B1 Eleanor Rigby picks up the rice in the church where a wedding has been

              Em
    Lives in a dream

                                                                   C
    Waits at the window, wearing the face that she keeps in a jar by the door
              Em
    Who is it for?

     Em7   Em6
C1 All the lonely people

            Emaug   Em
    Where do they all come from ?

     Em7   Em6
    All the lonely people

            Emaug   Em
    Where do they all belong ?

     Em   C
B2 Father McKenzie writing the words of a sermon that no one will hear

              Em
    No one comes near.

                                                                     C
    Look at him working. Darning his socks in the night when there's nobody there
              Em
    What does he care?
</pre>

<pre>
     Em7   Em6
C2 All the lonely people

           Emaug   Em
    Where do they all come from?

    Em7   Em6
    All the lonely people

               Emaug   Em
    Where do they all belong?
</pre>

<pre>
     C   Em
A2 Ah, look at all the lonely people

     C   Em
    Ah, look at all the lonely people
</pre>

<pre>
     Em   C
B3 Eleanor Rigby died in the church and was buried along with her name,

            Em
    Nobody came.

                                                                 C
    Father McKenzie wiping the dirt from his hands as he walks from the grave,

               Em
    No one was saved.
</pre>

<pre>
     Em7   Em6
C3 All the lonely people

           Emaug   Em
    Where do they all come from?

    Em7   Em6
    All the lonely people

           Emaug   Em
    Where do they all belong?
</pre>

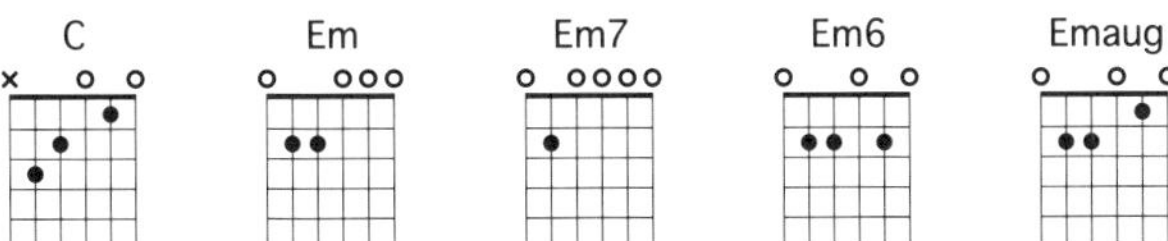

Every Little Thing

Words & Music by
John Lennon & Paul McCartney

Inst. ‖ A | D E ‖

A1
```
A                        D       E
When I'm walking beside her

A                  G    D
People tell me I'm lucky.

Bm      Bm/A         E/G#  A
Yes, I know I'm a lucky guy.

                    D     E
I remember the first time

A                  G    D
I was lonely without her.

Bm           Bm/A     E/G#        A
Can't stop thinking about her now.
```

B1
```
A            G                        G/A   (A)
Every little thing she does, she does for me,

G/A  (A)  A                  G
Yeah,     and you know the things she does,

            G/A (A)   G/A (A)
She does for me,      oooh.
```

A2
```
A                  D     E
When I'm with her I'm happy

A              G    D
Just to know that she loves me.

Bm      Bm/A       E/G#      A
Yes, I know that she loves me now.

                    D     E
There is one thing I'm sure of,

A            G    D
I will love her forever.

Bm    Bm/A         E/G#    A
For I know love will never die.
```



```
    A                G                        G/A   (A)
B2  Every little thing she does, she does for me,

    G/A  (A)  A                 G
    Yeah,     and you know the things she does,

              G/A (A)   G/A (A)
    She does for me,     oooh.
```

| **Inst.** | A | D E | A | G D | Bm Bm/A | E/G# A ‖ |

```
    A                G                        G/A   (A)
B3  Every little thing she does, she does for me,

    G/A  (A)  A                 G
    Yeah,     and you know the things she does,

              G/A (A)   G/A (A)
    She does for me,     oooh.
```

OUTRO

| A | D E ‖ Every little thing.

| A | D E ‖ Every little thing.

| A | D E ‖ Every little ...   *... fade out*

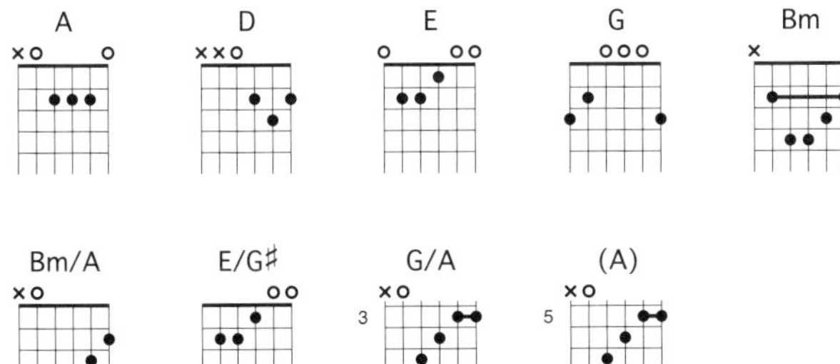

Everybody's Got Something To Hide Except For Me And My Monkey

Words & Music by
John Lennon & Paul McCartney

Inst. ‖: *E Esus4 A* | *E   Esus4* | *A*   :‖

E

A1 Come on, come on, come on, come on,

Come on is such a joy, come on is such a joy,

Come on take it easy, come on take it easy.

        A   *D*

B1 Take it easy, take it easy.

        B7

Everybody's got something to hide except for me and

        E

my monkey.

Inst. | *D   G* | *E   G* | *D*   ‖

E

A1 The deeper you go the higher you fly

The higher you fly the deeper you go

So come on come on

E

C1 Come on is such a joy, come on is such a joy,

Come on make it easy, come on make it easy.

|B2|
    A   *D*
Take it easy, take it easy.

    B7
Everybody's got something to hide except for me and

    E
my monkey.

Inst. | *D* *G* | *E* *G* | *D*   ‖

|A3|
  E
Your inside is out and your outside is in,

Your outside is in and your inside is out,

So come on come on

|C2|
  E
Come on is such a joy, come on is such a joy,

Come on make it easy, come on make it easy.

|B3|
    A   *D*
Make it easy, make it easy.

    B7
Everybody's got something to hide except for me and

    E
my monkey.

Inst. | *D* *G* | *E* *G* | *D*   ‖

|OUTRO| Come on, come on come on

Inst. | *C#* *(D)* *C#* *(D)* | *C#* *(D)* *C#* *(D)* | *C#* *(D)* *C#* *(D)* ‖
‖: *E* *Esus4* *A* | *E* *Esus4* *A* :‖   *... fade out*

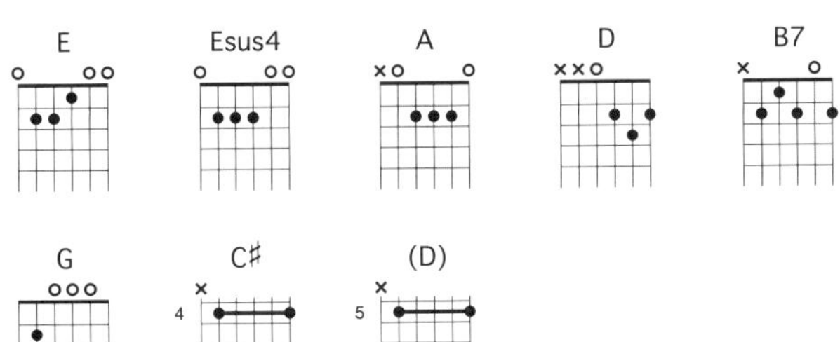

Fixing A Hole

Words & Music by
John Lennon & Paul McCartney

Inst. | *F* | *Caug* | *Fm7* | *Bb9* ||

A1
F   *Caug*   *Fm7*   *Fm6*
I'm fixing a hole where the rain gets in

Fm7   *Bb9*
And stops my mind from wandering

Fm7   *Bb9*   *(Fm7)*   *Bb7*
Where will it go

A2
F   *Caug*   *Fm7*   *Fm6*
I'm filling the cracks that ran through the door

Fm7   *Bb9*
And kept my mind from wandering

Fm7   *Bb9*   *(Fm7)*   *Bb7*
Where will it go

B1
F   *Gm/C*   *F*
And it really doesn't matter if I'm wrong

I'm right

Gm/C   *F*
Where I belong I'm right

Gm/C   *F*
Where I belong.

C   *G7*   *C*   *G7*
See the people standing there who disagree and never win

C   *G7*   *C*
And wonder why they don't get in my door.

F Caug Fm7 Fm6
A3 I'm painting my room in the colourful way

Fm7 Bb9
And when my mind is wandering

Fm7 Bb9
There I will go.

(Fm7) Bb9
Ooh-ooh uh-uh, hey, hey, hey.

Inst.

F Caug	*Fm7 Fm6*	*Fm7*	*Bb9*
Fm7	*Bb9*	*Fm7*	*Bb9*

F Gm/C
B2 And it really doesn't matter if

F
I'm wrong I'm right

Gm/C F
Where I belong I'm right

Gm/C F
Where I belong.

C G7 C
Silly people run around they worry me

G7 C G7 C
And never ask me why they don't get past my door.

F Caug Fm7 Fm6
A4 I'm taking the time for a number of things

Fm7 Bb9
That weren't important yesterday

Fm7 Bb9 (Fm7) Bb7
And I still go.

F Caug Fm7 Fm6
OUTRO ‖: I'm fixing a hole where the rain gets in

Fm7 Bb9
And stops my mind from wandering

Fm7 Bb9
Where it will go.

(Fm7) Bb9
Where it will go. :‖ *... fade out*

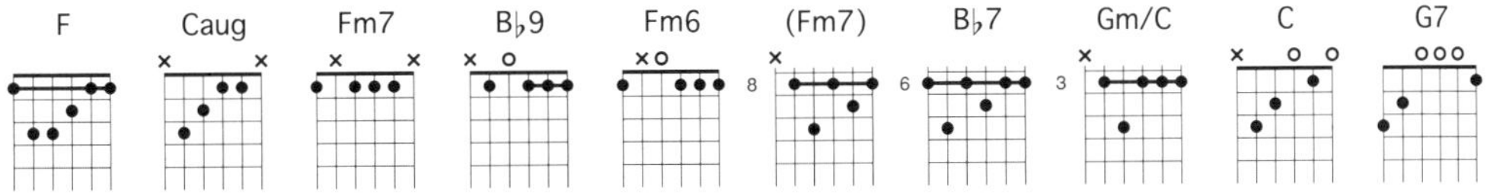

For No One

Words & Music by
John Lennon & Paul McCartney

** CAPO : 2 FRET.*

A1
A   *A/G#*
Your day breaks, your mind aches,

F#m   *F#m/E*   *D*   *G*
You find that all the words of kindness linger on

        A
When she no longer needs you

A2
A   *A/G#*
She wakes up, she makes up,

F#m   *F#m/E*   *D*   *G*
She takes her time and doesn't feel she has to hurry,

    A
She no longer needs you.

B1
    Bm   *F#7*
And in her eyes you see nothing,

Bm   *F#7*
No sign of love behind the tears cried for no one,

Bm   *Esus4* *E*
A love that should have lasted years.

A3
A   *A/G#*
You want her, you need her,

F#m   *F#m/E*   *D*   *G*
And yet you don't believe her when she said her love is dead,

    A
You think she needs you.

Inst. ‖ *A* *A/G#* | *F#m* *F#m/E* | *D* *G* | *A* ‖

B2

         Bm   *F#7*
And in her eyes you see nothing,

Bm   *F#7*
No sign of love behind the tears cried for no one,

Bm   *Esus4* *E*
A love that should have lasted years.

A4

A   *A/G#*
You stay home, she goes out,

F#m   *F#m/E*   *D*   *G*
She says that long ago she knew someone but now he's gone,

     A
She doesn't need him.

A5

A   *A/G#*
Your day breaks, your mind aches,

F#m   *F#m/E*   *D*   *G*
There will be time when all the things she said will fill your head,

A
You won't forget her.

B3

         Bm   *F#7*
And in her eyes you see nothing,

Bm   *F#7*
No sign of love behind the tears cried for no one,

Bm   *Esus4* *E*
A love that should have lasted years.

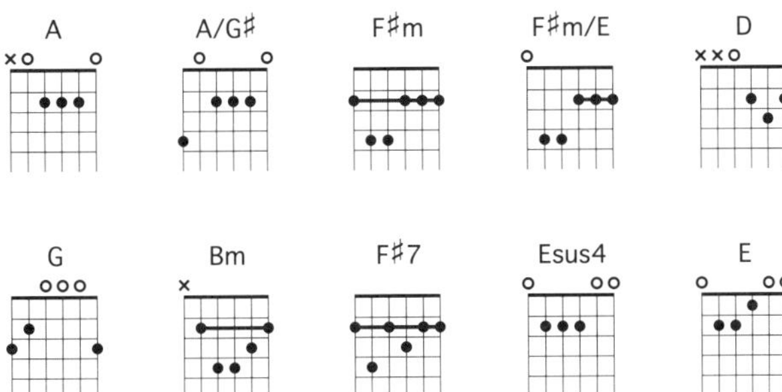

For You Blue

** CAPO : 5 FRET.*

Words & Music by
George Harrison

Inst. | A7 | D7 | B7 | E7 | E7 ‖

A1
    A7   *D7*   *A7*
Because you're sweet and lovely girl I love you,

   D7   *A7*
Because you're sweet and lovely girl it's true,

 E7   *D7*   *A7* *E7*
I love you more than ever girl I do.

A2
    A7   *D7*   *A7*
I want you in the morning girl I love you,

   D7   *A7*
I want you at the moment I feel blue,

   E7   *D7*   *A7* *E7*
I'm living every moment girl for you.

Inst. | A7 | D7 | A7 | A7 | D7 | D7 |
A7	A7	E7	D7	A7	E7
A7	D7	A7	A7
D7	D7	A7	A7
E7	D7	A7	E7 ‖

A7 *D7* *A7*
A3 I've loved you from the moment I saw you,

D7 *A7*
You looked at me 'all you had to do,

E7 *D7* *A7* *E7*
I feel it now I hope you feel it too.

A7 *D7* *A7*
A4 Because you're sweet and lovely girl I love you,

D7 *A7*
Because you're sweet and lovely girl it's true,

E7 *D7* *A7*
I love you more than ever girl I do.

E7 *A7*
Rhythm and blues!

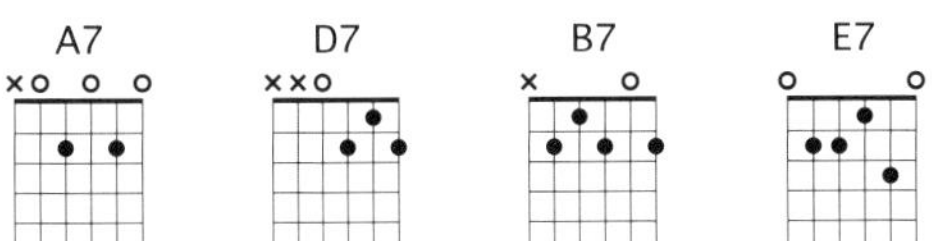

From Me To You

Words & Music by
John Lennon & Paul McCartney

`INTRO`
```
      C                    Am
Da da da da da dum dum da.

      C                    Am
Da da da da da dum dum da.
```

`A1`
```
        C                 Am
If there's anything that you want,

        C            G7
If there's anything I can do,

      F                 Am
Just call on me and I'll send it along

    C       G7     C   Am
With love from me to you.
```

`A2`
```
        C                 Am
I've got everything that you want,

      C                 G7
Like a heart that is oh, so true.

      F                 Am
Just call on me and I'll send it along

    C       G7     C   Am
With love from me to you.
```

`B1`
```
    Gm                C
I got arms that long to hold you

      F
And keep you by my side.

      D7
I got lips that long to kiss you

      G                Gaug
And keep you satisfied, oooh.
```

C   *Am*
A3 If there's anything that you want,

C   *G7*
If there's anything I can do,

F   *Am*
Just call on me and I'll send it along

C   *G7*   *C*   *Am*
With love from me to you.

C   *Am*
C1   From me,

C   *G7*
          To you.

F   *Am*
Just call on me and I'll send it along,

C   *G7*   *C*   *C7*
With love from me to you.

Gm   *C*
B2 I got arms that long to hold you

F
And keep you by my side.

D7
I got lips that long to kiss you

G   *Gaug*
And keep you satisfied, oooh.

C   *Am*
A4 If there's anything that you want,

C   *G7*
If there's anything I can do,

F   *Am*
Just call on me and I'll send it along

C   *G7*   *C*
With love from me to you.

Am   *Am(maj7)*   *C*   *Am*
To you,   to you,   to you.

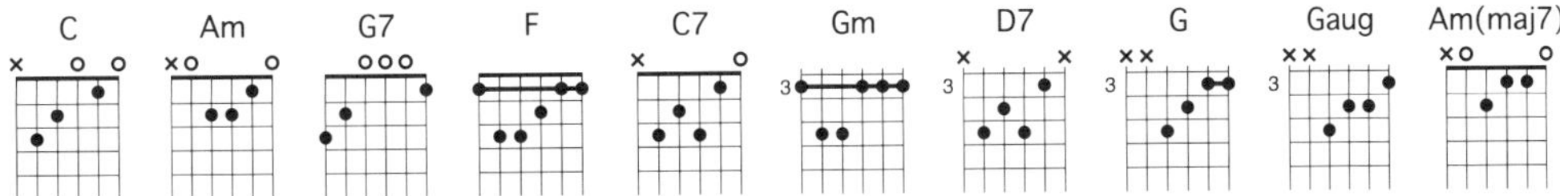

Get Back

Words & Music by
John Lennon & Paul McCartney

Inst. || *A5* | *A5* | *A5* | *A5* *G* *D/A* ||

A1
A5
Jojo was a man who thought he was a loner

D   *A5*
But he knew it couldn't last.

Jojo left his home in Tucson, Arizona

D   *A5*
For some California grass.

B1
A7   *D7*   *A5*   *G* *D/A*
Get back, get back, get back to where you once belonged.

A7   *D7*   *A5*
Get back, get back. get back to where you once belonged.

Get back Jojo.

Inst. || *A5* | *A5* | *D* | *A5* *G* *D/A* |
| *A5* | *A5* | *D* | *A5* *G* *D/A* |

B2
A7   *D7*   *A5*   *G* *D/A*
Get back, get back, get back to where you once belonged.

A7   *A5*   *D*
Get back, get back. get back to where you once belonged.

A5
Get back Jo.

Inst. || *A5* | *A5* | *D* | *A5* *G* *D/A* |
| *A5* | *A5* | *D* | *A5* *G* *D/A* |

A2 *A7*
Sweet Loretta Martin thought she was a woman

D　　　　　　　　　　*A5*
But she was another man

All the girls around her say she's got it coming

D　　　　　　　　　*A5*
But she gets it while she can

B3 *A7*　　　　　　　*D7*　　　　　　　　　*A5*　　　*G D/A*
Get back, get back, get back to where you once belonged.

　　A7　　　　　　　*D7*　　　　　　　　　*A5*
Get back, get back. get back to where you once belonged.

Get back Loretta.

Inst. | *A5* | *A5* | *D* | *A5 G D/A* |
| *A5* | *A5* | *D* | *A5 G D/A* |

B4 *A7*　　　　　　　*D7*　　　　　　　　　*A5*　　　*G D/A*
Get back, get back, get back to where you once belonged.

　　A7　　　　　　　*D7*　　　　　　　*D*
Get back, get back. get back to where you once belonged. Ooh.

Inst. | *A5* | *A5* | *D* | *A5 G D/A* |
| *A5* | *A5* | *D* | *A5 G D/A* ‖　*... fade out*

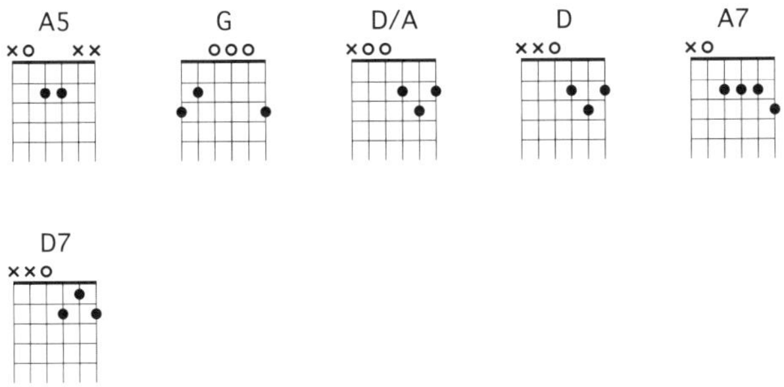

A5　　　G　　　D/A　　　D　　　A7

D7

Getting Better

Words & Music by
John Lennon & Paul McCartney

Inst. | F | F ‖

A1
```
      C                           Dm
It's getting better all the time

       G                         C/G
I used to get mad at my school,

        G                               C/G
The teachers who taught me weren't cool.

         G
You're holding me down, turning me round,

                           C/G
Filling me up with your rules.
```

B1
```
        C                       Dm
I've got to admit it's getting better

              Em              F
A little better all the time

        C                       Dm
I have to admit it's getting better

              Em            F
It's getting better since you've been mine.
```

Inst. | G | G C/G ‖

A2
```
      G           C/G         G     C/G
Me used to be a angry young man

      G          C/G        G    C/G
Me hiding me head in the sand

        G            C/G
You gave me the word

      G         C/G
I finally heard

        G         C/G        G    C/G
I'm doing the best that I can.
```

B2
    C   *Dm*   *Em*   *F*
I've got to admit it's getting better   a little better all the time

    C   *Dm*
I have to admit it's getting better

           Em   *F*
It's getting better since you've been mine.

F
Getting so much better all the time.

C1
 C   *Dm*   *Em*   *F*
It's getting better all the time, better, better, better.

 C   *Dm*   *Em*   *F*
It's getting better all the time, better, better, better.

Inst. | *C* | *G* ||

A3
 G
I used to be cruel to my woman,

                                       G   *C/G*
I beat her and kept her apart from the things that she loved.

G   *C/G*   *G*   *C/G*   *G*   *C/G*   *G* *C/G*
Man I was mean but I'm changing my scene and I'm doing the best that I can.

B3
    C   *Dm*   *Em*   *F*
I admit it's getting better,   a little better all the time

C   *Dm*
Yes I admit it's getting better

           Em   *F*
It's getting better since you've been mine.

F   *C*
Getting so much better all the time.

C2
 C   *Dm*   *Em*   *F*
It's getting better all the time, better, better, better.

 C   *Dm*   *Em*   *F*
It's getting better all the time, better, better, better.

F   *C*
Getting so much better all the time.

F   C   Dm   G   C/G   Em

Girl

Words & Music by
John Lennon & Paul McCartney

** CAPO : 8 FRET.*

A1
```
     Em          B7          Em      Em7
Is there anybody going to listen to my story
```

```
Am                          G    B7
All about the girl who came to stay?
```

```
          Em              B7          Em        Em7
She's the kind of girl you want so much it makes you sorry,
```

```
Am                      Em
Still, you don't regret a single day.
```

B1
```
     G     Bm    Am    D7
Ah, girl
```

```
G     Bm    Am    D7
Girl, girl.
```

A2
```
     Em          B7          Em      Em7
When I think of all the times I've tried so hard to leave her,
```

```
Am                          G    B7
She will turn to me and start to cry.
```

```
          Em          B7          Em      Em7
And she promises the earth to me and I believe her.
```

```
Am                      Em
After all this times I don't know why.
```

B2
```
     G     Bm    Am    D7
Ah, girl
```

```
G     Bm    Am    D7
Girl, girl
```

C1
```
Am                              E
She's the kind of girl who puts you down when friends are there,
```

```
        Am    E
You feel a fool.
```

```
Am                              E
When you say she's looking good, she acts as if it's understood.
```

```
        Am        C
She's cool, ooh, ooh, ooh
```


B3
G   Bm   Am   D7
Girl

G   Bm   Am   D7
Girl, girl

A3
          Em   B7   Em   Em7
Was she told when she was young the pain would lead to pleasure?

Am   G   B7
Did she understand it when they said,

          Em   B7   Em   Em7
That a man must break his back to earn his day of leisure?

 Am   Em
Will she still believe it when he's dead?

B4
          G   Bm   Am   D7
Ah, girl

G   Bm   Am   D7
Girl, girl

Inst. | *Em   B7* | *Em   Em7* | *Am* | *G   B7* |
           | *Em   B7* | *Em   Em7* | *Am* | *Em* ||

B5
          G   Bm   Am   D7
Ah, girl

G   Bm   Am   D7
Girl, girl   *... fade out*

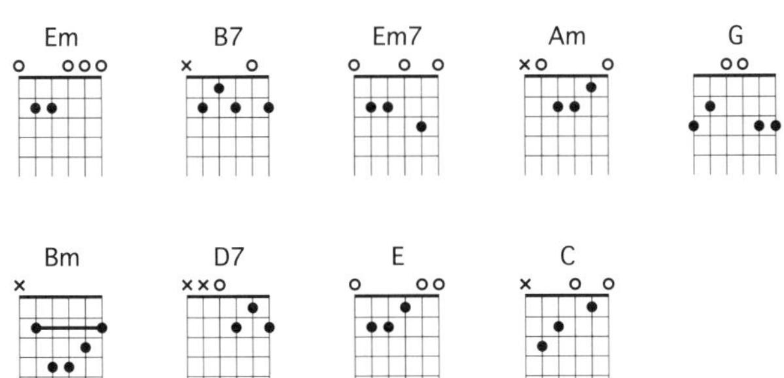

Glass Onion

Words & Music by
John Lennon & Paul McCartney

```
      Am              F7
A1  I told you about strawberry fields

      Am                   F7
    You know the place where nothing is real

      Am              Gm7            C7
    Well here's another place you can go

          Gm7            C7
    Where everything flows.

       F7                        D7
    Looking through the bent backed tulips

         F7                D7
    To see how the other half live

       F7                  G
    Looking through a glass onion.
```

```
      Am              F7
A2  I told you about the walrus and me-man

      Am                   F7
    You know that we're as close as can be-man

      Am              Gm7            C7
    Well here's another clue for you all

          Gm7          C7
    The walrus was Paul.

       F7                        D7
    Standing on the cast iron shore-yeah

    F7                          D7
    Lady Madonna trying to make ends meet-yeah

    F7                        G
    Looking through a glass onion.
```


A3

Am   *Amb6*
    Oh yeah,

Am6   *Am7*
Oh yeah, oh Yeah!

F7   *G*
Looking through a glass onion.

A4

Am   *F7*
I told you about the fool on the hill

Am   *F7*
I tell you man he living there still

Am   *Gm7*   *C7*
Well here's another place you can be

Gm7   *C7*
Listen to me.

F7   *D7*
Fixing a hole in the ocean

F7   *D7*
Trying to make a dove-tail joint-yeah

F7
Looking through a glass onion.   *... fade out*

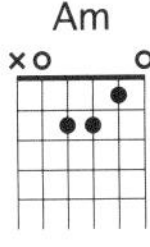

Am

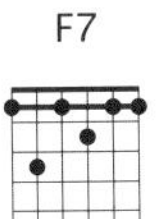

F7

Gm7

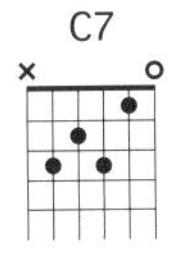

C7

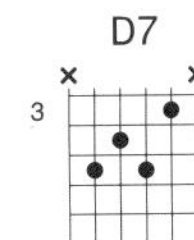

D7

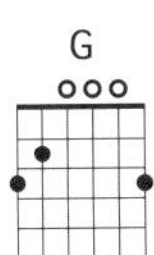

G

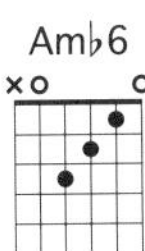

Amb6

Am6

Am7

Golden Slumbers

Words & Music by
John Lennon & Paul McCartney

Inst. | *Am* ||

Am7   *Dm*
A1 Once there was a way to get back homeward

G7   *C*
Once there was a way to get back home

E7   *Am*   *Dsus2*
Sleep pretty darling do not cry

G7   *C*
And I will sing a lullaby

C   *Fadd9*   *C*
B1 Golden slumbers fill your eyes

                 Fadd9   *C*
Smiles awake you when you rise

E7   *Am*   *Dsus2*
Sleep pretty darling do not cry

G7   *C*
And I will sing a lullaby

Am7   *Dm*
A2 Once there was a way to get back homeward

G7   *C*
Once there was a way to get back home

E7   *Am*   *Dsus2*
Sleep pretty darling do not cry

G7   *C*
And I will sing a lullaby

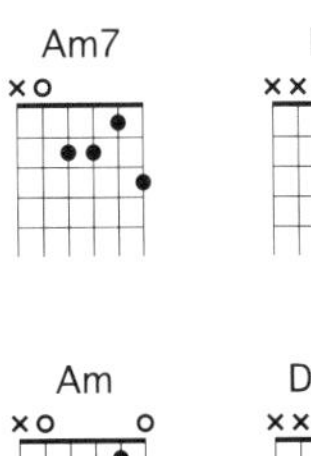

Am7

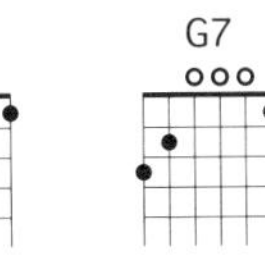

Dm

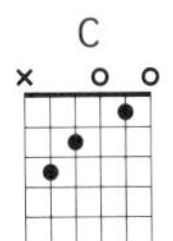

G7

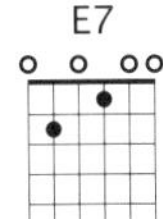

C

E7

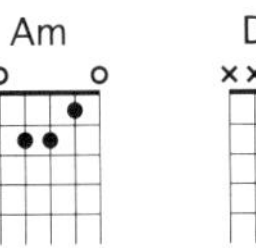

Am

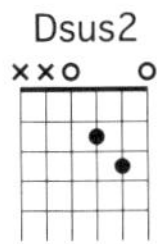

Dsus2

Fadd9

Good Day Sunshine

Words & Music by
John Lennon & Paul McCartney

Inst. | *E* | *E* | *E* | *E* ‖

A1
B　　　　*F#*　　　*B*　　　*F#*
Good day sunshine, good day sunshine,

E　　　　*E7*
Good day sunshine.

B1
　　　　　A　　*F#7*　　　　*B7*
I need to laugh and when the sun is out

E7　　　　　　　　*A*
I've got something I can laugh about

　　　　　F#7　　　*B7*
I feel good in a special way

E7　　　　　　　　*A*
I'm in love and it's a sunny day

A2
B　　　　*F#*　　　*B*　　　*F#*
Good day sunshine, good day sunshine,

E　　　　*E7*
Good day sunshine.

B2
　　　　　A　　*F#*　　　*B7*
We take a walk, the sun is shining down

E7　　　　　　　　*A*
Burns my feet as they touch the ground

Inst. | *D B7* | *E7* | *A7* | *D* ‖

A3
B　　　　*F#*　　　*B*　　　*F#*
Good day sunshine, good day sunshine,

E　　　　*E7*
Good day sunshine

B3

       A   *F#7*   *B7*
Then we'd lie beneath the shady tree

E7   *A*
I love her and she's loving me

              F#7   *B7*
She feels good, she knows she's looking fine

E7   *A*
I'm so proud to know that she is mine.

A4

B   *F#*   *B*   *F#*
Good day sunshine, good day sunshine,

E   *E7*
Good day sunshine.

A5

B   *F#*   *B*   *F#*
Good day sunshine, good day sunshine,

E   *E7*
Good day sunshine.

OUTRO

F
‖: Good day sunshine. :‖   *... fade out*

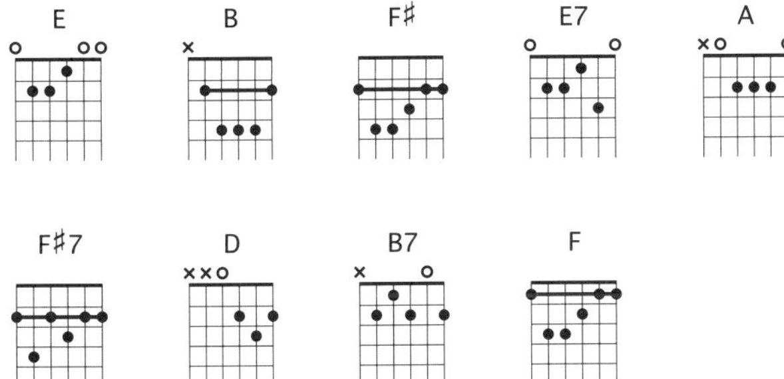

Good Morning, Good Morning

Words & Music by
John Lennon & Paul McCartney

|INTRO| *A D*   *A*   *D*
Good morning, good morning,

     A   *D*
Good morning, good morning,

     A
Good morning, ah!

|A1| *A*   *Em* *G*   *A*
Nothing to do to save his life call his wife in

     Em *G*   *A*
Nothing to say but what a day how's your boy been

D   *E*
Nothing to do it's up to you

     A   *Em* *G*
I've got nothing to say but it's O.K.

     A   *D*
Good morning, good morning,

     A
Good morning, ah!

|A2| *A*   *Em*   *G*   *A*
Going to work don't want to go feeling low down

     Em   *G*   *A*   *D*
Heading for home you start to roam then you're in town

|B1| *A*   *D*   *A*
Everybody knows there's nothing doing

     D   *A*
Everything is closed it's like a ruin

     D   *A*
Everyone you see is half asleep.

     D   *A*
And you're on your own you're in the street

<pre>
     A   Em   G   A
A3 After a while you start to smile now you feel cool.

               Em   G   A
    Then you decide to take a walk by the old school.

    D   E
    Nothing has changed it's still the same

            A   Em   G
    I've got nothing to say but it's O.K.

            A   D
    Good morning, good morning,

            A
    Good morning, ah!
</pre>

Inst. ┃ *A Em G* ┃ *G   A* ┃ *A Em G* ┃ *G   A* ┃ *A   D* ┃┃

<pre>
     A   D   A
B2 People running round it's five o'clock.

                   D   A
    Everywhere in town is getting dark.

                 D   A
    Everyone you see is full of life.

                D   A
    It's time for tea and meet the wife.
</pre>

<pre>
     A   Em   G   A
A4 Somebody needs to know the time, glad that I'm here.

               Em   G   A
    Watching the skirts you start to flirt now you're in gear.

    D   E
    Go to a show you hope she goes.

            A   Em   G
    I've got nothing to say but it's O.K.

            A   D   A
    Good morning, good morning, good!
</pre>

<pre>
                A   D   A   D
OUTRO ┃: Good morning, good morning, good!   :┃ ... fade out
</pre>

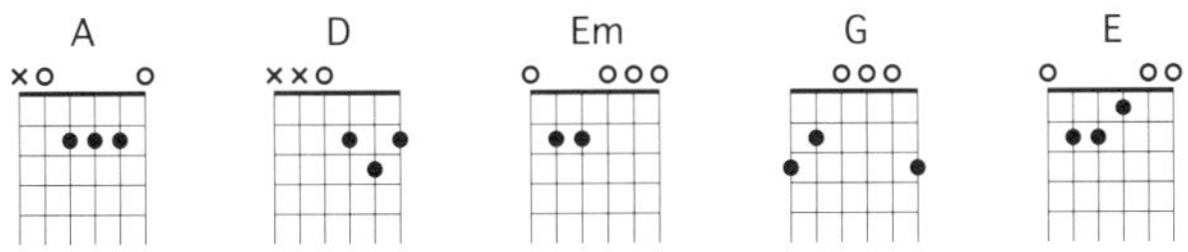

Good Night

Words & Music by
John Lennon & Paul McCartney

Inst. | Gmaj7 C/G | Gmaj7 C/G | G   Am/G |
| G   Am/G | G   Bm7 | Am7   D7 ||

G   Bm7   Am7
A1 Now it's time to say good night

Bm7   Am7   Am/G   D7/F#
Good night sleep tight

G   Bm7   Am7
Now the sun turns out his light

Bm7   Am7   Am/G   D7/F#
Good night sleep tight

Gmaj7   D7/G   Gmaj7   D7/G
Dream sweet dreams for me

G   C/G   G   C/G
Dream sweet dreams for you.

G   Bm7   Am7
A2 Close your eyes and I'll close mine

Bm7   Am7   Am/G   D7/F#
Good night sleep tight

G   Bm7   Am7
Now the moon begins to shine

Bm7   Am7   Am/G   D7/F#
Good night sleep tight

Gmaj7   D7/G   Gmaj7   D7/G
Dream sweet dreams for me

G   C/G   G   C/G
Dream sweet dreams for you.

Inst. ‖ *G Am7* | *A7 Dm7* | *G7 C/G* | *D7/F# Am7 D7* ‖

|A3|
G　　　　*Bm7*　　　*Am7*
Close your eyes and I'll close mine

Bm7　　*Am7*　*Am/G*　*D7/F#*
Good night sleep tight

G　　　　*Bm7*　　　*Am7*
Now the sun turns out his light

Bm7　　*Am7*　*Am/G*　*D7/F#*
Good night sleep tight

Gmaj7　　　　　*D7/G*　　　*Gmaj7*　*D7/G*
Dream sweet dreams for me

G　　　　　*C/G*　　　　*G*　　*C/G*
Dream sweet dreams for you.

Inst. ‖ *G Bm7* | *Am7 D7* | *G Bm7* | *Am7 D7* | *G*　　　‖

Gmaj7 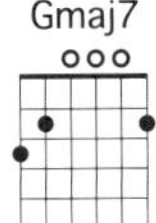　C/G 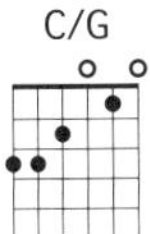　G 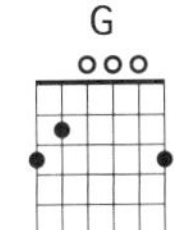　Am/G 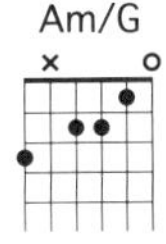　Bm7 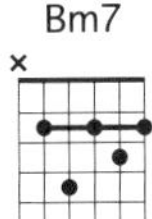

Am7 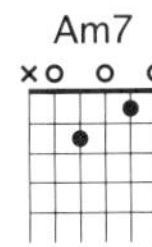　D7 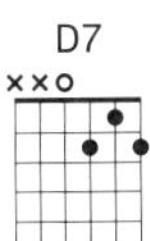　D7/F♯ 　D7/G 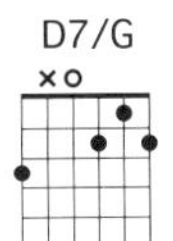　A7 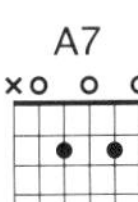

Dm7 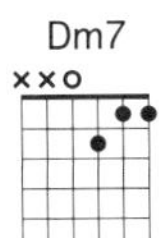　G7 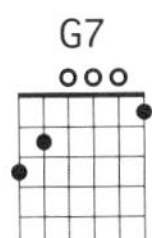

Got To Get You Into My Life

Words & Music by
John Lennon & Paul McCartney

Inst. | *G* | *G* | *G* | *G* ||

A1
G
I was alone, I took a ride,

                                  F/G
I didn't know what I would find there

G   *F/G*
Another road where maybe I could see another kind of mind there

B1
Bm   *Bm(maj7)*   *Bm7*   *Bm/G#*
Ooh,   then I suddenly see you,

Bm   *Bm(maj7)*   *Bm7*   *Bm/G#*
Ooh,   did I tell you I need you

C   *C/B*   *Am7* *D7*   *G*
Every single day of my life

A2
G
You didn't run, you didn't lie

                                  F/G
You knew I wanted just to hold you

G
And had you gone you knew in time we'd meet again

                  F/G
For I had told you

B2
Bm   *Bm(maj7)*   *Bm7*   *Bm/G#*
Ooh,   you were meant to be near me

Bm   *Bm(maj7)*   *Bm7*   *Bm/G#*
Ooh,   and I want you hear me

C   *C/B*   *Am7* *D7*   *G*
Say we'll be together every day

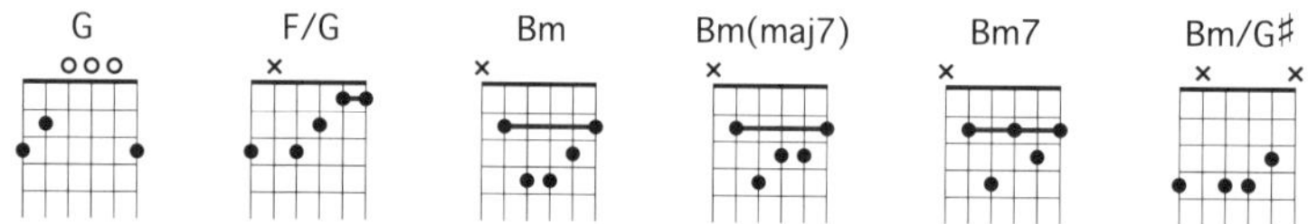

C1
```
G                    C   D
Got to get you into my life
```

Inst. | G | G ‖

A3
```
G
What can I do, what can I be,
```
```
                          F/G
When I'm with you I want to stay there
```
```
G
If I'm true I'll never leave
```
```
                        F/G
And if I do I know the way there
```

B3
```
Bm    Bm(maj7)   Bm7        Bm/G#
Ooh,      then I suddenly see you,
```
```
Bm    Bm(maj7)   Bm7        Bm/G#
Ooh,      did I tell you I need you
```
```
C       C/B    Am7 D7     G
Every single day of my life
```

C2
```
G                    C   D
Got to get you into my life
```

Inst. | G | G | G F/G | C | G |
```
     G                    C   D
I've got to get you into my life
```

OUTRO
```
G
I was alone, I took a ride,
```

I didn't know what I would find there

Another road where maybe I could see another kind of mind there

Then suddenly I see you,

Did I tell you I need you, every single day,...

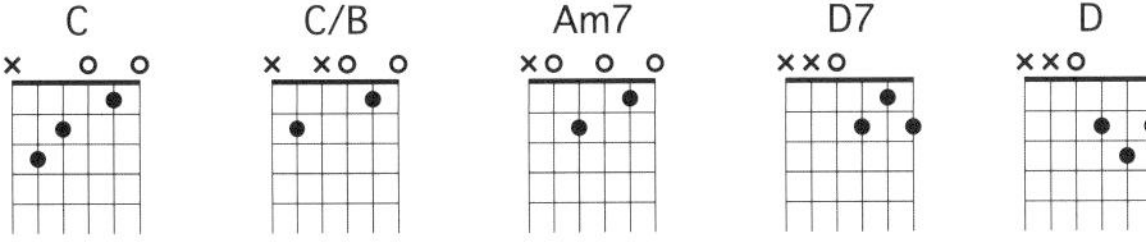

Happiness Is A Warm Gun

Words & Music by
John Lennon & Paul McCartney

INTRO
   Am7 *Am6* *Em(add9)* *Em*
She's not a girl who misses much

Am7   *Am6* *Em(add9)* *Em*
Do do do do do do do do, oh yeah.

A1
Dm13
She's well acquainted with the touch of the velvet hand

        Am
Like a lizard on a window pane.

   Dm7
The man in the crowd with the multicoloured mirrors

   Am
On his hobnail boots

Dm7
Lying with his eyes while his hands are busy

    Am
Working overtime

Dm7
A soap impression of his wife which he ate

     Am
And donated to the Nation Trust.

Inst. ‖ *A7* | *A7* | *C* *Am* ‖

A2
A7
I need a fix 'cause I'm going down

Down to the bits that I left uptown

C   *Am*
I need a fix cause I'm going down

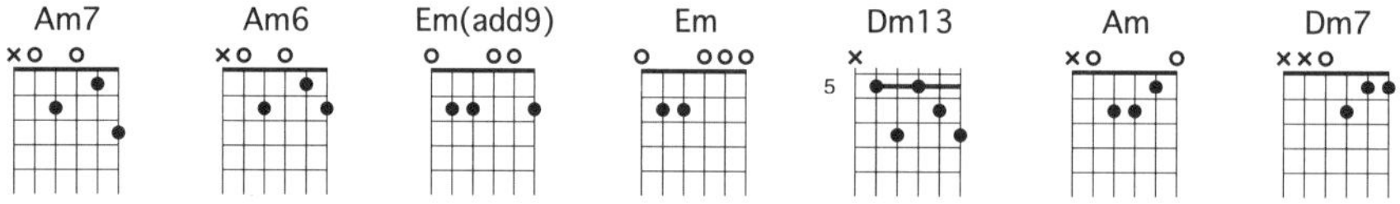

Am7   Am6   Em(add9)   Em   Dm13   Am   Dm7

A7　　　　　　　*C*
B1 Mother Superior jump the gun

A7　　　　　　　*G*
Mother Superior jump the gun

A7　　　　　　　*C*
Mother Superior jump the gun

A7　　　　　　　*G*
Mother Superior jump the gun.

A7　　　　　　　*C*
Mother Superior jump the gun

A7　　　　　　　*G*
Mother Superior jump the gun.

C　　　*Am*　　*F*　　　　　*G*
C1 Happiness is a warm gun

C　　　*Am*　　*F*　　　　　*G*
Happiness is a warm gun, momma.

C　　　*Am*　　*F*　　*G*
When I hold you in my arms

C　　　*Am*　　*F*　　*G*
And I feel my finger on your trigger

C Am　　*F*　　　　　　*G*
I know nobody can do me no harm

C　　　　　*Am*　　*F*　　　*G*
Because happiness is a warm gun, momma

C　　　*Am*　　*F*　　　　　*G*
C2 Happiness is a warm gun, yes it is

Fm
Happiness is a warm, yes it is

　　　　C　　　　　　*Am F*　　*G*
Gun.　　　　(Happiness… bang, bang, shoot, shoot)

　　　　　　　　　　C　　　　　*Am*
Well don't you know that happiness

　　F　　　　　　*G*　　*C*
Is a warm gun, momma.

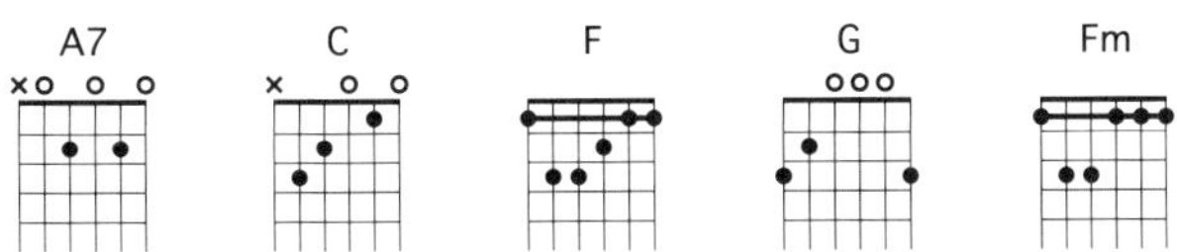

Hello Goodbye

Words & Music by
John Lennon & Paul McCartney

A1
F6   *C*
You say yes, I say no.

G7   *Am*   *G7*   *Am*
You say stop and I say go go go,

    G7   *G*   *G7*   *F/G*
Oh no.   You say goodbye and I say hello

B1
C C/B   *Am*   *Am/G*
   Hello hello

      F   *Ab*
I don't know why you say goodbye, I say hello

C C/B   *Am*   *Am/G*
   Hello hello

      F   *Bb9*   *C*
I don't know why you say goodbye, I say hello

A2
F6   *C*
I say high, you say low.

G7   *Am*   *G7*   *Am*
You say why and I say I don't know,

    G7   *G*   *G7*   *F/G*
Oh no.   You say goodbye and I say hello

B2
C C/B   *Am*   *Am/G*
   Hello hello

      F   *Ab*
I don't know why you say goodbye, I say hello

C C/B   *Am*   *Am/G*
   Hello hello

      F   *Bb9*   *C*
I don't know why you say goodbye, I say hello.

F6   C   G7   Am   G   F/G   C/B

A3
F6   C   G7
Why why why why why why

      Am   G7   Am
Do you say goodbye goodbye?

      G7   G   G7   F/G
Oh no.   You say goodbye and I say hello

B3
C C/B   Am   Am/G
  Hello hello

            F   Ab
I don't know why you say goodbye, I say hello.

C C/B   Am   Am/G
  Hello hello

            F   Bb9   C
I don't know why you say goodbye, I say hello.

A4
F6   C
You say yes I say no

G7   Am   G7   Am
You say stop and I say go go go,

      G7   G   G7   F/G
Oh no.   You say goodbye and I say hello

B4
C C/B   Am   Am/G
  Hello hello

            F   Ab
I don't know why you say goodbye, I say hello

C C/B   Am   Am/G
  Hello hello

            F   Bb9   C
I don't know why you say goodbye, I say hello

B5
C/B   Am   Am/G
  Hello hello

            F   Ab   Ab   Ab/G   Ab/Gb   F
I don't know why you say goodbye, I say hello

      C
hello.

OUTRO
C
‖:Hela heba helloa CHA CHA, hela... :‖   *... fade out*

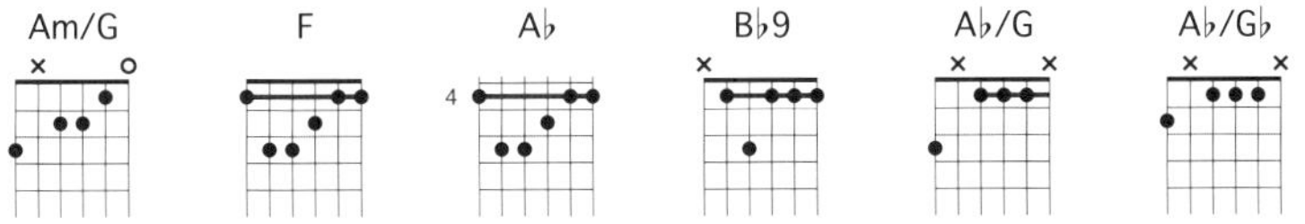

Help!

Words & Music by
John Lennon & Paul McCartney

INTRO
Bm
Help, I need somebody,

G
Help, not just anybody,

E   *A*
Help, you know I need someone,   Help!

A1
A   *C#m*
When I was younger, so much younger than today,

F#m   *D*   *G*   *A*
I never needed anybody's help in any way.

A   *C#m*
But now these days are gone, I'm not so self assured,

F#m   *D*   *G*   *A*
Now I find I've changed my mind and opened up the doors.

B1
Bm
Help me if you can, I'm feeling down

          G
And I do appreciate you being round.

E
Help me, get my feet back on the ground,

              A | *A* *Asus2* | *A* *Asus2* *A* ‖
Won't you please, please help me.

A2
A   *C#m*
And now my life has changed in oh so many ways,

F#m   *D*   *G*   *A*
My independence seems to vanish in the haze.

A   *C#m*
But every now and then I feel so insecure,

F#m   *D*   *G*   *A*
I know that I just need you like I've never done before.

Bm
[B2] Help me if you can, I'm feeling down

      G
And I do appreciate you being round.

E
Help me, get my feet back on the ground,

      A | *A* *Asus2* | *A* *Asus2* *A* ‖
Won't you please, please help me.

A   *C#m*
[A3] When I was younger, so much younger than today,

F#m   *D*   *G*   *A*
I never needed anybody's help in any way.

A   *C#m*
But now these days are gone, I'm not so self assured,

F#m   *D*   *G*   *A*
Now I find I've changed my mind and opened up the doors.

Bm
[B3] Help me if you can, I'm feeling down

      G
And I do appreciate you being round.

E
Help me, get my feet back on the ground,

      A   *F#m*
Won't you please, please help me,

      A   *A6*
Help me, help me, ooh.

Bm   G   E   A   C♯m

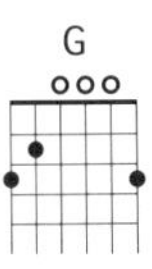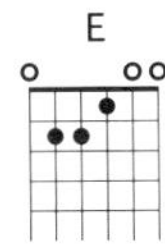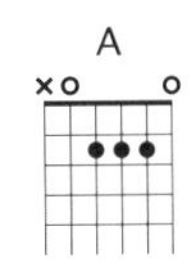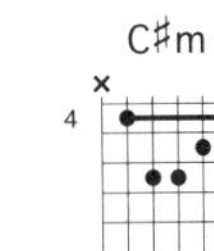

F♯m   D   Asus2   A6

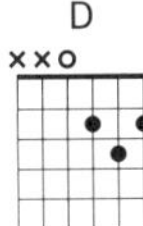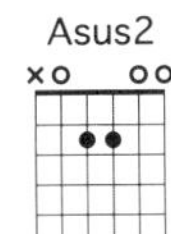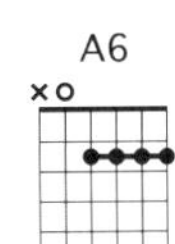

Helter Skelter

Words & Music by
John Lennon & Paul McCartney

Inst. | *(E7)* ‖

(E7)   *(E6)*
A1 When I get to the bottom I go back to the top of the slide

                                              (Eaug)
Where I stop and I turn and I go for a ride

                                                      G
Till I get to the bottom and I see you again.

                  E
Yeah, yeah, yeah!

            E
A2 Do you, don't you want me to love you

I'm coming down fast but I'm miles above you

                  G
Tell me tell me tell me come on tell me the answer

        A   *E*
You may be a lover but you ain't no dancer.

        A   *E*
B1 Helter Skelter, Helter Skelter,

        A   *E*
Helter Skelter. yeah!

Inst. | *E* | *E*   ‖

            E
A3 Will you, won't you want me to make you

I'm coming down fast but don't let me break you

G
Tell me tell me tell me the answer

          A   *E*
You may be a lover but you ain't no dancer. Look out!

B2
   A   *E*
Helter Skelter, Helter Skelter,

   A   *E*
Helter Skelter, yeah!

   E
Look out, cause here she comes.

Inst. | *A* | *E* | *A* | *E*   ‖

A4
      (E7)   *(E6)*
When I get to the bottom I go back to the top of the slide

                              (Eaug)
And I stop and I turn and I go for a ride

                                      G
And I get to the bottom and I see you again

        E
Yeah, yeah, yeah!

A5
   E
Well do you, don't you want me to make you

I'm coming down fast but don't let me break you

G
Tell me tell me tell me the answer

     A   *E*
You may be a lover but you ain't no dancer.

Look out

B3
   A   *E*
Helter Skelter, Helter Skelter,

   A   *E*
Helter Skelter.

Look out, Helter Skelter.

She's coming down fast!

Yes she is Yes she is. coming down fast…

Inst.   ‖: *E* | *E*   :‖   *...fade out*

Her Majesty

Words & Music by
John Lennon & Paul McCartney

| Inst. | ‖ *D* | ‖ |

D   *D/C#*   *D/B*   *D/A*
Her Majesty's a pretty nice girl,

       E7   *A*   *D*
But she doesn't have a lot to say

D   *D/C#*   *D/B*   *D/A*
Her Majesty's a pretty nice girl

       E7   *A*
But she changes from day to day

Bm   *Bsus2*
I want to tell her that I love her a lot

    D7   *G*
But I gotta get a bellyful of wine

Gm6   *D*   *B7*
Her Majesty's a pretty nice girl

   E7   *A6*   *D*
Someday I'm going to make her mine,

  B7
Oh yeah,

   E7   *A6*   *D*
Someday I'm going to make her mine.

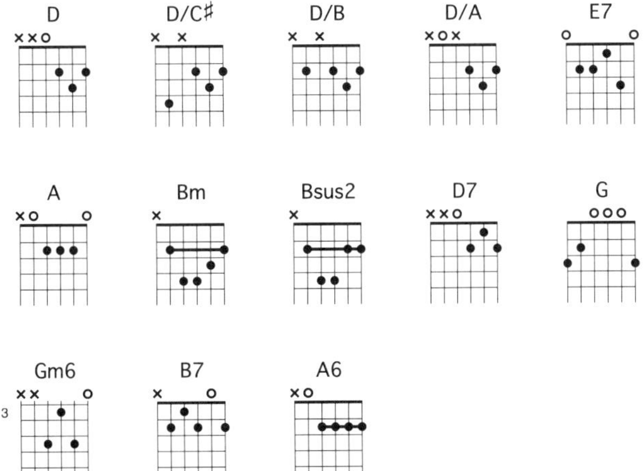

D
D/C♯
D/B
D/A
E7
A
Bm
Bsus2
D7
G
Gm6
B7
A6

Here Comes The Sun

** CAPO : 7 FRET.*

Words & Music by
George Harrison

Inst. ‖: D | D | G | A7 :‖

A1
```
D      Dsus2   D
Here comes the sun,

G               E7
Here comes the sun,

          D   Dsus2   D
And I say it's all   -   right.
```

Inst. | Bmadd11 Asus4 | G6 Asus4 A7 ‖

B1
```
D      Dsus2  D            G               A7        A7sus4
Little dar - ling, it's been a long cold lonely winter,

D      Dsus2  D            G                 A7        A7sus4
Little dar - ling, it feels like years since it's been here.
```

A2
```
D      Dsus2    D
Here comes the sun,

G               E7
Here comes the sun,

          D   Dsus2    D
And I say  it's all   -   right.
```

Inst. | Bmadd11 Asus4 | G6 Asus4 A7 | D | A7 ‖

B2
```
D      Dsus2  D                G             A7        A7sus4
Little dar - ling, the smiles returning to the faces,

D      Dsus2  D                G             A7        A7sus4
Little dar - ling, it seems like years since it's been here.
```

A3
```
D      Dsus2    D
Here comes the sun,

G               E7
Here comes the sun,

          D   Dsus2    D
And I say it's all   -   right. | Bmadd11  Asus4 | G6  A | D | A7 ‖
```


Inst. | *F* | *C* | *G/B* *G* | *D* | *A7* ||

C1
F   *C*   *G/B* *G*   *D*   *A7*
Sun, sun, sun, here it comes…

F   *C*   *G/B* *G*   *D*   *A7*
Sun, sun, sun, here it comes…

F   *C*   *G/B* *G*   *D*   *A7*
Sun, sun, sun, here it comes…

F   *C*   *G/B* *G*   *D*   *A7*
Sun, sun, sun, here it comes…

F   *C*   *G/B* *G*   *D*   *A7*
Sun, sun, sun, here it comes…

Inst. | *A7* | *A7sus4* | *A* | *A7sus4* *A* ||

B3
D   *Dsus2* *D*   *G*   *A7*   *A7sus4*
Little dar - ling, I feel that ice is slowly melting,

D   *Dsus2* *D*   *G*   *A7*   *A7sus4*
Little dar - ling, it seems like years since it's been clear.

A4
D   *Dsus2*   *D*
Here comes the sun,

G   *E7*
Here comes the sun,

                D *Dsus2*   *D*
And I say it's all - right.

Inst. || *Bmadd11* *Asus4* | *G6* *Asus4* *A7* ||

A5
D   *Dsus2*   *D*
Here comes the sun,

G   *E7*
Here comes the sun,

D   *Dsus2* *D*
It's all - right.

Inst. || *Bmadd11* *Asus4* | *G6* *Asus4* *A7* ||

D   *Dsus2* *D*
It's all - right.

Inst. || *Bmadd"* *Asus4* | *G6* *Asus4* *A7* |
         | *F*   *C* | *G/B*   *G* | *D/A* ||

Here, There And Everywhere

Words & Music by
John Lennon & Paul McCartney

|A3|
G   *Am*
Everywhere,

Bm   *C*   *G*   *Am*
Knowing that love is to share

Bm   *C*   *F#m7*   *B7*
Each one believing that love never dies

F#m7   *B7*   *Em*   *Am*   *Am7*   *D7*
Watching her eyes and hoping I'm always there

|B2|
   F7   *Bb*   *Gm*
I want her everywhere,

      Cm   *D7*   *Gm*
And if she's beside me, I know I need never care

Cm   *D7*
But to love her is to need her

|A4|
G   *Am*
Everywhere,

Bm   *C*   *G*   *Am*
Knowing that love is to share,

Bm   *C*   *F#m7*   *B7*
Each one believing that love never dies,

F#m7   *B7*   *Em*   *Am*   *Am7*   *D7*
Watching her eyes and hoping I'm always there.

|OUTRO|
     G   *Am*
I will be there

    Bm   *C*
And everywhere,

G   *Am*   *Bm*   *C*   *G*
Here, there and everywhere.

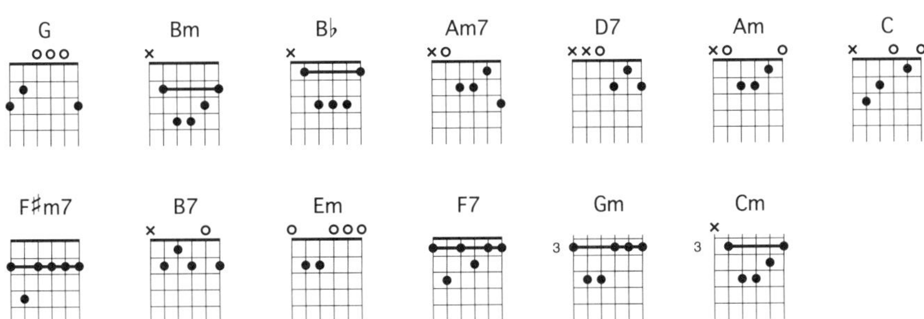

Hey Bulldog

Words & Music by
John Lennon & Paul McCartney

Inst. | B7 | B7 | B7 | B7 | B7 | B7 ||

A1
B7 / F#m7
Sheep dog standing in the rain,

B7 / F#m7
Bullfrog, doing it again.

A / F#m7 / E / E7
Some Kind of happiness is measured out in miles.

A / F#m7 / B7
What makes you think you're something special when you smile?

A2
B7 / F#m7
Child-like, no one understands,

B7 / F#m7
Jack knife in your sweaty hands,

A / F#m7 / E / E7
Some kind of innocence is measured out in years,

A / F#m7 / B7
You don't know what it's like to listen to your fears

B1
Bm / Bmaug / Bm6
You can talk to me,

Bm7 / E / Emaug
You can talk to me,

Em6 / Em7
You can talk to me,

Bm / Em
if you're lonely, you can talk to me.

Inst. | B7 | B7 | B7 | B7 |
| B7 | F#m7 | B7 | F#m7 |
| A F#m7 | E E7 | A F#m7 | B7 ||

|A3| **B7**   **F#m7**
Big man, walking in the park,

B7   **F#m7**
Wigwam, frightened of the dark.

A   **F#m7**   **E**   **E7**
Some kind of solitude is measured out in you.

A   **F#m7**   **B7**
You think you know me but you haven't got a clue.

|B2| **Bm**   **Bmaug**   **Bm6**
You can talk to me,

Bm7   **Em**   **Emaug**
You can talk to me,

Em6   **Em7**
You can talk to me,

         Bm   **Em**
if you're lonely, you can talk to me.

Inst. | **B7** | **B7** | **B7** | **B7** | **B7** |

|OUTRO| **F#m7**   **B7**
          Hey Bull-dog.

F#m7   **B7**
Hey Bull-dog.   *... fade out*

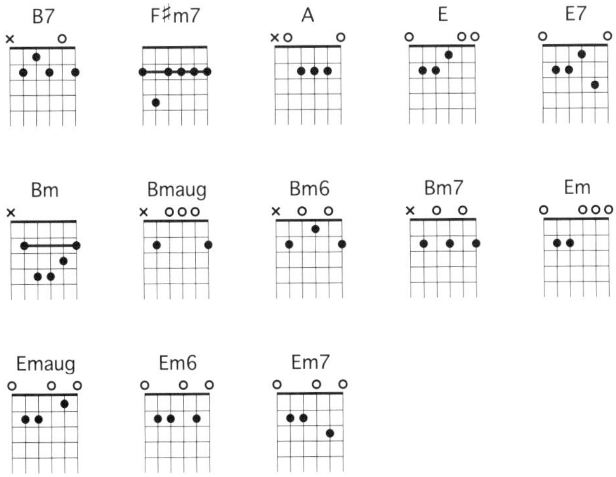

Hey Jude

Words & Music by
John Lennon & Paul McCartney

** CAPO : 1 FRET.*

|A1|
```
      E                    B
Hey Jude, don't make it bad.

        B7                  E
Take a sad song and make it better.

      A                    E
Remember to let her into your heart,

            B7              E
Then you can start to make it better.
```

|A2|
```
      E                    B
Hey Jude, don't be afraid.

        B7                  E
You were made to go out and get her.

      A                    E
The minute you let her under your skin,

        B7                 E
Then you begin to make it better.
```

|B1|
```
E7                          A         A/G#    A/F#
And anytime you feel the pain, hey Jude, refrain,

        A/E      B7          E          E7
Don't carry the world upon your shoulders.

                        A       A/G#    A/F#
For well you know that it's a fool who plays it cool

    A/E      B7          E
By making his world a little colder.

        E7      B7
Na na na, na na, na na na na.
```


A3
```
     E                    B
Hey Jude, don't let me down.

         B7                      E
You have found her, now go and get her.

     A                       E
Remember to let her into your heart,

             B7                 E
Then you can start to make it better.
```

B2
```
E7                  A        A/G#      A/F#
So let it out and let it in, hey Jude, begin,

         A/E         B7        E        E7
You're waiting for someone to perform with.

                        A        A/G#         A/F#
And don't you know that it's just you, hey Jude, you'll do,

     A/E            B7                E
The movement you need is on your shoulder.

             E7      B7
Na na na, na na, na na na na.
```

A4
```
     E                    B
Hey Jude, don't make it bad.

         B7                    E
Take a sad song and make it better.

     A                        E
Remember to let her under your skin,

             B7
Then you'll begin to make it

E
Better better better better better better, oh.
```

OUTRO
```
     E            D
:Na      na na nananana,

A                 E
Na na na na    hey Jude...  :    ... fade out
```

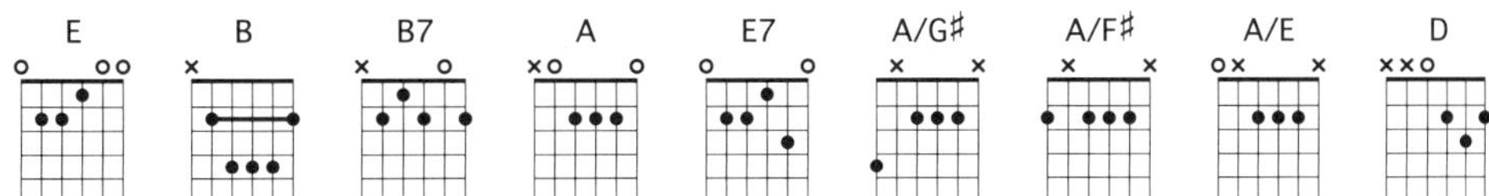

Hold Me Tight

Words & Music by
John Lennon & Paul McCartney

F   *Bb7*
A3 Hold me tight,

G7   *C7*   *F*   *Bb7*
Tell me I'm the only one, and then I might,

G7   *C7*
Never be the only one,

    F   *F7*   *Bb7*   *Bbm7*
So hold me tight, tonight, tonight,

     F   *Bbm7*   *F*   *Ab7*
It's you,   you, you, you.

Ab7   *F7*   *Ab7*   *F7*
B2 Don't know what it means to hold you tight,

Bb7   *Gm*   *G7*
Being here alone tonight with you,

   C7
It feels so right now,

F   *Bb7*
A4 Hold me tight,

G7   *C7*   *F*   *Bb7*
Let me go on loving you, tonight, tonight,

G7   *C7*
Making love to only you,

    F   *F7*   *Bb7*   *Bbm7*
So hold me tight, tonight, tonight,

     F   *Bbm7*   *F*   *Ab7*   *F*
It's you,   you, you, you.

Ab7   *F*
You. —

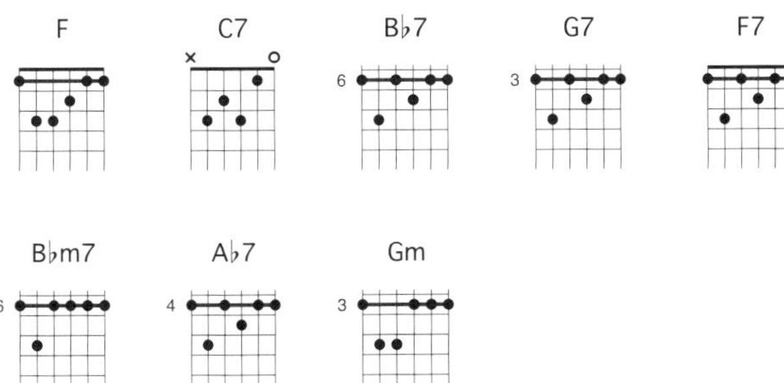

Honey Pie

Words & Music by
John Lennon & Paul McCartney

INTRO
```
Em    A6      Am/D
She was a working girl.

Cm                    G
North of England way.

Em       A6       Am/D  Cm         G
Now she's hit the big time in the U.S.A.

A7
And if she could only hear me,

D7
This is what I'd say.
```

A1
```
G                                  Eb7
Honey Pie, you are making me crazy,

E7              A7
I'm in love but I'm lazy

D7                     G     Eb7   D7
So won't you please come home.
```

A2
```
     G                             Eb7
Oh, Honey Pie, my position is tragic,

E7                    A7
Come and show me the magic

D7                    G     F#    F
Of your Hollywood song.
```

B1
```
Em            C#m7b5        G
You became a legend of the silver screen,

G7           C
And now the thought of meeting you

E7                        Am    D7
Makes me weak in the knee.
```

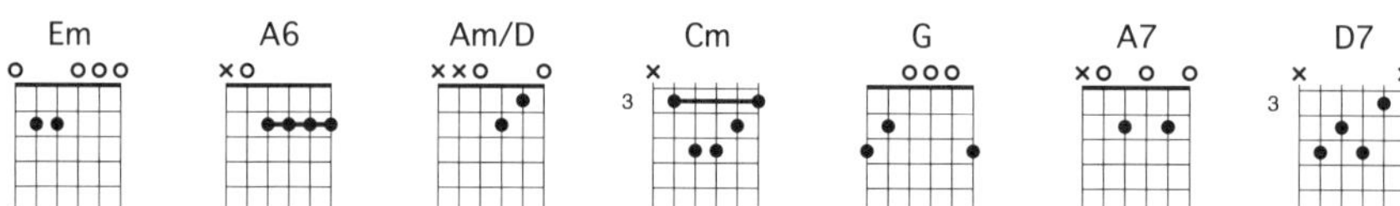

A3
G   Eb7
Oh, Honey Pie, you are driving me frantic,

E7   A7
Sail across the Atlantic

D7   G
To be where you belong.

Eb7   D7   G
Honey Pie, come back to me.

Inst. | G | G | Eb7 | E7 | A7 | D7 ||

A4
G   Eb7
I like it Like That

G   Eb7
I like this kind of, hot kind of music,

E7
Hot kind of music,

A7
Play it to me,

D7   G   F#   F
Play it to me, Hollywood blues.

B2
Em   C#m7b5   G   G7
Will the wind that blew her boat across the sea

C   E7   Am   D7
Kindly send her sailing back to me.

A5
G   Eb7
Now, Honey Pie, you are making me crazy

E7   A7
I'm in love but I'm lazy

D7   G
So won't you please come home?

Eb7   D7   G
Come, come back to me Honey Pie,

Inst. | G | Eb7 | E7 | A7 |
| D7 | G | Eb7 | D7 | G ||

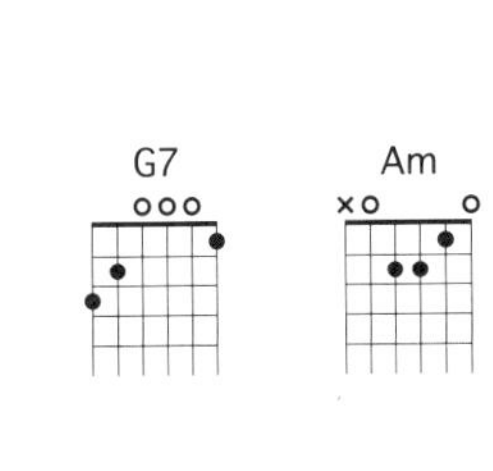

I Am The Walrus

Words & Music by
John Lennon & Paul McCartney

Intro. | B | B A A6 | G F F6 | E | E7 | D | D7 ||

A1
```
A              A/G
```
I am he as you are he
```
     C           D            A      A/G
```
As you are me and we are all together.
```
C
```
See how they run like pigs from a gun,
```
     D              A
```
see how they fly. I'm crying.

A2
```
A                    A/G       Dadd9/F#
```
Sitting on a cornflake,
```
F            G        A      A/G
```
Waiting for the van to come.
```
F
```
Corporation T-shirt, stupid bloody Tuesday.
```
B7
```
Man, you been a naughty boy, you let your face grow long.

B1
```
        C                 D
```
I am the eggman, they are the eggmen.
```
        E
```
I am the walrus, goo goo g'joob.

A3
```
A          A/G
```
Mister City Policeman sitting
```
C       D           A      A/G
```
Pretty little policemen in a row.
```
C
```
See how they fly like Lucy in the Sky,
```
     D              A
```
See how they run. I'm crying,

Dsus4
I'm crying.

    A
I'm crying,

    E   *D*   *D7*
I'm crying.

A4
 A   *A/G*   *Dadd9/F#*
Yellow matter custard,

 F   *G*   *A*   *A/G*
dripping from a dead dog's eye.

 F
Crabalocker fishwife, pornographic priestess,

 B7
Boy, you been a naughty girl you let your knickers down.

B2
         C   *D*
I am the eggman, they are the eggmen.

        E
I am the walrus, goo goo g'joob.

Inst. | *B* *A* | *G* *F* | *E* ||

C1
 B   *A*   *G*   *F*   *E*
Sitting in an English garden waiting for the sun.

 F   *B7*
If the sun don't come, you get a tan

From standing in the English rain.

B3
         C   *D*
I am the eggman, they are the eggmen.

        E   *D*
I am the walrus, goo goo g'joob, goo goo g'joob.

A5
<pre>
A   A/G
Expert textpert choking smokers,

C   D   A
Don't you think the joker laughs at you?

          A/G
(Ha ha ha! Hee hee hee! Ha ha ha!)

C
See how they smile like pigs in the sty,

   D   A
See how they snide. I'm crying.
</pre>

A6
<pre>
A   A/G   Dadd9/F#
Semolina pilchard,

F   G   A   A/G
Climbing up the Eiffel Tower.

F
Elementary penguin singing Hare Krishna.

    B7
Man, you should have seen them kicking Edgar Allan Poe.
</pre>

B4
<pre>
          C   D
I am the eggman, they are the eggmen.

           E
I am the walrus,

Goo goo g'joob

D
Goo goo goo g'joob.

C
Goo goo g'joob

               B7
Goo goo goo, g'joob goo.

B7
Chooga, chooga, chooga.

Jooba, jooba, jooba.
</pre>

Inst. ‖: A | G | F | E | D | C | B7 :‖   *... fade out*

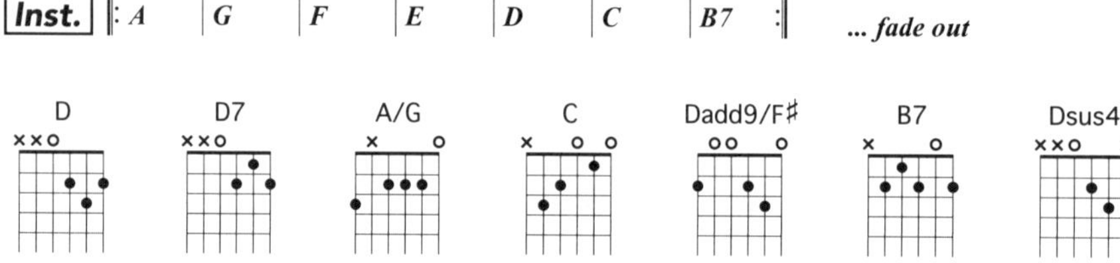

I Call Your Name

Words & Music by
John Lennon & Paul McCartney

Inst. | *F#7* | *B7* | *E7* | *B7* ‖

A1
E7
I call your name,

C#7
But you're not there,

F#7
Was I to blame

B7
For being unfair,

B1
E7
Oh I can't sleep at night,

C#7
Since you've been gone.

F#7
I never weep at night,

A   *Am*   *E7*
I can't go on.

C1
A7
Don't you know I can't take it?

C#m
I don't know who can.

F#7
I'm not going to make it,

C7   *B7*
I'm not that kind of man.

|B2| Oh, I can't sleep at night,   *E7*

But just the same   *C#7*

I never weep at night   *F#7*

I call your name,   *A Am   E7*

Inst. | *E7* | *E7* | *C#7* | *C#7* |
| *F#7* | *A Am* | *E7* | *E7* |

|C2| Don't you know I can't take it?   *A7*

I don't know who can.   *C#m*

I'm not going to make it,   *F#7*

I'm not that kind of man.   *C7   B7*

|B3| Oh, I can't sleep at night,   *E7*

But just the same,   *C#7*

I never weep at night,   *F#7*

I call your name,   *A   Am   E7*

‖: I call your name, I call your name. :‖   *A7   E7   A7   E7*   *... fade out*

F#7   B7   E7   B7   C#7

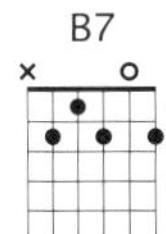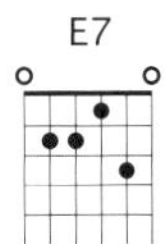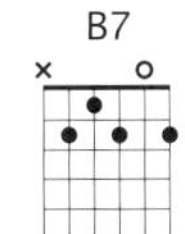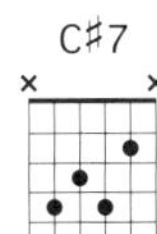

A   Am   A7   C#m   C7

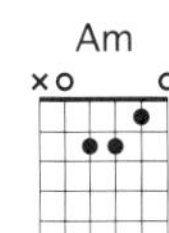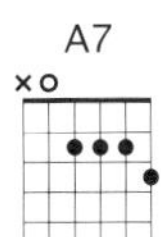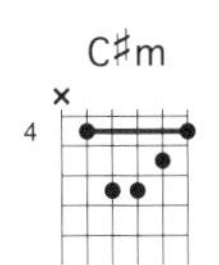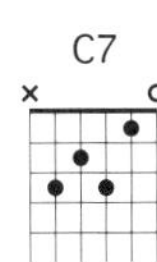

I Don't Want To Spoil The Party

Words & Music by
John Lennon & Paul McCartney

Inst. | G | G | Dsus4 | Dsus4 |
| D7 | D7 | G | G ||

A1
    G
I don't want to spoil the party so I'll go,

                            D7
I would hate my disappointment to show,

    Em   *B7*   *Am*   *D*
There's nothing for me here so I will disappear,

    G   *Fadd9*   *G*
If she turns up while I'm gone please let me know.

A2
    G
I've had a drink or two and I don't care,

                          D7
There's no fun in what I do if she's not there,

    Em   *B7*   *Am*   *D*
I wonder what went wrong I've waited far too long,

    G   *Fadd9*   *G*
I think I'll take a walk and look for her.

B1
        G
Though tonight she's made me sad,

Em *A* *C* *D7*
I   still love her,

    G
If I find her I'll be glad,

Em *A* *C* *D7*
I   still love her.

                    G
A3 I don't want to spoil the party so I'll go,

                                                     D7
   I would hate my disappointment to show,

                 Em   *B7*   *Am*   *D*
   There's nothing for me here so I will disappear,

                 G   *Fadd9*   *G*
   If she turns up while I'm gone please let me know.

Inst. | *G* | *G* | *G* | *G* | *G* | *G* |
| *D7* | *D7* | *Em* | *B7* | *Am* | *D* |
| *G* | *Fadd9* | *G* ||

                        G
B2 Though tonight she's made me sad,

Em   *A*   *C*   *D7*
I   still love her,

              G
If I find her I'll be glad,

Em   *A*   *C*   *D7*
I   still love her.

                        G
A4 So, I've had a drink or two and I don't care,

                                                     D7
   There's no fun in what I do if she's not there,

                 Em   *B7*   *Am*   *D*
   I wonder what went wrong I've waited far too long,

                 G   *Fadd9*   *G*
   I think I'll take a walk and look for her.

Inst. | *G* | *G* | *D7sus4* | *D7sus4* |
| *D7* | *D7* | *G* ||

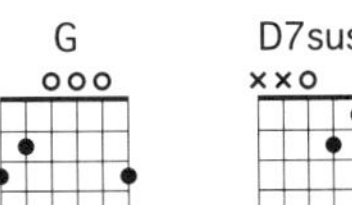

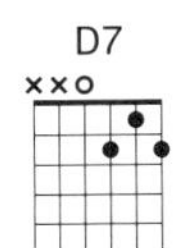

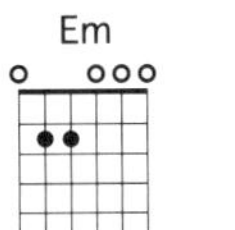

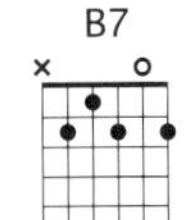

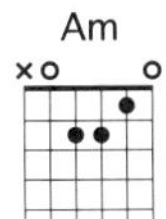

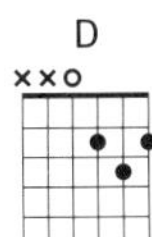

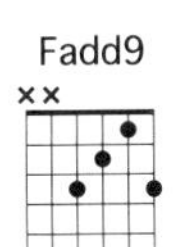

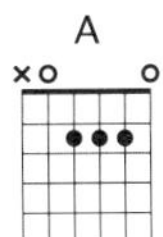

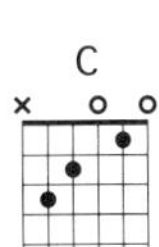

I Feel Fine

Words & Music by
John Lennon & Paul McCartney

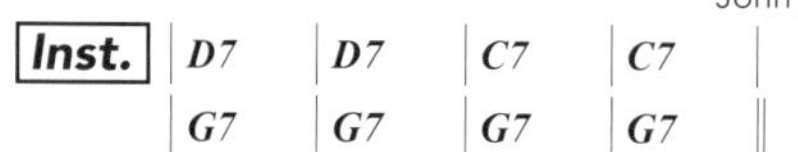


```
        G
A1  Baby's good to me, you know,

    She's happy as can be, you know,
         D7                    C7           G7
    She said so. I'm in love with her and I feel fine.


        G
A2  Baby says she's mine, you know,

    She tells me all the time, you know,
         D7                    C7           G7
    She said so. I'm in love with her and I feel fine.


    G      Bm        C           D7
B1  I'm so glad that she's my little girl.

    G      Bm          Am          D7
    She's so glad, she's telling all the world


        G
A3  That her baby buys her things, you know.

    He buys her diamond rings, you know,
         D7
    She said so.

                      C7          G7
    She's in love with me and I feel fine, mmm.
```


Inst. | G7 | G7 | G7 | G7 |
| D7 | D7 | D7 | D7 |
| C7 | C7 | G7 | G7 | G7 | G7 ‖

A4
G7
Baby says she's mine, you know,

She tells me all the time, you know,

D7   *C7*   *G7*
She said so. I'm in love with her and I feel fine.

B2
G   *Bm*   *C*   *D7*
I'm so glad that she's my little girl.

G   *Bm*   *Am*   *D7*
She's so glad, she's telling all the world

A5
          G7
That her baby buys her things, you know.

He buys her diamond rings, you know,

    D7
She said so.

         C7   *G7*
She's in love with me and I feel fine,

D7   *C7*   *G7*
She's in love with me and I feel fine, mmm, mmm.

Inst. ‖: G7 | G7 | G7 | G7 :‖   *... fade out*

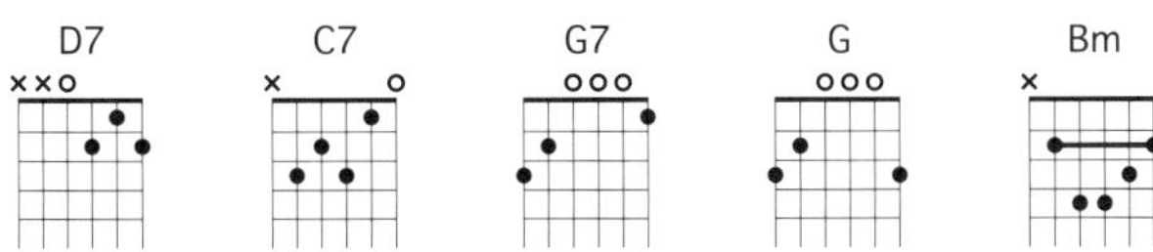

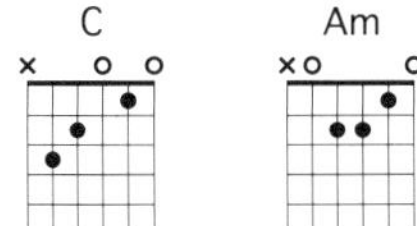

I Me Mine

Words & Music by
George Harrison

Inst. ‖ Am   C | D7 | G   E7 ‖

A1
Am C   D7   G   E7   Am
All   through the day, I me mine, I me mine, I me mine.

Am C   D7   G   E7   Am
All   through the night, I me mine, I me mine, I me mine.

Dm
Never frightened of leaving it

F6
Everyone's weaving it,

E7b9   E
Coming on strong all the time,

Am Am(maj7)   Am7   Am6
All   through the day,

Fmaj7
I me mine.

B1
A7
I-me-me mine, I-me-me mine,

D7   A7   E7
I-me-me mine, I-me-me mine.

A2
Am C   D7   G   E7   Am
All   I can hear, I me mine, I me mine, I me mine.

Am C   D7   G   E7   Am
Even those tears, I me mine, I me mine, I me mine.

Dm
No-one's frightened of playing it

F6
Everyone's saying it,

E7b9   E
Flowing more freely than wine,

Am Am(maj7)   Am7   Am6
All   through the day,

Fmaj7
I me mine.

A7

B2 I-me-me mine, I-me-me mine,

D7   *A7*   *E7*

I-me-me mine, I-me-me mine.

Am *C*   *D7* *G*   *E7*   *Am*

A3 All I can hear, I me mine, I me mine, I me mine.

Am *C*   *D7*   *G*   *E7*   *Am*

Even those tears, I me mine, I me mine, I me mine.

     Dm

No-one's frightened of playing it

F6

Everyone's saying it,

E7b9   *E*

Flowing more freely than wine,

Am *Am(maj7)*   *Am7* *Am6*

All through your life,

   Fmaj7

I me mine.

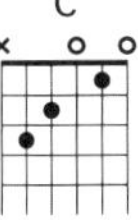
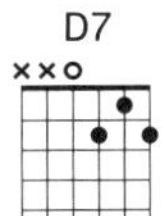
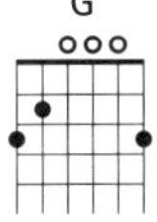
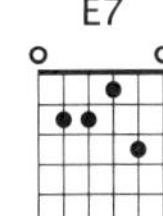

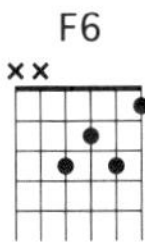
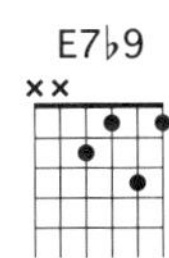
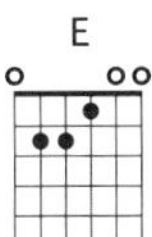

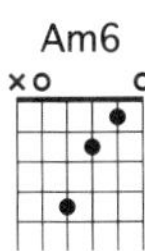
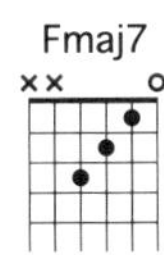
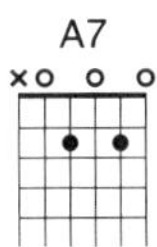

I Need You

Words & Music by
George Harrison

* 반음 낮추어 튜닝합니다.

Inst. ‖ A Asus2 │ Asus4 A ‖

A1
```
A                D                 A        Asus2  Asus4   A
You don't realise how much I need you,

A                D                 A     A7   Asus4    A
Love you all the time and never leave you.

        F#m                 C#m       F#m          Bm
Please come on back to me. I'm lonely as can be.

A       Asus2   Asus4   A
I need you.
```

A2
```
A                D                 A    Asus2  Asus4    A
Said you had a thing or two to tell me.

A                D                 A    A7    Asus4    A
How was I to know you would upset me?

    F#m      C#m        F#m              Bm
I didn't realise as I looked in your eyes.

        A    Asus2   Asus4    A
You told me.
```

B1
```
                D
Oh yes, you told me,

        E                        A
You don't want my loving anymore.

                D              E
That's when it hurt me, and feeling like this

    B7                   E7
I just can't go on anymore.
```

|A3|
  A   *D*   *A*   *Asus2* *Asus4* *A*
Please remember how I feel about you,

  A   *D*   *A* *A7* *Asus4* *A*
I could never really live without you.

    F#m   *C#m*
So, come on back and see

    F#m   *Bm*
Just what you mean to me,

   A   *Asus2*   *Asus4*   *A*
I need you.

|B2|
             D
But when you told me,

    E   *A*
You don't want my loving anymore.

      D   *E*
That's when it hurt me, and feeling like this

  B7   *E7*
I just can't go on anymore.

|A4|
  A   *D*   *A* *Asus2* *Asus4* *A*
Please remember how I feel about you,

  A   *D*   *A* *A7* *Asus4* *A*
I could never really live without you.

    F#m   *C#m*
So, come on back and see

    F#m   *Bm*
Just what you mean to me,

   A   *Asus2*   *Asus4*   *A*
I need you.

|OUTRO|
    F#m   *Dmaj7*
I need you, I need you.

Inst. | *A Asus2* | *Asus4 A* ‖

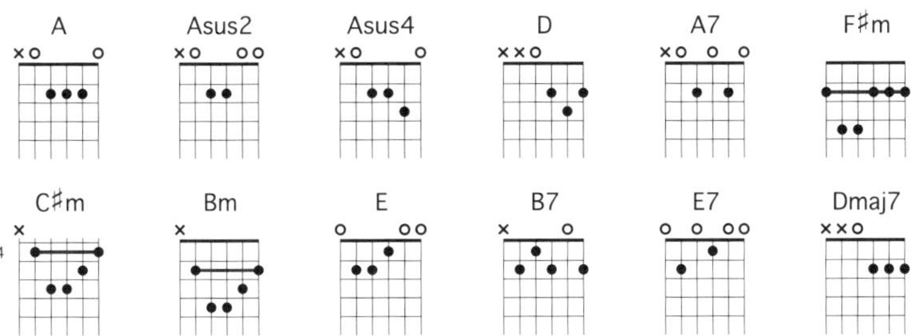

I Saw Her Standing There

Words & Music by
John Lennon & Paul McCartney

One - two - three - four!

Inst. | E7 | E7 | E7 | E7 ‖

A1
        E7
Well, she was just seventeen,

  A7   *E7*
You know what I mean,

                          B7
And the way she looked was way beyond compare.

  E7   *A7*
So how could I dance with another

C   *E7*   *B7*   *E7*
Ooh,when I saw her standing there.

A2
    E7
Well she looked at me,

  A7   *E7*
And I, I could see

                     B7
That before too long, I'd fall in love with her.

E7   *A7*
She wouldn't dance with another,

C   *E7*   *B7*   *E7*
Ooh, when I saw her standing there.

B1
    A7
Well, my heart went boom,

When I crossed that room,

        B7   *A7*
And I held her hand in mine...

                         E7
[A3] Well, we danced through the night,

              A7   *E7*
And we held each other tight,

                                      B7
And before too long I fell in love with her.

       E7   *A7*
Now I'll never dance with another,

C   *E7*   *B7*   *E7*
Ooh, since I saw her standing there.

Inst. | *E7* | *E7* | *E7* | *E7* | *E7* | *E7* |
       | *B7* | *B7* | *E7* | *E7* | *A7* | *A7* |
       | *E7* | *B7* | *E7* | *E7* ||

              A7
[B2] Well, my heart went boom,

When I crossed that room,

                       B7   *A7*
And I held her hand in mine...

              E7
[A4] Oh, we danced through the night,

              A7   *E7*
And we held each other tight,

                                      B7
And before too long I fell in love with her.

       E7   *A7*
Now I'll never dance with another,

C   *E7*   *B7*   *E7*
Oh, since I saw her standing there,

                       B7   *E7*
Oh, since I saw her standing there,

                            B7   *A7*   *E7*   *E9*
Yeah, well since I saw her standing there.

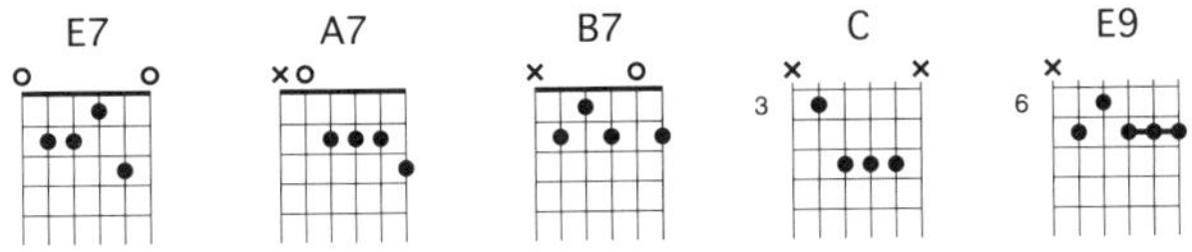

I Should Have Known Better

Words & Music by
John Lennon & Paul McCartney

Inst. | *G D* | *G D* | *G D* | *G D* ‖

A1
G D G D   *G*   *D*   *G*   *D*
I ——— should have known better with a girl like you,

        G   *D*   *Em*
That I would love everything that you do

        C   *D*   *G   D   G*
And I do, hey, hey, hey, and I do.

A2
D   *G D G D*   *G*   *D*   *G*   *D*
Whoa, oh, I ——— never realised what a kiss could be,

        G   *D*   *Em*
This could only happen to me,

              C   *B7*
Can't you see, can't you see?

B1
Em   *C*   *G*   *B7*
That when I tell you that I love you, oh,

Em   *G*   *G7*
  You're gonna say you love me too,   oh,

C   *D*   *G*   *Em*
  And when I ask you to be mine,

C   *D*   *G*   *D* *G*
  You're gonna say you love me too.

A3
D   *G D G D*   *G*   *D*   *G*   *D*
So, oh, I ——— should have realised a lot of things before.

        G   *D*   *Em*
If this is love, you've got to give me more,

              C   *D*   *G*   *D* *G* *D*
Give me more, hey hey hey, give me more.

```
Inst. | G  D | G  D | G  D | G  D |
      | G  D | Em   | C    | D    ||
      | G  D | G  D ||
```


A4 I   never realised what a kiss could be,

This could only happen to me,

Can't you see, can't you see?

B2 That when I tell you that I love you, oh,

You're gonna say you love me too,   oh,

And when I ask you to be mine,

You're gonna say you love me too.

OUTRO You love me too.

You love me too,

You love me too.   ... fade out

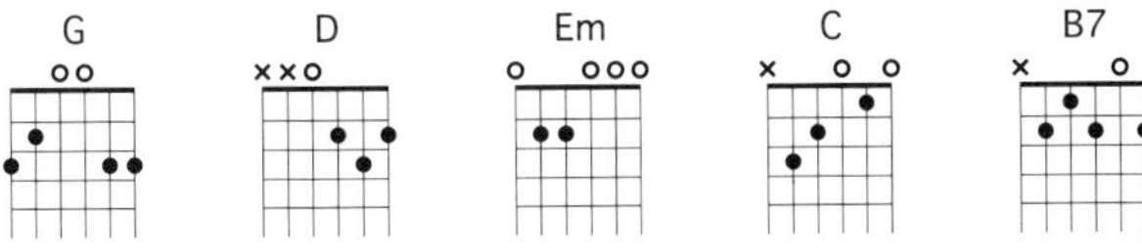

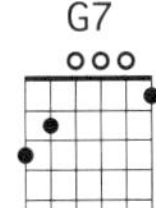

I Wanna Be Your Man

Words & Music by
John Lennon & Paul McCartney

```
    E       E7      E       E7      E           E7          E           E7
A1  I wanna be your lover baby, I wanna be your man,

    E       E7      E       E7      E           E7
    I wanna be your lover baby, I wanna be your man.
```

```
    E           E7      E       E7      E           E7      E           E7
A2  Love you like no other baby, like no other can,

    E           E7      E       E7      E           E7
    Love you like no other baby, like no other can.
```

```
                    F#7         B7
B1  I wanna be your man,

                        E       C#7
    I wanna be your man,

                    F#7         B7
    I wanna be your man,

                        E       E7
    I wanna be your man,
```

```
    E           E7      E       E7      E           E7          E       E7
A3  Tell me that you love me baby, let me understand,

    E       E7      E       E7      E           E7
    Tell me that you love me baby, I wanna be your man.
```

```
    E           E7      E       E7      E           E7          E       E7
A4  I wanna be your lover baby, I wanna be your man,

    E       E7      E       E7      E           E7
    I wanna be your lover baby, I wanna be your man.
```



```
                   F#7       B7
[B2] I wanna be your man,

                    E      C#7
     I wanna be your man,

                   F#7       B7
     I wanna be your man,

                    E    E7
     I wanna be your ma - an. wow.
```

Inst. | E E7 | E E7 | E E7 | E E7 |
   | E E7 | E E7 | E E7 | E E7 |
   | E E7 | E E7 | E E7 | E E7 ‖

```
     E        E7      E     E7   E       E7       E      E7
[A5] I wanna be your lover baby, I wanna be your man,

     E        E7      E     E7   E       E7
     I wanna be your lover baby, I wanna be your man.
```

```
     E        E7      E     E7   E       E7    E      E7
[A6] Love you like no other baby, like no other can.

     E        E7      E     E7   E       E7
     Love you like no other baby, like no other can.
```

```
                   F#7       B7
[B3] I wanna be your man,

                    E      C#7
     I wanna be your man,

                   F#7       B7
     I wanna be your man,

                    E    E7
     I wanna be your ma - an. wow.
```

```
        E E7 E        E7        E
[OUTRO]         I wanna be your man

        E E7 E        E7        E
                I wanna be your man        ... fade out
```

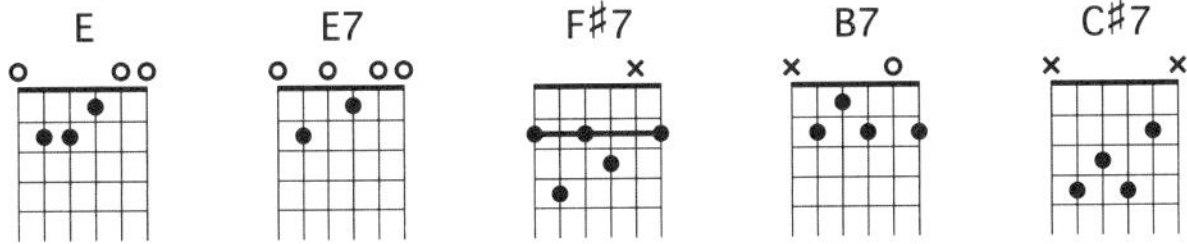

I Want To Hold Your Hand

Words & Music by
John Lennon & Paul McCartney

Inst. | C   D | D   C   D | D   C   D | D | D   ‖

                  G   D   Em   B7
A1 Oh yeah, I'll tell you something, I think you'll understand.

              G   D   Em   B7
When I say that something, I wanna hold your hand.

        C   D   G   Em
B1 I wanna hold your hand,

        C   D   G
I wanna hold your hand.

              G   D   Em   B7
A2 Oh please, say to me, you'll let me be your man

              G   D   Em   B7
And please, say to me, you'll let me hold your hand.

        C   D   G   Em
B2 Now let me hold your hand,

        C   D   G
I wanna hold your hand.

        Dm   G   C   Am
C1 And when I touch you I feel happy inside.

        Dm   G   C
It's such a feeling that my love

                  D   C   D   C   D
I can't hide, I can't hide, I can't hide.

A3   *G*   *D*   *Em*   *B7*
Yeah, you got that something, I think you'll understand.

      G   *D*   *Em*   *B7*
When I'll say that something, I wanna hold your hand,

B3 *C*   *D*   *G*   *Em*
I wanna hold your hand,

    C   *D*   *G*
I wanna hold your hand.

C2 *Dm*   *G*   *C*   *Am*
And when I touch you I feel happy inside.

Dm   *G*   *C*
It's such a feeling that my love

      D   *C*   *D*   *C*   *D*
I can't hide, I can't hide, I can't hide.

A4   *G*   *D*   *Em*   *B7*
Yeah, you got that something, I think you'll understand.

      G   *D*   *Em*   *B7*
When I feel that something I want to hold your hand,

B4 *C*   *D*   *G*   *Em*
I want to hold your hand,

    C   *D*   *B7*
I want to hold your hand,

    C   *D*   *C*   *G*
I want to hold your hand.

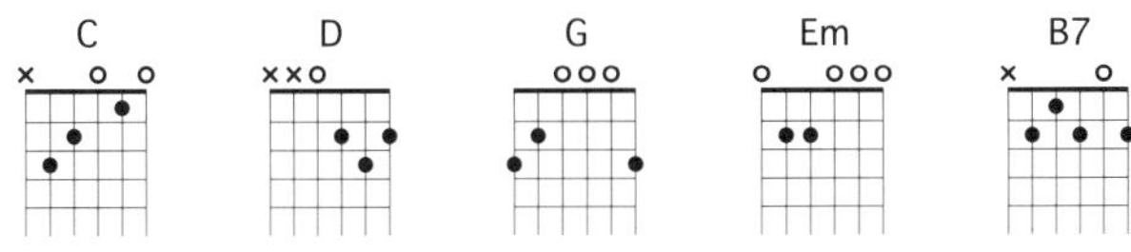

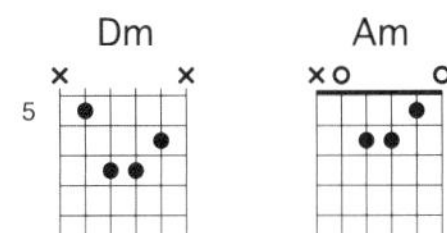

I Want To Tell You

Words & Music by
George Harrison

Inst. | A7 | A7sus4 | A7 | A7sus4 ||

A1
A
I want to tell you,

B7
My head is filled with things to say.

E7b9
When you're here

A7
All those words, they seem to slip away.

A2
A
When I get near you,

B7
The games begin to drag me down.

E7b9
It's all right,

A7
I'll make you maybe next time around.

B1
Bm *Bdim* *A*
But if I seem to act unkind,

B7 *Bm*
It's only me, it's not my mind,

Bdim *A* *Asus4*
That is confusing things.

A3
A
I want to tell you

B7
I feel hung up but I don't know why,

E7b9 *A7*
I don't mind, I could wait forever, I've got time.

Bm   *Bdim*   *A*
B2 Sometimes I wish I knew you well,

                    B7   *Bm*
Then I could speak my mind and tell you,

Bdim   *A*   *Asus4*
Maybe you'd understand.

A
A4 I want to tell you,

                     B7
I feel hung up but I don't know why.

E7b9
I don't mind, I could wait forever,

A7
I've got time,

I've got time,

I've got time.   *... fade out*

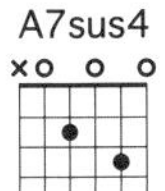

A7

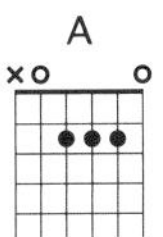

A7sus4

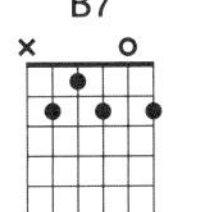

A

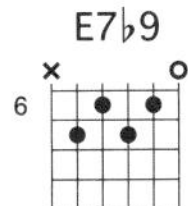

B7

E7b9

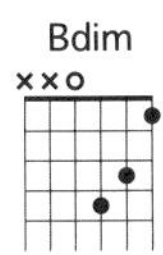

Bm

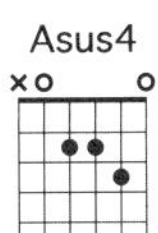

Bdim

Asus4

I Want You(She's So Heavy)

Words & Music by
John Lennon & Paul McCartney

Inst. | Dm | Dm/F | E7b9 | Bb7 | Aaug ‖

A1
    Am7
I want you, I want you so bad,

        C
I want you, I want you so bad,

  D   *F*   *G*   *Am7*
It's driving me mad, it's driving me mad.

    Dm7
I want you, I want you so bad, babe,

       F
I want you, I want you so bad,

  C   *Bb7*   *G5 G#5* *A5*
It's driving me mad, it's driving me mad.

Inst. | E7b9 | E7b9 | E7b9 | E7b9 | E7b9 | E7b9 ‖

A2
    Am7
I want you, I want you so bad, babe,

       C
I want you, I want you so bad,

  D   *F*   *G*   *Am7*
It's driving me mad, it's driving me mad.

    Dm7
I want you, I want you so bad,

      F
I want you, I want you so bad,

  C   *Bb7*
It's driving me mad,

  G5 G#5 *A5*
It's driving me...

Dm   Dm/F   E7♭9   B♭7   Aaug   Am7   C

Inst. | E7b9 | E7b9 | E7b9 | E7b9 | E7b9 | E7b9 ‖

          Dm   *Dm/F*   *E7b9*

B1 She's so…

Bb7   *Aaug*
Heavy.

Dm   *Dm/F*   *E7b9*   *Bb7*   *Aaug*
Heavy, (heavy, heavy.)

Inst. | Am7 | Am7 | Am7 | Am7 | Am7 | Am7 |
| Am7 C | D F | G | Am7 | Am7 ‖
| Dm7 | Dm7 | Dm7 | Dm7 | Dm7 | Dm7 |
| Dm7 F | C Bb | G5 G#5 A5 ‖

Inst. | E7b9 | E7b9 | E7b9 | E7b9 | E7b9 | E7b9 ‖

          Dm   *Dm/F*   *E7b9*

B2 She's so…

Bb7   *Aaug*
Heavy.   She's so

Dm   *Dm/F*   *E7b9*   *Bb7*   *Aaug*
Heavy, (heavy, heavy.)

        Am7

A3 I want you, I want you so bad,

                               C
I want you, I want you so bad,

   D   *F*   *G*   *Am7*
It's driving me mad, it's driving me mad.

        Dm7
I want you, I want you so bad, babe,

                              F
I want you, I want you so bad,

   C   *Bb7*   *G5 G#5*   *A5*
It's driving me mad, it's driving me mad.

Inst. | E7b9 | E7b9 | E7b9 | E7b9 | E7b9 | E7b9 |

OUTRO ‖: Dm | Dm/F | E7b9 | Bb7 | Aaug :‖

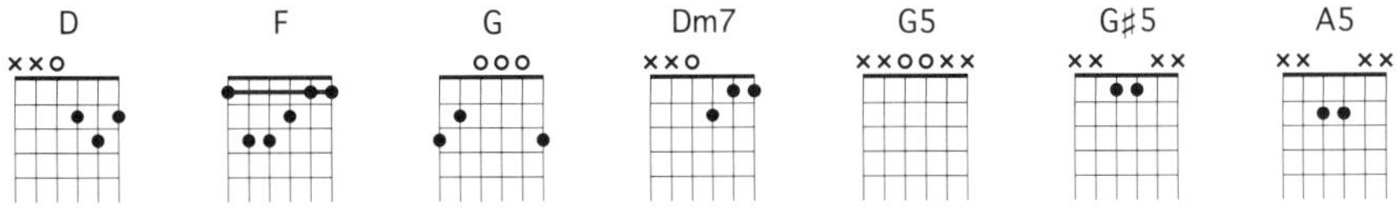

D   F   G   Dm7   G5   G♯5   A5

I Will

Words & Music by
John Lennon & Paul McCartney

|A1|
       F   *Dm*   *Gm7*   *C7*
Who knows how long I've loved you?

    F   *Dm*   *Am*
You know I love you still,

F7   *Bb*   *C7*   *Dm*   *F*
Will I wait a lonely lifetime?

     Bb   *C7* *F* *Dm* *Gm7*   *C7*
If you want me to, I will.

|A2|
    F *Dm* *Gm7*   *C7*
For if I ever saw you,

   F   *Dm*   *Am*
I didn't catch your name.

F7   *Bb*   *C7*   *Dm*   *F*
But it never really mattered,

    Bb   *C7*   *F*   *F7*
I will always feel the same.

|B1|
Bb   *Am7* *Dm*
Love you forever and forever,

Gm7   *C7*   *F*   *F7*
Love you with all my heart,

Bb   *Am7*   *Dm*
Love you whenever we're together,

G7   *C7*
Love you when we're apart.

|A3|
                 F   Dm   Gm7   C7
And when at last I find you,

                  F   Dm   Am
Your song will fill the air.

           Bb   C7   Dm   Bbm   F
Sing it loud so I can hear you,

           Bb   C7   Dm   Bbm   F7
Make it easy to be near you,

            Bb   C7
For the things you do

      Dm Bbm   F   Fdim
Endear you to me

Gm7   C7   Db7
Oh, you know I will,

          F   F7
I will.

|Inst.| | *Bb   Am* | *Dm* | *Gm7   C7* | *F*   ‖

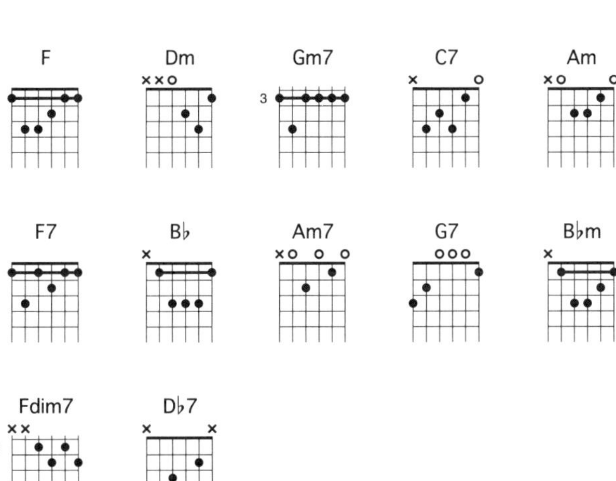

I'll be back

Words & Music by
John Lennon & Paul McCartney

Inst. | A | A ||

Am   G6   Fmaj7
A1 You know if you break my heart I'll go,

    E   A
But I'll be back again.

      Am   G6   Fmaj7
'Cause I told you once before goodbye,

    E   A
But I came back again.

             F#m
B1 I love you so,

                 Bm
Oh I'm the one who wants you,

                 E
Yes, I'm the one who wants you,

D   E   D   E
Oh - ho, oh - ho.

Am   G6   Fmaj7
A2 You could find better things to do,

      E   A
Than to break my heart again,

      Am   G6   Fmaj7
This time I will try to show you

        E   A
That I'm not trying to pretend.

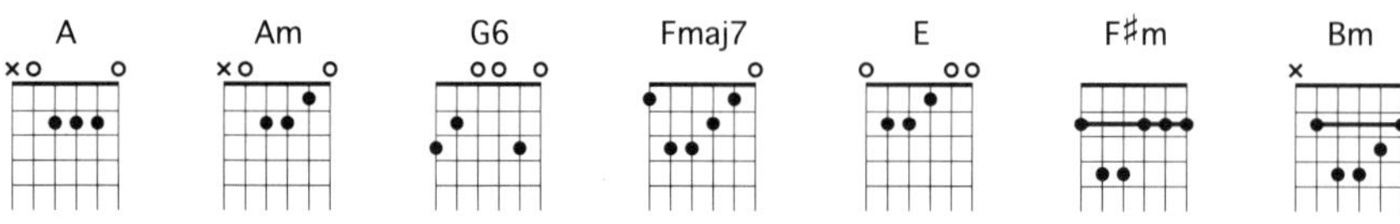

B2

Bm   Bm(maj7)   Bm7
I

                                C#m
Thought that you would realise,

       F#m
That if I ran away from you,

      B7
That you would want me too,

       D   *E*
But I've got a big surprise,

D   *E*   *D*   *E*
Oh - ho,   oh - ho.

A3

Am   *G6*   *Fmaj7*
You could find better things to do,

       E   *A*
Than to break my heart again,

      Am   *G6*   *Fmaj7*
This time I will try to show that I'm

      E   *A*
Not trying to pretend.

B3

         F#m
I wanna go,

            Bm
But I hate to leave you,

                     E
You know I hate to leave you,

D   *E*   *D*   *E*
Oh - ho,   oh - ho.

OUTRO

Am   *G6*   *Fmaj7*
You, if you break my heart I'll go,

      E   *A*
But I'll be back again.

Inst. ‖: *A* |*A* |*Am* |*Am* :‖   *... fade out*

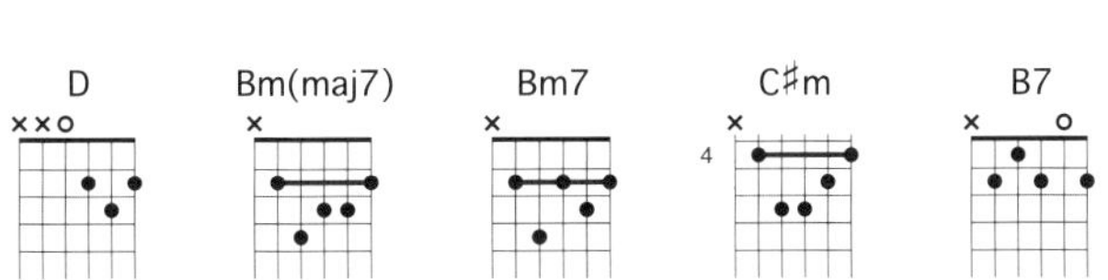

I'll Cry Instead

Words & Music by
John Lennon & Paul McCartney

Inst. | G   C6 ‖

G C6   G   C6
A1   I've got every reason

G   C6   G   C6   G   C6
On earth to be mad,

G   C6   G   C6   D7
'Cause I've just lost the only girl I had.

C7
If I could get my way,

I'd get myself locked up today,

G   C6   D7   G   C6   G   C6
But I can't,   so I cry instead.

G   C6
A2 I've got a chip on my shoulder

G   C6   G   C6   G   C6
That's bigger than my feet,

G   C6   G   C6   D7
I can't talk to people that I meet.

C7
If I could see you now,

I'd try to make you sad somehow,

G   C6   D7   G   C6   G   C6
But I can't,   so I cry instead.

Bm   A7
B1 Don't want to cry when there's people there, I get shy when

D
They start to stare, I'm gonna hide myself away,

E7   A   D
But I'll come back again someday.

|A3| And when I do,

        G

      C6   *G*   *C6*   *G* *C6* *G* *C6*
You'd better hide all the girls,

G   *C6*   *G*   *C6*   *D7*
I'm gonna break their hearts all round the world.

   C7
Yes, I'm gonna break them in two,

Show you what your loving man can do,

   G   *D7*   *G*   *C6* *G* *C6*
Until then I'll cry instead.

          Bm   *A7*
|B2| Don't want to cry when there's people there, I get shy when

         D
They start to stare, I'm gonna hide myself away,

  E7   *A*   *D*
But I'll come back again someday.

      G
|A4| And when I do,

      C6   *G*   *C6*   *G* *C6* *G* *C6*
You'd better hide all the girls,

G   *C6*   *G*   *C6*   *D7*
I'm gonna break their hearts all round the world.

   C7
Yes, I'm gonna break them in two,

Show you what your loving man can do,

   G   *D7*   *G*   *C6* *G*
Until then I'll cry instead.

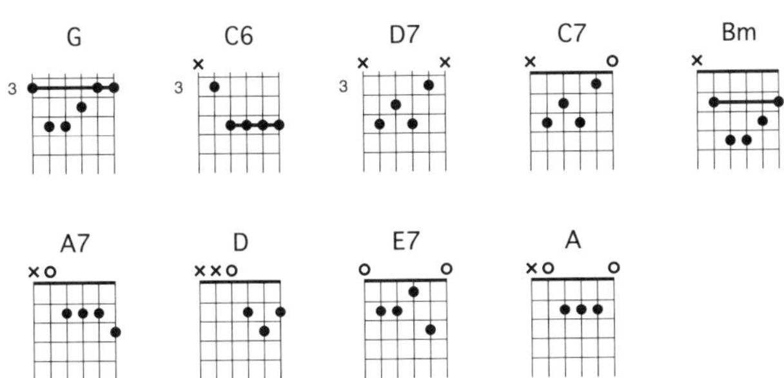

I'll Follow The Sun

Words & Music by
John Lennon & Paul McCartney

Inst. | C | F C ‖

A1
G   F
One day you'll look

C   D
To see I've gone.

C   Em/B
For tomorrow may rain, so

D G   C F C
I'll follow the sun.

A2
G   F
Someday you'll know

C   D
I was the one,

C   Em/B
But tomorrow may rain, so

D G   C C7
I'll follow the sun.

B1
          Dm
And now the time has come

Fm   C
And so my love I must go.

C7   Dm
And though I lose a friend,

Fm   C Dm
In the end you'll know, oooh.

A3 *G   F*
One day you'll find

C   D
   That I have gone.

    C   Em/B
But tomorrow may rain, so

D   G   C   F   C
I'll follow the sun.

Inst. | *G* | *F* | *C* | *D*   ‖

    C   Em/B
Yes, tomorrow may rain, so

D   G   C   C7
I'll follow the sun.

    Dm
B2 And now the time has come

  Fm   C
And so my love I must go.

C7   Dm
And though I lose a friend,

Fm   C   Dm
In the end you'll know, oooh.

G   F
A4 One day you'll find

C   D
   That I have gone,

    C   Em/B
But tomorrow may rain, so

D   G   C   F   C
I'll follow the sun.

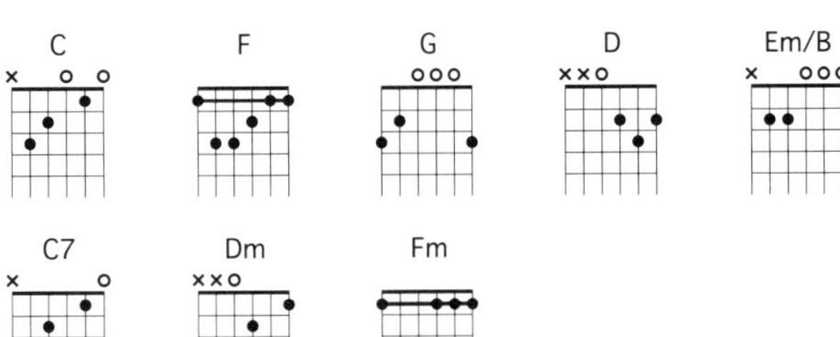

I'll Get You

Words & Music by
John Lennon & Paul McCartney

INTRO Oh yeah, oh yeah,

Oh yeah, oh yeah.

A1 Imagine, I'm in love with you,

It's easy 'cause I know.

I've imagined, I'm in love with you.

Many, many, many times before.

It's not like me to pretend,

But I'll get you in the end,

Yes I will, I'll get you in the end,

Oh yeah, oh yeah.

A2 I think about you night and day,

I need you 'cause it's true.

When I think about you, I can say,

I'm never, never, never, never blue.

So I'm telling you, my friend,

That I'll get you, I'll get you in the end.

B1
```
   G                           A
Yes I will, I'll get you in the end,

   D         A
Oh yeah, oh yeah.
```

C1
```
                G
Well, there's gonna be a time,

        D
Well I'm gonna change your mind.

       E7                          A
So you might as well resign yourself to me,

Oh yeah.
```

A3
```
D
Imagine, I'm in love with you,

   G           A
It's easy 'cause I know,

      D              Bm
I've imagined, I'm in love with you,

G                         A
Many, many, many times before.

        D           Am
It's not like me to pretend,

        D                       Bm
But I'll get you, I'll get you in the end,

   G                      A
Yes I will, I'll get you in the end,

     D         A
Oh yeah, oh yeah.

     D        A         D
Oh yeah, oh yeah, oh yeah.
```

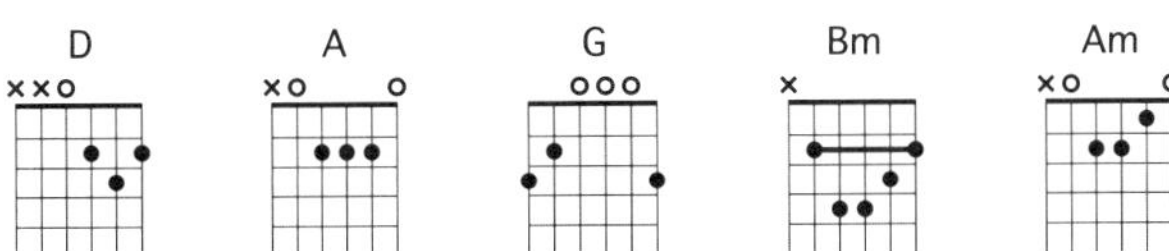

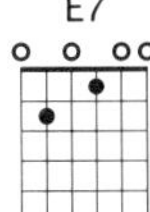

I'm A Loser

Words & Music by
John Lennon & Paul McCartney

B2
```
    Am   D
I'm a lo - ser,

    Am                    D
And I lost someone who's near to me,

      G    Em
I'm a lo - ser,

         Am            Fmaj7   D
And I'm not what I appear to be.
```

Inst.
```
‖: G        | D        | Fadd9    | G        :‖
 | Am       | D        | Am       | D        |
 | G        | Em       | Am       | Fmaj7  D ‖
```

A3
```
   G              D            Fadd9            G
     What have I done to deserve such a fate?

 G   D         Fadd9      G
I realise I have left it too late.

 G           D                  Fadd9      G
And so it's true, pride comes before a fall,

 G           D          Fadd9            G
I'm telling you so that you won't lose all.
```

B3
```
    Am   D
I'm a lo - ser,

    Am                    D
And I lost someone who's near to me,

      G    Em
I'm a lo - ser,

         Am            Fmaj7   D
And I'm not what I appear to be.
```

Inst.
```
‖: G        | D        | Fadd9    | G        :‖
 | Am       | D        | Am       | D        |
 | G        | Em       ‖       ... fade out
```

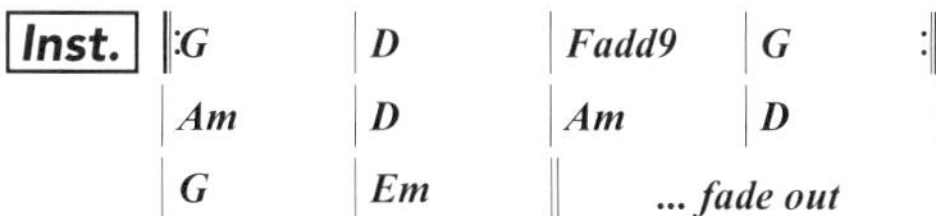

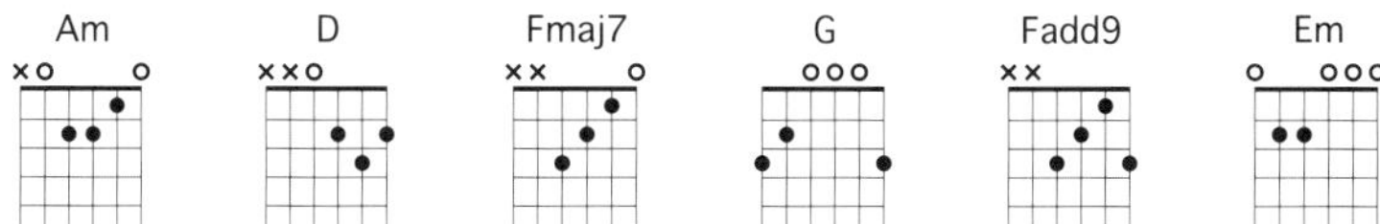

I'm Down

Words & Music by
John Lennon & Paul McCartney

|A1| You tell lies thinking I can't see.

G
You don't cry 'cause you're laughing at me.

    C7
|B1| I'm down, (I'm really down)

    G
I'm down, (down on the ground)

    C7
I'm down, (I'm really down)

D7   *G*
How can you laugh when you know I'm down?

D7   *G*
(How can you laugh) when you know I'm down?

    G
|A2| Man buys ring, woman throws it away,

    G
Same old thing happens everyday.

    C7
|B2| I'm down, (I'm really down)

    G
I'm down, (down on the ground)

    C7
I'm down, (I'm really down)

D7   *G*
How can you laugh when you know I'm down?

D7   *G*
(How can you laugh) when you know I'm down?

Inst. | | G | | G | | G | | G | | C7 | | C7 | |
| | G | | G | | D7 | | D7 | | G | | G | ||

A3
G
We're all alone and there's nobody else,

G
You still moan keep your hands to yourself.

B3
C7
I'm down, (I'm really down)

G
I'm down, (down on the ground)

C7
I'm down, (I'm really down)

D7   *G*
How can you laugh when you know I'm down?

D7   *G*
(How can you laugh) when you know I'm down?

Inst. | | G | | G | | G | | G | | C7 | | C7 | |
| | G | | G | | D7 | | D7 | | G | | D7 | ||

B4
G
||:Oh babe, you know that I'm down, (I'm really down)

Oh yes I'm down, (I'm really down)

C7
I'm down on the ground, (I'm really down)

G
I'm down (I'm really down)

D7   *C7*
Ah, baby, I'm upside down.

G   *D7*
Oh yeah, yeah, yeah, yeah, yeah. :|| *...fade out*

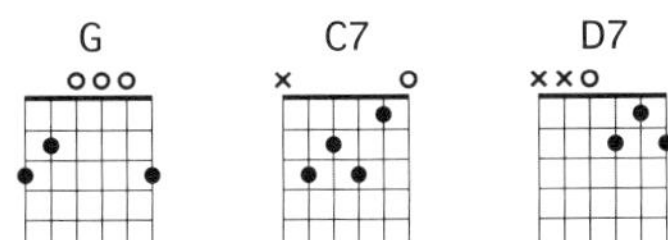

I'm Happy Just To Dance With You

Words & Music by
John Lennon & Paul McCartney

Inst. | C#m | F#m G# | C#m | F#m G# ‖

A1
C#m
Before this dance is through,

F#m   G#
I think I'll love you too,

A6   B6   E6   B7
I'm so happy when you dance with me.

B1
E   G#m   F#m   B
I don't wanna kiss or need to hold your hand,

E   G#m   F#m   B
If it's funny, try and understand

A   F#m   E   C#m
There is really nothing else I'd rather do,

A   Baug   E   B7
'Cause I'm happy just to dance with you.

B2
E   G#m   F#m   B
I don't need to kiss or hold you tight,

E   G#m   F#m   B
I just wanna dance with you all night.

A   F#m   E   C#m
In this world there's nothing I would rather do,

A   Baug   E
'Cause I'm happy just to dance with you.

C1
C#m   F#m   G#
Just to dance with you.

C#m   F#m   G#
It's everything I need.

C#m
Before this dance is through,

F#m   G#
I think I'll love you too,

A6   B6   E6   B7
I'm so happy when you dance with me.

```
        E               G#m      F#m     B
```
B3 If somebody tries to take my place,

```
          E                      G#m      F#m    B
```
Let's pretend we just can't see his face.

```
        A                        F#m           E    C#m
```
In this world there's nothing I would rather do,

```
          A              Baug         E
```
'Cause I'm happy just to dance with you.

```
          C#m                  F#m    G#
```
C2 Just to dance with you.

```
      C#m           F#m    G#
```
It's everything I need.

```
          C#m
```
Before this dance is through,

```
      F#m          G#
```
I think I'll love you too,

```
        A6                 B6            E6     B7
```
I'm so happy when you dance with me.

```
        E               G#m      F#m     B
```
B4 If somebody tries to take my place

```
        E                      G#m      F#m    B
```
Let's pretend we just can't see his face

```
        A                        F#m           E    C#m
```
In this world there's nothing I would rather do

```
          A              Baug         C#m
```
I've discovered I'm in love with you.

```
F#m     G#
```
Oh - oh,

```
            A              Baug         C#m
```
'Cause I'm happy just to dance with you

```
F#m     G#     A6     B6
```
Oh - oh, oh - oh,

```
E6
```
Oh!

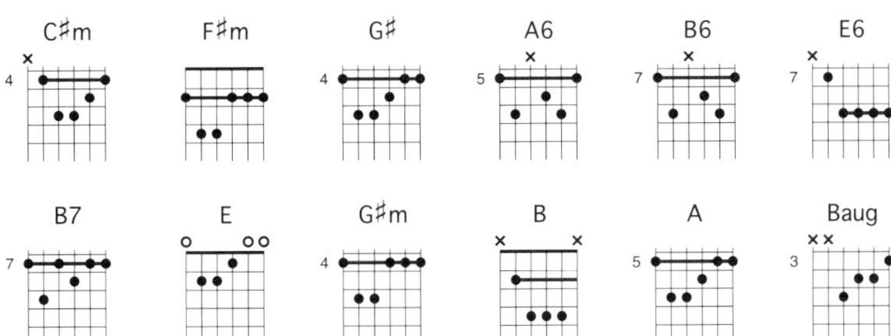

I'm Looking Through You

** CAPO : 1 FRET.*

Words & Music by
John Lennon & Paul McCartney

Inst. | (G) | Gmaj9 | G C | G C | G C ‖

A1
```
G       C    G/B   Am        Em              D
I'm look - ing through you,   where did you go?

G       C    G/B   Am        Em              D
I thought I - knew you,    what did I know?

Em7                  Asus4  Am      G     C      D
You don't look differ - ent, but you have changed,

G    C    G/B   Am         C                G    C
I'm look - ing   through you,   you're not the same.
```

Inst. | G C | G C ‖

A2
```
G       C   G/B    Am        Em          D
Your lips are   mo - ving,   I cannot hear,

G       C   G/B    Am        Em                  D
Your voice is   soo - thing, but the words aren't clear.

Em7                    Asus4  Am      G       C  D
You don't sound   differ - ent, I've learned the game.

G    C    G/B   Am         C                G    C
I'm look - ing   through you,   you're not the same.
```

Inst. | G C | G C | G ‖

B1
```
C                          G
Why, tell me why, did you not treat me right?

C                      Dsus4          D
Love has a nasty habit of disappearing overnight
```

A3
```
G        C     G/B   Am    Em          D
```
You're think - ing of me, the same old way,

```
G    C    G/B   Am        Em        D
```
You were a - bove me, but not today.

```
Em7        Asus4   Am      G     C     D
```
The only differ - ence is you're down there,

```
G    C    G/B   Am        C               G     C
```
I'm look - ing through you, and you're nowhere.

Inst. ‖ G C ‖ G C ‖ G   ‖

B2
```
C                            G
```
Why, tell me why, did you not treat me right?

```
C                      Dsus4        D
```
Love has a nasty habit of disappearing overnight.

A4
```
G    C    G/B   Am       Em          D
```
I'm look - ing through you,   where did you go?

```
G   C      G/B   Am       Em          D
```
 I thought I - knew you, what did I know?

```
Em7          Asus4   Am      G    C    D
```
You don't look differ - ent,   but you have changed,

```
G    C    G/B   Am       C               G     C
```
I'm look - ing through you, you're not the same.

OUTRO
```
G          C          G        C
```
Yeah! Well, baby, you've changed.

```
G    C         G       C
```
 Ah,   I'm looking through you,

```
G    C         G          C    G    C
```
Yeah,   I'm looking through you.   *...fade out*

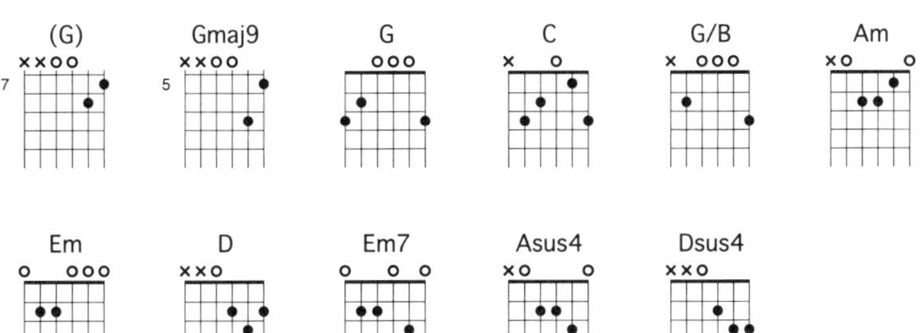

185

I'm Only Sleeping

Words & Music by
John Lennon & Paul McCartney

** 반음 낮추어 튜닝합니다.*

A1
Em   *Am*
When I wake up early in the morning,

G   C   G   B7
Lift my head, I'm still yawning.

Em   *Am*
When I'm in the middle of a dream,

G   C   G   C
Stay in bed, float upstream. (float upstream.)

B1
G   *Am*
Please, don't wake me, no, don't shake me,

Bm   *Am*   *Cmaj7*
Leave me where I am - I'm only sleeping.

A2
Em   *Am*
Everybody seems to think I'm lazy,

G   C   G   B7
I don't mind, I think they're crazy.

Em   *Am*
Running everywhere at such a speed,

G   C   G   C
Till they find there's no need. (there's no need)

B2
G   *Am*   *Bm*
Please, don't spoil my day, I'm miles away,

              Am   *Cmaj7*
And after all I'm only sleeping.

| *Em* | *Em* ||

C1
| Dm | | E7 | | Am | Am/G |

Keeping an eye on the world going by my window

F
Taking my time

E7   **Am**
Lying there and staring at the ceiling,

G   **C**   **G**   **B7**
Waiting for a sleepy feeling.

Inst. | *Em* | *Am* | *G*   *C* | *G*   *C* | *C*   ‖

B3
G   **Am**   **Bm**
Please, don't spoil my day, I'm miles away,

     Am   **Cmaj7**
And after all I'm only sleeping. | *Em* | *Em*   ‖

C2
Dm   **E7**   **Am**   **Am/G**
Keeping an eye on the world going by my window,

F
Taking my time.

A3
Em   **Am**
When I wake up early in the morning

G   **C**   **G**   **B7**
Lift my head, I'm still yawning

Em   **Am**
When I'm in the middle of a dream

G   **C**   **G**   **C**
Stay in bed, float up stream (float up stream)

B4
G   **Am**
Please, don't wake me, no, don't shake me,

Bm   **Am**   **Cmaj7**
Leave me where I am, I'm only sleeping | *Em* | *Em* | *Em*   ‖

Em   Am   G   C   B7   Bm

Cmaj7   Dm   E7   Am/G   F

I'm So Tired

Words & Music by
John Lennon & Paul McCartney

                A   G#7   D   E7
A1| I'm so tired, I haven't slept a wink,

        A   F#7   D   E7
I'm so tired,   my mind is on the blink.

        A   Eaug
I wonder should I get up

                        Dm
And fix myself a drink?

No, no, no.

                A   G#7   D   E7
A2| I'm   so   tired I don't know what to do,

        A   F#m   D   E7
I'm   so   tired, my mind is set on you.

        A   Eaug   F#m   Dm
I wonder should I call you, but I know what you'd do.

        A
B1| You'd say I'm putting you on,

But it's no joke, it's doing me harm,

                E
You know I can't sleep, I can't stop my brain,

You know it's three weeks, I'm going insane,

                D
You know I'd give you everything I've got

                        A
for a little peace of mind.

A3 I'm so tired, I'm feeling so upset,
A   G#7   D   E7

Although   I'm so tired,   I'll have another cigarette,
A   F#m   D   E7

And   curse Sir Walter Raleigh,
A   Eaug

He was such a stupid get..
F#m   Dm

B2 You'd say I'm putting you on,
A

But it's no joke, it's doing me harm,

You know I can't sleep, I can't stop my brain,
E

You know it's three weeks, I'm going insane,

You know I'd give you everything I've got
D

for a little peace of mind.
A

C1 I'd give you everything I've got
D

For a little peace of mind.
A

I'd give you everything I've got
D

For a little peace of mind.
A

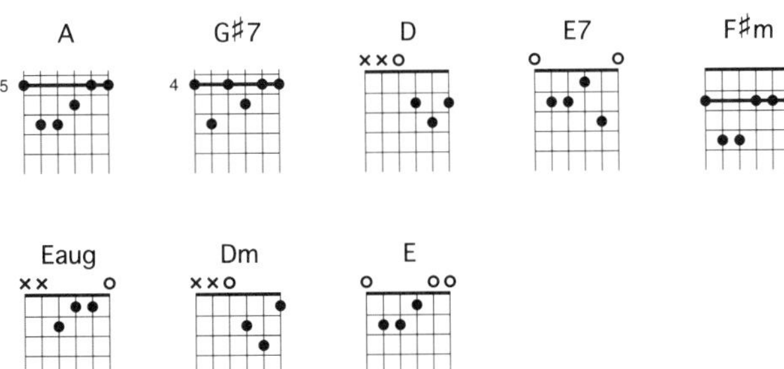

I've Just Seen A Face

Words & Music by
John Lennon & Paul McCartney

Inst. | F#m | F#m | F#m | F#m | D |
| D | D | D | E | E ||

A1
A
I've just seen a face,

                                      F#m
I can't forget the time or place where we just met.

                                       F#m7   *D*
She's just the girl for me and want all the world to see we've met.

         E   *A*
Mmm mm mm mm - mm mm.

A2
A
Had it been another day I might have looked the other way

    F#m
And I'd have never been aware. but as it is I'll dream of her tonight,   *F#m7* *D*

      E   *A*
Da da da da - da da.

B1
E   *D*
Falling, yes I am falling,

           A   *D*   *A*
And she keeps calling me back again.

A3
A
I have never known the like of this,

                 F#m
I've been alone and I have missed things and kept out of sight

               F#m7   *D*
But other girls were never quite like this,

      E   *A*
Da da da da - da da.

B2
E   D
Falling, yes I am falling,

               A   D   A
And she keeps calling me back again.

Inst. | A | A | A | A | F#m | F#m |
| F#m | F#m | F#m7 | D | D | E | A | |

B3
E   D
Falling, yes I am falling,

          A   D   A
And she keeps calling me back again.

A4
A
I've just seen a face,

                            F#m
I can't forget the time or place where we just met.

                              F#m7   D
She's just the girl for me and want all the world to see we've met.

         E   A
Mm mm mm, da - da da.

B4
E   D
Falling, yes I am falling,

          A   D   A
And she keeps calling me back again.

B5
E   D
Falling, yes I am falling,

          A   D   A
And she keeps calling me back again.

OUTRO
       E   D
Oh, falling, yes I am falling,

          A   D   D A E A
And she keeps calling   me back again.

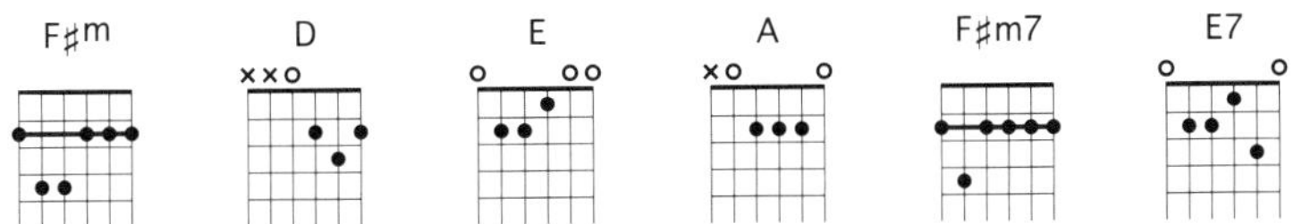

If I fell

Words & Music by
John Lennon & Paul McCartney

|C1| *D7*   *G*
'Cause I couldn't stand the pain

          Gm7   *D*   *A*
And I would be sad if our new love was in vain

          D   *Em7* *F#m7*   *Em7*
|B3| So I hope you see that I

            A
Would love to love you,

D   *Em7* *F#m7*   *Em7*
And that   she will cry

            A   *D7*
When she learns we are two.

|C2| *D7*   *G*
'Cause I couldn't stand the pain

          Gm7   *D*   *A*
And I would be sad if our new love was in vain.

          D   *Em7* *F#m7*   *Em7*
|B4| So I hope you see that I

            A
Would love to love you,

D   *Em7* *F#m7*   *Em7*
And that   she will cry

            A   *D7*
When she learns we are two.

          Gm7   *D*   *Gm7*   *D*
If I fell in love with you.

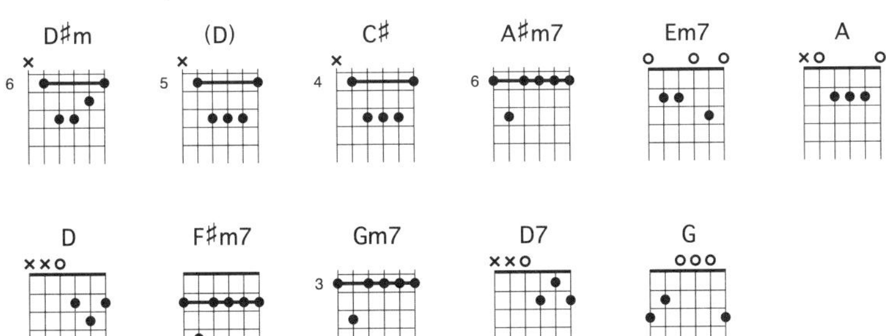

If I Needed Someone

Words & Music by
George Harrisson

Inst. | *A7* | *A7* | *A7* | *A7* |

A1
A
If I needed someone to love,

                                      G/A
You're the one that I'd be thinking of,

          A7
If I needed someone.

A2
A
If I had some more time to spend,

                              G/A
Then I guess I'd be with you my friend,

          A7
If I needed someone.

B1
Em   *F#7*
Had you come some other day

                   Bm
It might not have been like this,

Em   *F#7*   *Bm*   *E7sus4*   *E*
But you see now I'm too much in love.

A3
A
Carve your number on my wall,

                              G/A
And maybe you will get a call from me,

          A7
If I needed someone.

Inst. | *A* | *A* | *A* | *A* |
| *G/A* | *G/A* | *A7* | *A7* ‖

A4
A
If I had some more time to spend,

G/A
Then I guess I'd be with you my friend,

A7
If I needed someone.

B2
Em　　　　　　　　*F#7*
Had you come some other day,

Bm
Then It might not have been like this,

Em　　　　　　　*F#7*　　　　　*Bm*　　*E7sus4*　　*E7*
But you see now I'm too much in love.

A5
A
Carve your number on my wall,

G/A
And maybe you will get a call from me,

A7
If I needed someone.

OUTRO
A7　　　　　*A*
Ah,　　ah.

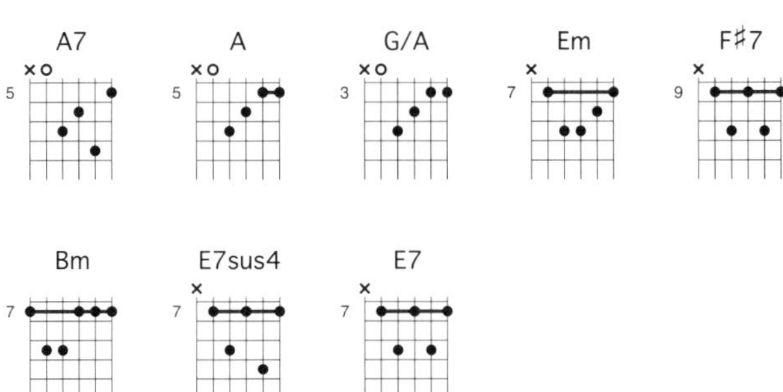

If You've Got Trouble

Words & Music by
John Lennon & Paul McCartney

Inst. | 2 DRUMS | E7 | E7 |

A1
E7 ..... B7sus4 ..... E7
If you've got trouble then you've got less trouble than me.

B7sus4 ..... E7
You say you're worried, you can't be as worried as me.

A7 ..... B7sus4
You're quite contend to be bad

A7 ..... B7sus4
With all the vantage you had over me

E7 ..... B7sus4 ..... E7
Just cause you're troubled, then don't bring your troubles to me.

A2
E7 ..... B7sus4 ..... E7
I don't think it's funny when you ask for money and things.

B7sus4 ..... E7
Especially when you're standing there wearing diamond and rings.

A7 ..... B7sus4
You think I'm soft in the head

A7 ..... B7sus4
Well try someone softer instead pretty thing,

E7 ..... B7sus4 ..... E7
It's not so funny when you know what money can bring.

B1
A ..... E
You better leave me alone,

A ..... E ..... B ..... E
I don't need a thing from you,

A ..... E
You better take yourself home,

A ..... E ..... B ..... E
Go and count a ring or two.

A3 *E7*   *B7sus4*   *E7*
If you've got trouble then you've got less trouble than me.

             B7sus4   *E7*
You say you're worried, you can't be as worried as me.

A7   *B7sus4*
You're quite contend to be bad,

A7   *B7sus4*
With all the advantage you had over me,

E7   *B7sus4*   *E7*
Just 'cause you're troubled then don't bring your troubles to me.

(Ah rock on, anybody.)

Inst. | E | E | E | E | A7 | A7 |
    | E | E | B7 | A7 | E | E ||

B1 *A*   *E*
 You better leave me alone,

A   *E*   *B*   *E*
I don't need a thing from you,

A   *E*
 You better take yourself home,

A   *E*   *B*   *E*
Go and count a ring or two.

A4 *E7*   *B7sus4*   *E7*
If you've got trouble then you've got less trouble than me.

             B7sus4   *E7*
You say you're worried, you can't be as worried as me.

A7   *B7sus4*
You're quite contend to be bad,

A7   *B7sus4*
With all the advantage you had over me,

E7   *B7sus4*   *E7*
Just 'cause you're trouble then don't bring your troubles to me,

E7   *B7sus4*   *E7*
Just 'cause you're trouble then don't bring your troubles to me.

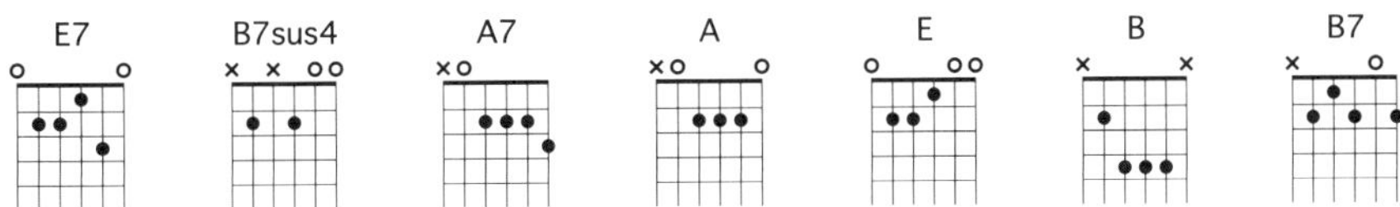

In My Life

Words & Music by
John Lennon & Paul McCartney

Inst. ‖: A | E | A | E :‖

A1
            A   *E*   *F#m*   *A/G*
There are places I remember

        D *Dm*   *A*
All my life,   though some have changed,

         A   *E*   *F#m*   *A/G*
Some forever not for better,

           D   *Dm*   *A*
Some have gone   and some remain.

B1
        F#m   *D*
All these places have their moments,

      G   *A*
With lovers and friends I still can recall,

       F#m   *B*
Some are dead and some are living,

  Dm7   *A*
In my life I've loved them all.

Inst. ‖: A | E :‖

A2
        A   *E*   *F#m*   *A/G*
But of all these friends and lovers,

       D *Dm*   *A*
There is no one compares with you,

       A   *E*   *F#m*   *A/G*
And these memories lose their meaning

     D   *Dm*   *A*
When I think of love as something new.

<pre>
                F#m   D
[B2] Though I know I'll never lose affection

          G   A
For people and things that went before,

    F#m   B
I know I'll often stop and think about them,

    Dm7   A
In my   life I love you more.
</pre>

Inst. | A   E | F#m A/G | D Dm | A |
           | A   E | F#m A/G | D Dm | A ||

<pre>
                F#m   D
[B3] Though I know I'll never lose affection

          G   A
For people and things that went before,

    F#m   B
I know I'll often stop and think about them,

    Dm7   A
In my   life I love you more
</pre>

| A | E ||

<pre>
    Dm7   A
In my   life I love you more
</pre>

[OUTRO] | A | E | A ||

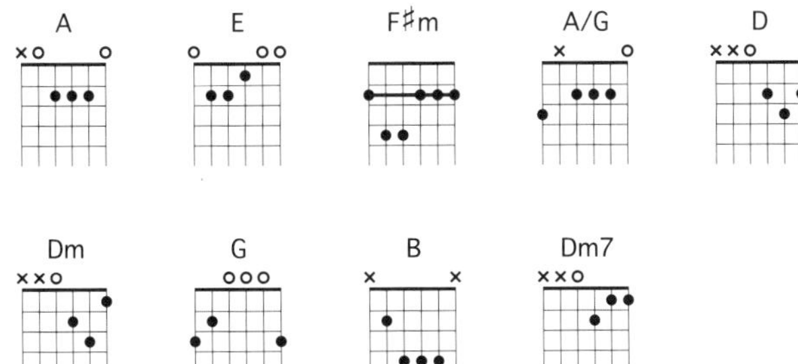

It Won't Be Long

Words & Music by
John Lennon & Paul McCartney

A1
C#m
It won't be long yeah, yeah, yeah.

E
It won't be long yeah, yeah, yeah.

C#m
It won't be long yeah, yeah, yeah.

A　*A7(b9)*　*E*
Till I belong to you.

B1
E　　　　　　　*C*　　　　　*E*
Every night when everybody has fun,

C　　　　　*E*
Here am I sitting all on my own.

A2
C#m
It won't be long yeah, yeah, yeah.

E
It won't be long yeah, yeah, yeah.

C#m
It won't be long yeah, yeah, yeah.

A　*A7(b9)*　*E*
Till I belong to you.

C1
E　　　*D#aug*
Since you left me I'm so alone,

D6　　　　　　*C#7*
Now you're coming, you're coming home,

A　　　　　　　*B*
I'll be good like I know I should,

F#m　　　　　　　　　*B*
You're coming home, you're coming home.

B2
E   C   E
Every night the tears come down from my eyes,

         C   E
Every day I've done nothing but cry.

A3
        C#m
It won't be long yeah, yeah, yeah.

        E
It won't be long yeah, yeah, yeah.

        C#m
It won't be long yeah, yeah, yeah.

    A   A7(b9)   E
Till I belong to you.

C2
        E   D#aug
Since you left me I'm so alone,

       D6   C#7
Now you're coming, you're coming on home,

A   B
I'll be good like I know I should,

        F#m   B
You're coming home, you're coming home.

B3
     E   C   E
So, every day we'll be happy, I know,

        C   E
Now I know that you won't leave me no more.

A4
        C#m
It won't be long yeah, yeah, yeah.

        E
It won't be long yeah, yeah, yeah.

        C#m
It won't be long yeah, yeah, yeah.

    A   G6   F#7   Fmaj7   Emaj7
Till I belong to you.

C#7   B   F#m   G6   F#7   Fmaj7   Emaj7

It's All Too Much

Words & Music by
George Harrison

Inst. ‖: *C G* | *Gadd9   G* | *C G Gadd9* | *G* :‖ *3회 반복

INTRO
C/G G   Gadd9   G
    It's all too much,

C/G G   Gadd9   G
    It's all too much

A1
G
When I look into your eyes, your love is there for me.

And the more I go inside, the more there is to see.

B1
C/G   G   Gadd9   G
It's all too much for me   to take

C/G   G   Gadd9   G
The love that's shining all   around you

C/G   G   Gadd9   G
Everywhere, it's what you make

C/G   G   Gadd9   G
For us to take, it's all too   much

A2
G
Floating down the stream of time, of life to life with me

Makes no difference where you are or where you'd like to be

B2
C/G   G   Gadd9   G
It's all too much for me to take

C/G   G   Gadd9   G
The love that's shining all   around here

C/G   G   Gadd9   G
All the world's a birthday cake,

C/G   G   Gadd9   G
So take a piece but not too much

Inst. ‖: *C/G* | *Gadd9* *G* | *C/G G Gadd9* | *G* :‖ *G* ‖   **4회 반복*

A3 *G*
Sail me on a silver sun, for I know that I'm free

Show me that I'm everywhere, and get me home for tea

B3
  C/G *G* *Gadd9* *G*
It's all to much for me to see

   C/G   *G* *Gadd9* *G*
The love that's shining all   around here

   C/G *G* *Gadd9* *G*
The more I am, the less I know

   C/G *G* *Gadd9*   *G*
And what I do is all too much

B4
   C/G *G*   *Gadd9* *G*
It's all too much for me to take

   C/G   *G* *Gadd9* *G*
The love that's shining all   around you

C/G *G* *Gadd9*   *G*
Everywhere, it's what you make

   C/G *G* *Gadd9*   *G*
For us to take, it's all too much

OUTRO
C/G G *Gadd9* *G* *C/G G* *Gadd9* *G*
  It's too much,

C/G G *Gadd9* *G* *C/G G* *Gadd9* *G*
  It's too much

Inst. ‖: *C/G G* | *Gadd9 G* | *C/G G Gadd9* | *G* :‖

    C/G   *G*   *Gadd9* *G C/G G Gadd9 G*
With your long blonde hair and your eyes of blue…

    C/G   *G*   *Gadd9* *G C/G G Gadd9 G*
With your long blonde hair and your eyes of blue…

Inst. ‖: *C/G G* | *Gadd9 G* | *C/G G Gadd9* | *G* :‖ *… fade out*

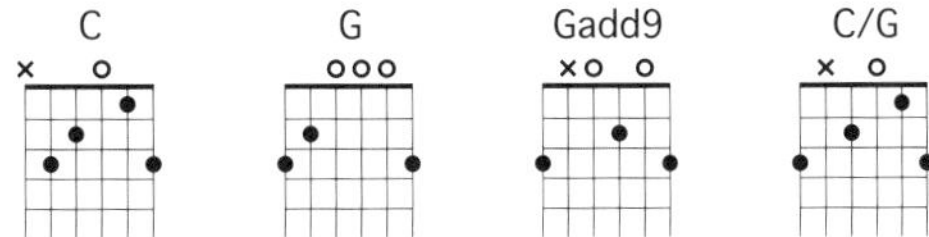

It's Only Love

Words & Music by
John Lennon & Paul McCartney

** CAPO : 5 FRET.*

Inst. | G | Em | G | Em ||

G Bm   F C   Dsus4 D Dsus4 D

A1 I get high when I see you go by,

Daug
My oh my,

G   Bm   F C   Dsus4 D Dsus4 D
When you sigh, my, my inside just flies,

Daug
Butterflies.

C   D   G   Em
Why am I so shy when I'm beside you?

     F   D
B1 It's only love and that is all,

      G   Em
Why should I feel the way I do?

     F   D
It's only love, and that is all,

     C   D
But it's so hard loving you.

G Bm   F   C   Dsus4 D Dsus4 D
A2 Is it right that you and I should fight

Daug
Every night?

G   Bm   F   C   Dsus4 D Dsus4 D
Just the sight of you makes night time bright,

Daug
Very bright.

C   D   G   Em
Haven't I the right to make it up girl?

<code>B2</code>
$\quad$ *F* $\qquad\qquad$ *D*
It's only love and that is all,

$\qquad\qquad$ *G* $\qquad\qquad$ *Em*
Why should I feel the way I do?

$\qquad$ *F* $\qquad\qquad$ *D*
It's only love, and that is all,

$\qquad\qquad$ *C* $\qquad$ *D*
But it's so hard loving you,

$\qquad\qquad$ *C* $\qquad$ *D*
Yes it's so hard loving you,

$\qquad$ *G*
Loving you.

Inst. | *Em* | *G* | *Em* | *G* | *Em* | *G* |

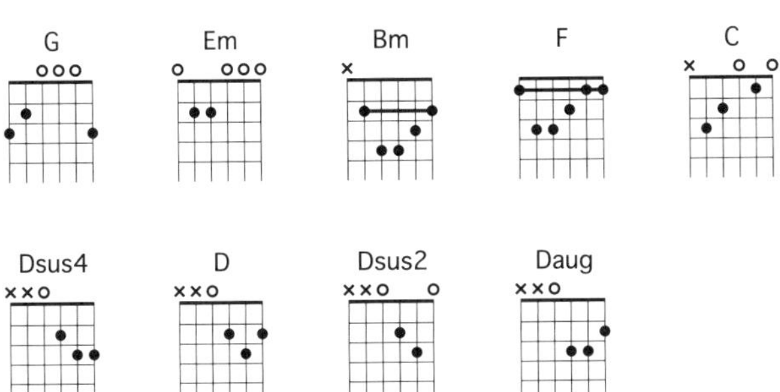

Julia

CAPO : 2 FRET.

Words & Music by
John Lennon & Paul McCartney

A1
```
C                Am7          Em
Half of what I say is meaningless,

C           Am7            Em G  C
But I say it just to reach you, Ju - lia.
```

B1
```
C    Am7 Gm7  Gm9    A7          F9  Fm7
Ju - lia, Ju - lia,   oceanchild, calls me

C           Am7        Em G  C
So I sing a song of love, Ju  -  lia.
```

B2
```
C    Am7 Gm7        Gm9    A7           F9  Fm7
Ju - lia, sea - shell eyes, windy smile, calls me,

C           Am7        Em G  C
So I sing a song of love, Ju  -  lia.
```

C1
```
Bm                     C
Her hair of floating sky is shimmering,

Am7         Am6
Glimmering,

Em7   Em6   Emaug  (Em)
In the sun.
```

B3
```
C    Am7 Gm7  Gm9  A7             F9     Fm7
Ju - lia, Ju - lia,   morning moon, touch me,

C           Am7        Em G  C
So I sing a song of love, Ju  -  lia.
```

A2
```
C                Am7           Em
When I cannot sing my heart,

C           Am7             Em G  C
I can only speak my mind, Ju  -  lia.
```


B4

<pre>
C   Am7   Gm7   Gm9   A7   F9   Fm7
Ju - lia, sleeping sand, silent cloud, touch me,

C   Am7   Em G C   Am7
So I sing a song of love, Ju - lia.
</pre>

OUTRO

<pre>
Gm7   Gm9   A7
Mm…

F9   Fm7
Calls me,

C   Am7   Em   C
So I sing a song of love for Ju - lia.

Em   C
Ju - lia.

Em G Cmaj7/G
Ju - lia.
</pre>

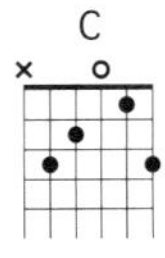

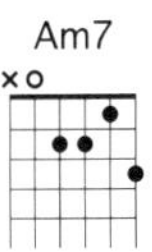

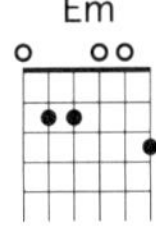

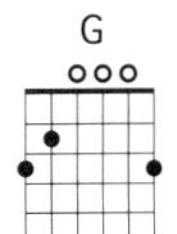

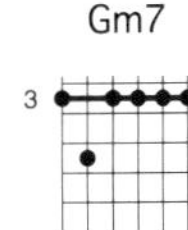

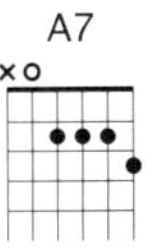

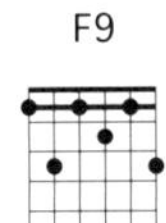

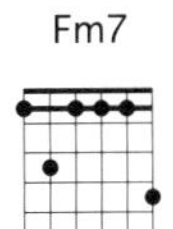

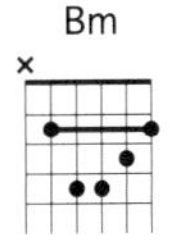

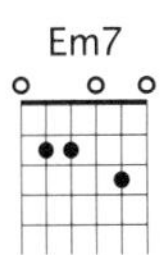

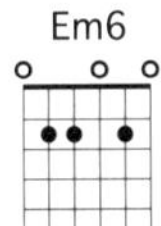

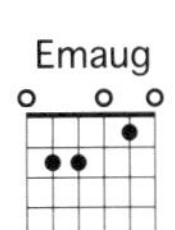

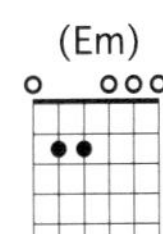

Emaug

(Em)

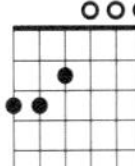

Lady Madonna

Words & Music by
John Lennon & Paul McCartney

Inst. ‖ A D | A D | A D | F G A ‖

A   D   A   D
A1 Lady Madonna, children at your feet.

A   D   F   G   A
Wonder how you manage to make ends meet.

A   D   A   D
Who finds the money when you pay the rent?

A   D   F   G   A
Did you think that money was heaven sent?

Dm7   G7
B1 Friday night arrives without a suitcase.

C   Am7
Sunday morning creep in like a nun.

Dm7   G7
Monday's child has learned to tie his bootlace.

C   Bm7   E7sus4   E7
See how they run.

A   D   A   D
A2 Lady Madonna, baby at your breast.

A   D   F   G   A
Wonder how you manage to feed the rest.

Inst. ‖ A D | A D | A D | F G A |
 | Dm7 | G7 | C | Am7 | Dm7 | G7 ‖

C   Bm7   E7sus4   E7
See how they run.

A3
```
A          D    A            D
```
Lady Madonna, lying on the bed,

```
A              D              F  G    A
```
Listen to the music playing in your head.

Inst. ‖ *A D* | *A D* | *A D* | *F G A* ‖

B2
```
Dm7                              G7
```
Tuesday afternoon is never - ending.

```
C                                Am7
```
Wednesday morning papers didn't come.

```
Dm7                                   G7
```
Thursday night you stockings needed mending.

```
C    Bm7       E7sus4     E7
```
See how they run.

A4
```
A          D    A              D
```
Lady Madonna, children at your feet,

```
A                  D        F    G    (A)  (Asus2/4) (Adim) (A)
```
Wonder how you manage to make ends meet.

Inst. ‖ *(A)   (Asus2/4)* | *(Adim) (Asus2/4) A* ‖

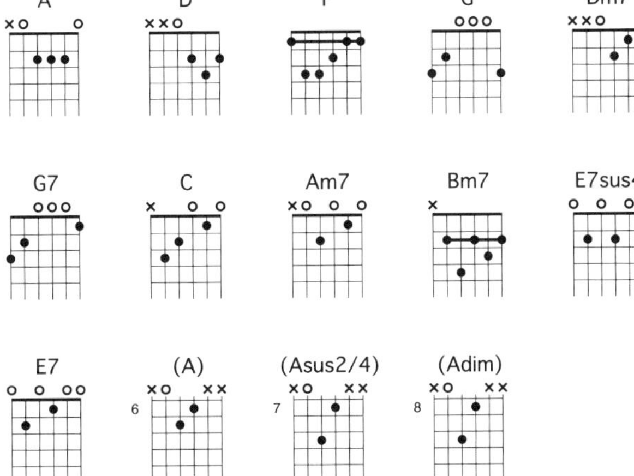

Let It Be

Words & Music by
John Lennon & Paul McCartney

Inst. ‖ C G │ Am Fmaj7 F6 │ C G │ F C ‖

        C   *G*
A1 When I find myself in times of trouble,

Am   *Fmaj7*   *F6*
Mother Mary comes to me,

C   *G*   *F* *C*
Speaking words of wisdom, let it be.

     C   *G*
And in my hour of darkness

      Am   *Fmaj7*   *F6*
She is standing right in front of me,

C   *G*   *F* *C*
Speaking words of wisdom, let it be.

     Am   *C/G* *F*   *C*
B1 Let it be, let it be, let it be, let it be

              G   *F* *C*
Whisper words of wisdom, let it be.

     C   *G*
A2 And when the broken hearted people

Am   *Fmaj7*   *F6*
Living in the world agree,

C   *G*   *F* *C*
There will be an answer, let it be.

     C   *G*
For though they may be parted there is

Am   *Fmaj7*   *F6*
Still a chance that they will see.

C   *G*   *F* *C*
There will be an answer, let it be.

B2
<pre>
      Am   C/G   F   C
Let it be, let it be, let it be, let it be,

                    G   F   C
There will be an answer, let it be.

      Am   C/G   F   C
Let it be, let it be, let it be, let it be,

                 G   F   C
Whisper words of wisdom, let it be.
</pre>

Inst. ‖ *F C* | *G F C* | *F C* | *G F C* ‖
‖: *C G* | *Am F* | *C G* | *F C* :‖

B3
<pre>
      Am   C/G   F   C
Let it be, let it be, let it be, let it be

                 G   F   C
Whisper words of wisdom, let it be.
</pre>

A3
<pre>
        C   G
And when the night is cloudy,

          Am   Fmaj7   F6
There is still a light that shines on me,

C   G   F   C
Shine on until tomorrow, let it be.

      C   G
I wake up to the sound of music

Am   Fmaj7   F6
Mother Mary comes to me,

C   G   F   C
Speaking words of wisdom, let it be.
</pre>

B4
<pre>
       Am   C/G   F   C
‖:Let it be, let it be, let it be, let it be.

                    G   F   C
There will be an answer, let it be. :‖

       Am   C/G   F   C
Let it be, let it be, let it be, let it be

                 G   F   C
Whisper words of wisdom, let it be.
</pre>

Inst. ‖ *F C* | *G F C* ‖

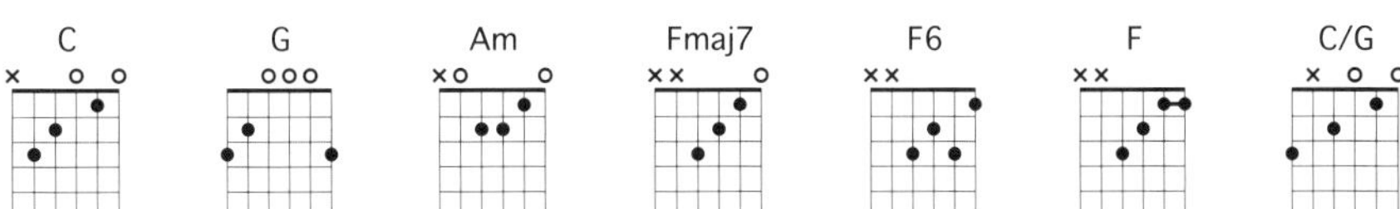

Little Child

Words & Music by
John Lennon & Paul McCartney

Inst. | *E7* | *A* | *E7* | *E7* ‖

[A1]
      E7
Little child, little child,

                  A   *E7*
Little child, won't you dance with me?

B7   *A7*
I'm so sad and lonely,

F#7   *B*
Baby take a chance with me.

[A2]
      E7
Little child, little child,

                  A   *E7*
Little child, won't you dance with me?

B7   *A7*
I'm so sad and lonely,

F#7   *B7*   *E*
Baby take a chance with me.

[B1]
      E   *B7*
If you want someone to make you feel so fine,

        E7
Then we'll have some fun when you're mine, all mine,

      F#7   *B*
So come on, come on, come on.

[A3]
      E7
Little child, little child,

                  A   *E7*
Little child, won't you dance with me?

B7   *A7*   *F#7*   *B7*   *E*
I'm so sad and lonely, baby take a chance with me.


```
Inst.  |E7    |E7    |E7    |E7    |A7    |A7    |
       |E7    |E7    |B7    |A7    |F#7   |B7    ||
```

          E
B2 When you're by my side,

            B7
You're the only one,

        E7
Don't run and hide,

Just come on, come on,

          F#7   *B*
So come on, come on, come on.

          E7
A4 Little child, little child,

                            A   *E7*
Little child, won't you dance with me?

B7   *A7*
I'm so sad and lonely,

F#7   *B7*   *E*   *C#7*
Baby take a chance with me, oh yeah,

F#7   *B7*   *E*   *C#7*
Baby take a chance with me, oh yeah,

F#7   *B7*   *E*   *C#7*
Baby take a chance with me, oh yeah,   *... fade out*

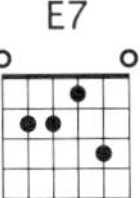 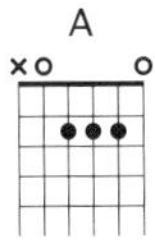 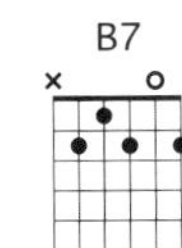 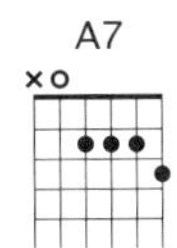 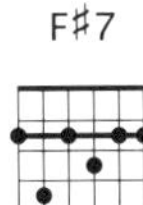

 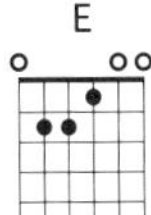 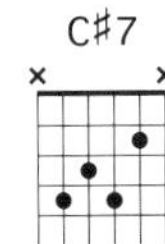

Long Long Long

Words & Music by
George Harrison

** CAPO : 3 FRET.*

Inst. | *Em G* | *Em D* | *A* ‖

A1
```
              G   F#m   Em   D    Em/G   D
It's been a long long long time.

A                        Em        D    A
How could I ever have lost you,

Em        D      A
   When I loved you?

            G   F#m   Em   D    Em/G   D
It took a long long long time.

A                        Em           D    A
Now I'm so happy I found you,

Em        D      A    A7
   How I love you.
```

B1
```
G            D            A           Em
So many tears I was searching,

G            D          A    Em  G   A
   So many tears I was wasting,  oh, oh!
```

A2
```
            G   F#m   Em   D    Em/G   D
Now I can see you,   be you

A                     Em          D    A
How can I ever misplace you?

Em     D     A
How I want you,

Em     D     A
How I love you.

Em              D           A
Your know that I need you.

Em    D    A
Oh I love you.
```

Inst. | *A* | *A* | *Asus4* | *Asus4* ‖

Love Me Do

Words & Music by
John Lennon & Paul McCartney

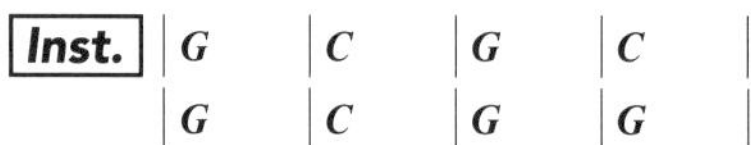

Inst. | G | C | G | C |
| G | C | G | G ‖

A1
G *C*
Love, love me do.

G *C*
You know I love you,

G *C*
I'll always be true,

G
So please, love me do.

C *G* *C*
Oh, love me do.

A2
G *C*
Love, love me do.

G *C*
You know I love you,

G *C*
I'll always be true,

G
So please, love me do.

C *G* *C*
Oh, love me do.

B1
D
Someone to love,

C *G*
Somebody new.

D
Someone to love,

C *G*
Someone like you.

A3
|G   C|
Love, love me do.

     G   *C*
You know I love you,

     G   *C*
I'll always be true,

             G
So please, love me do.

C   *G*   *C*
Oh, love me do.

Inst. ‖: *D* | *D* | *C* | *G* :‖
         | *G* | *G* | *G* | *G* ‖

A4
G   *C*
Love, love me do.

     G   *C*
You know I love you,

     G   *C*
I'll always be true,

             G
So please, love me do.

C   *G*   *C*
Oh, love me do.

OUTRO
     G   *C*
Yeah, love me do.

     G   *C*
Whoa, oh, love me do.

     G   *C*
Yeah, love me do.

     C   *C*
Whoa, oh, love me do.   *... fade out*

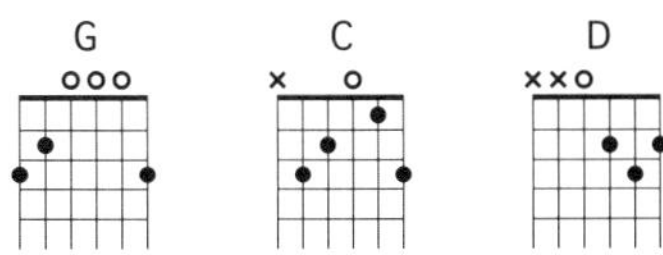

Love You To

Words & Music by
George Harrison

Inst. ‖: C5 | C5 | C5 | C5 :‖

A1
C6   C5
Each day just goes so fast,

C6   C5
I turn around, it's past,

C6 C5 C7   C6 C7 C5
You don't get time to hang a sign on me.

B1
Bb   C5 Bb C5
Love me while you can,

Bb   C5 Bb C5
Before I'm dead old man.

A2
C6   C5
A lifetime is so short,

C6   C5
A new one can't be bought,

C6   C5   C7   C6 C7 C5
And what you've got means such a lot to me.

B2
Bb   C5 Bb C5
Make love all day long.

Bb   C5 Bb C5
Make love singing songs.

Inst. ‖: C5 | C5 | C5 | C5 | C5 :‖

B3
Bb   C5 Bb C5
Make love all day long.

Bb   C5 Bb C5
Make love singing songs.

C6   *C5*
A3 There's people standing round,

C6   *C5*
Who'll screw you in the ground,

C6   *C5*   *C7*   *C6*
They'll fill you in with all the their sins,

C7   *C5*
You'll see.

Bb   *C5*   *Bb*   *C5*
B4 I'll make love to you,

Bb   *C5*   *Bb*   *C5*
If you want me to.

Inst. ‖: *C5* | *C5* | *C5* | *C5* | *C5* :‖   *... fade out*

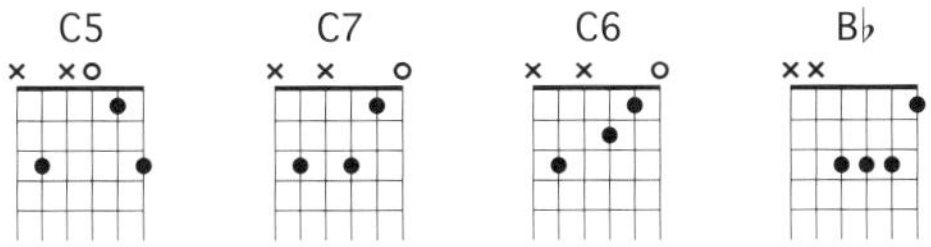

C5   C7   C6   Bb

Lovely Rita

Words & Music by
John Lennon & Paul McCartney

*반음 낮추어 튜닝합니다.

Inst. | B | A | E | B ‖

INTRO
B   A
Lovely Rita meter maid.

E   B
Lovely Rita meter maid.

A1
E   D   A
Lovely Rita meter maid.

E   B7
Nothing can come between us,

C#m   F#   B7
When it gets dark I tow your heart away.

B1
E   A
Standing by a parking meter,

D   G
When I caught a glimpse of Rita,

E   B7
Filling in a ticket in her little white book.

B2
E   A
In a cap she looked much older,

D   G
And the bag across her shoulder

E   B7
Made her look a little like a military man.

Inst. | E C#m F#m B ‖

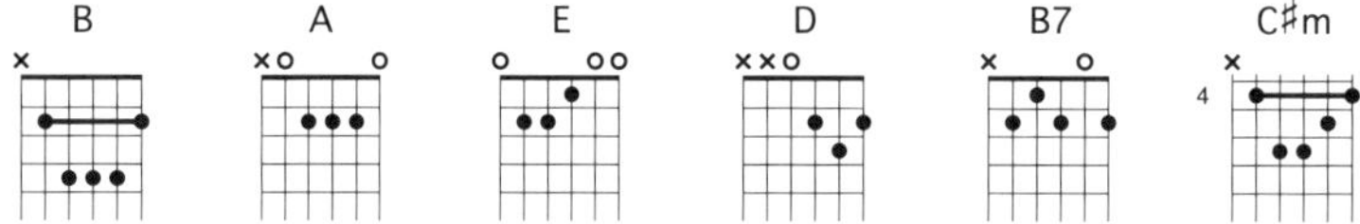

E　　　　　*D*　　*A*
A2 Lovely Rita meter maid,

E　　　　　　　　*B7*
May I enquire discreetly,

C#m　　　　　　　*F#*　　　　　　　　*B7*
When are you free, to take some tea with me?

Bsus4　　*B*
Ah.

Inst. ‖ *E D A* | *E B7* | *C#m F#* | *B B7* ‖

E　　　　　　　*A*
B3 Took her out and tried to win her,

D　　　　　　　*G*
Had a laugh and over dinner,

E　　　　　　　　　　*B7*
Told her I would really like to see her again,

E　　　　　　　*A*
B4 Got the bill and Rita paid it,

D　　　　　　　*G*
Took her home I nearly made it,

E　　　　　　　　*B7*
Sitting on the sofa with a sister or two.

Inst. ‖ *E C#m F#m B* ‖

E　　　　*D*　　*A*
A3 Oh, lovely Rita meter maid,

E　　　　　　　　*B7*
Where would I be without you,

C#m　　　　　　　*F#*　　　　　　*B*
Give us a wink and make me think of you.

B　　　　*A*　　　　*E*　　　　*B*
OUTRO Lovely Rita meter maid, Lovely Rita meter maid.

B　　　　*A*　　　　*E*　　　　*B*
Lovely Rita meter maid, Lovely Rita meter maid.

Inst. ‖: *Am* | *Am* | *Am* | *Am* :‖
　　　　　　| *Am* | *Am* | *Am* ‖

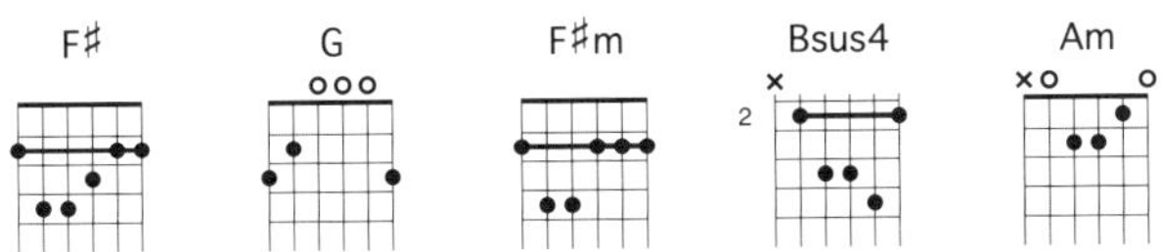

Lucy In The Sky With Diamonds

Words & Music by
John Lennon & Paul McCartney

Inst. | (A5) | (A5/G) | (A5/F#) | (Dm/F) ‖

A   A7   A6   F6
A1 Picture yourself in a boat on a river,

        A   A7   A6   F
With tangerine trees and marmalade skies.

A   A7   A6   F6
Somebody calls you, you answer quite slowly,

      A   A7   A6   Dm   Dm/C
A girl with kaleidoscope eyes.

Bb   C
B1 Cellophane flowers of yellow and green,

F   Bb
Towering over your head.

C   G
Look for the girl with the sun in her eyes,

          D
And she's gone.

G   C   D
C1 Lucy in the sky with diamonds.

G   C   D
Lucy in the sky with diamonds.

G   C   D   D   A
Lucy in the sky with diamonds. Ah - ah.

A   A7   A6   F6
A2 Follow her down to a bridge by a fountain,

      A   A7   A6   F
Where rocking horse people eat marshmallow pies,

A   A7   A6   F6
Everyone smiles as you drift past the flowers,

      A   A7   A6   Dm   Dm/C
That grow so incredibly high.

B2
Bb   C
Newspaper taxis appear on the shore,

F   Bb
Waiting to take you away.

C   G
Climb in the back with your head in the clouds,

      D
And you're gone.

C2
G   C   D
Lucy in the sky with diamonds.

G   C   D
Lucy in the sky with diamonds.

G   C   D D A
Lucy in the sky with diamonds. Ah - ah.

A3
A   A7   A6   F6
Picture yourself on a train in a station,

   A   A7   A6   F
With plasticine porters with looking glass ties,

A   A7   A6   F6
Suddenly someone is there at the turnstile,

   A   A7   A6 Dm
The girl with the kaleidoscope eyes.

C3
G   C   D
‖: Lucy in the sky with diamonds.

G   C   D
Lucy in the sky with diamonds.

G   C   D D A
Lucy in the sky with diamonds. Ah - ah. :‖ *... fade out*

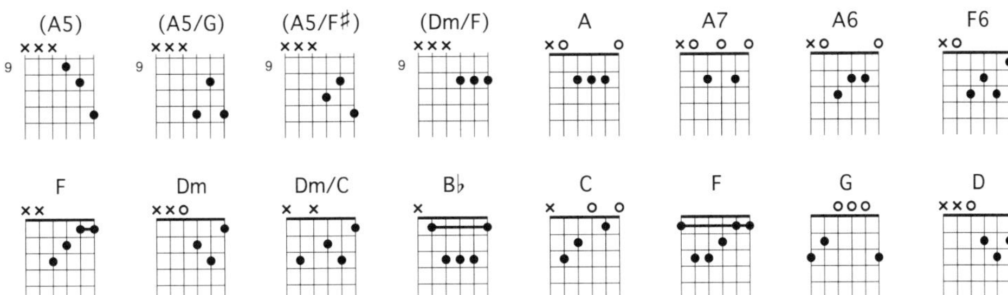

Magical Mystery Tour

Words & Music by
John Lennon & Paul McCartney

<pre>
Inst. |D |A ||
</pre>

       E
(Roll up, roll up for the Magical Mystery Tour, step right this way!)

       E   G   A
A1 Roll up,   roll up for the Mystery Tour.

       E   G   A
    Roll up,   roll up for the Mystery Tour.

       E
    Roll up,   (and that's an invitation),

       G   A
    Roll up,   for the Mystery Tour.

       E
    Roll up   (to make a reservation),

       G   A
    Roll up,   for the Mystery Tour.

       D   D/C   G/B   Gm/Bb
B1 The Magical Mystery Tour is waiting to take you away,

       D/A   A
    Waiting to take you away.

       E   G   A
A2 Roll up,   roll up for the Mystery Tour.

       E   G   A
    Roll up,   roll up for the Mystery Tour.

       E
    Roll up,   (we've got everything you need),

       G   A
    Roll up,   for the Mystery Tour.

       E
    Roll up   (satisfaction guaranteed),

       G   A
    Roll up,   for the Mystery Tour.

D   *D/C*   *G/B*   *Gm/Bb*
B2 The Magical Mystery Tour is hoping to take you away,

D/A   *A*
Hoping to take you away.

Inst. | *B* | *B* | *F#m7* | *F#m7* |
      | *B* | *B* | *F#m7* | *F#m7* *G#m7* | *A* | *B7* ‖

E   *G*   *A*
A3 Ah,   The Magical Mystery Tour.

E   *G*   *A*
Roll up,   roll up for the Mystery Tour.

E
Roll up,   (and that's an invitation),

G   *A*
Roll up,   for the Mystery Tour.

E
Roll up   (to make a reservation),

G   *A*
Roll up,   for the Mystery Tour.

D   *D/C*   *G/B*   *Gm/Bb*
B3 The Magical Mystery Tour is coming to take you away,

D/A   *A6*
Coming to take you away.

D   *D/C*   *G/B*   *Gm/Bb*
B4 The Magical Mystery Tour is dying to take you away,

D/A   *A6*
Dying to take you away.

Inst. | *D* | *D* ‖
      ‖: *Dm7* | *Dm7* | *Dm7* | *Dm7* :‖   *... fade out*

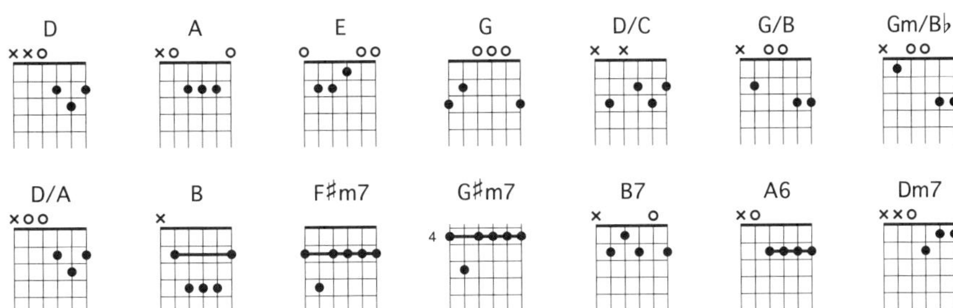

Maxwell's Silver Hammer

Words & Music by
John Lennon & Paul McCartney

A1
```
D            D/C#      B7                          Em                          Em7
```
Joan was quizzical, studied pataphysical science in the home.

```
A7                                          D             A7
```
Late nights all alone with a test-tube, oh-oh-oh-oh...

```
D            D/C#      B7                          Em                          Em7
```
Maxwell Edison majoring in medicine, calls her on the phone

```
A7                                    D        A7
```
"Can I take you out to the pictures Jo-o-o-an?"

```
     E7                              A7
```
But as she's getting ready to go, a knock comes on the door.

B1
```
D                                           E7
```
Bang, bang, Maxwell's silver hammer came down upon her head,

```
A7                                  Em        A7          D   A  D
```
Clang, Clang, Maxwell's silver hammer made sure that she was dead.

Inst. ‖ D F#/C# | Bm D7/A | G | D   ‖

A2
```
D            D/C#      B7
```
Back in school again Maxwell plays the fool again,

```
Em                Em7
```
Teacher gets annoyed.

```
A7                              D        A7
```
Wishing to avoid an unpleasant sce-ee-ee-ene,

```
D            D/C#      B7
```
She tells Max to stay when the class has gone away,

```
Em                Em7
```
So he waits behind,

```
A7                              D        A7
```
Writing fifty times, I must not be so-o-o-oo.

```
     E7
```
But when she turns her back on the boy,

```
     A7
```
He creeps up from behind.

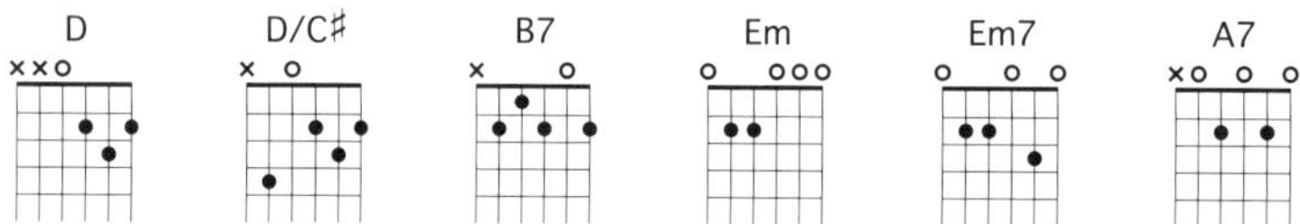

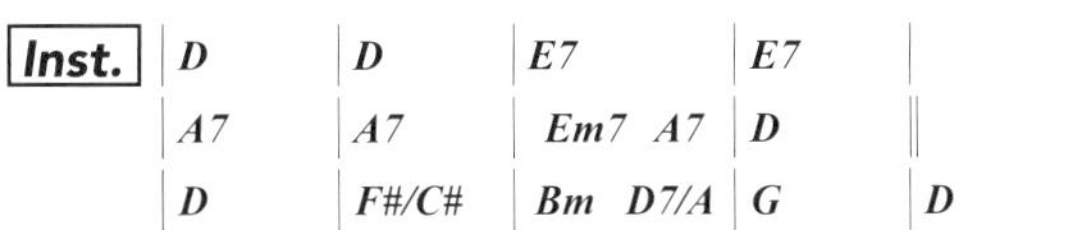


```
Inst.   |D        |D        |E7       |E7       |
        |A7       |A7       | Em7  A7 |D        ||
        |D        |F#/C#    | Bm   D7/A |G      |D        ||
```

D   D/C#   B7
[A3] P.C. Thirty-One said, "We've caught a dirty one,"

Em   Em7
Maxwell stands alone,   Painting testimonial pictures,

D   A7
Oh, oh-oh oh.

D   D/C#   B7
[C1] Rose and Valerie screaming from the gallery,

Em   Em7
Say he must go free.

     A7   D   A7
The judge does not agree and he tells them so-o-o-oo.

          E7
But as the words are leaving his lips

     A7
A noise comes from behind

D   E7
[B3] Bang, bang, Maxwell's silver hammer came down upon his head,

A7   Em   A7
Clang, Clang, Maxwell's silver hammer made sure that he was dead.

             D
Wo-wo-wo-woh,

```
Inst.   |D     |E7   |E7   |A7   |A7   |Em7 A7|D  A  D|
```

D   F#/C#   Bm   D7/A   G   D   A   D
Sil - ver   ham - mer   man.

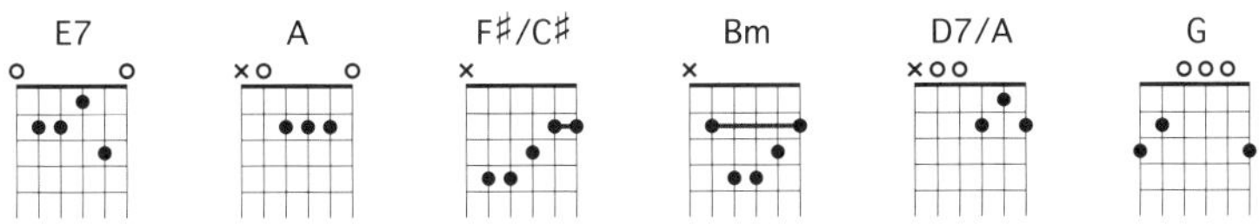

Martha My Dear

Words & Music by
John Lennon & Paul McCartney

** CAPO : 3 FRET.*

Inst. | *C   B7* | *Em Em7 A* | *D* | |
| *G Fadd9* | *G7 Fmaj7* | *G7 Fmaj7* | *C   G* ‖

* 첫 마디는 4분의 5박으로, C코드 한마디 후에
B7 한박자를 추가한다는 느낌으로 연주합니다.

A1
C
Martha my dear,

B7　　　*Em*　　*Em7*　　*A*
Though I spend my days in conversation,

D　　　　　　　*G*
Please remember me.

Fadd9　　　*G7*
Martha my love,

Fmaj7　　　*G7*
Don't forget me,

Fmaj7　　　*G7*
Martha my dear.

A2
Bm7　　　　　　　　*Emadd9*
Hold your head up you silly girl,

D
Look what you've done.

Asus4　　　　　　*A*
When you find yourself in the thick of it,

Asus4　　　　　*A*　　　　*F#7*　*Bm7*
Help yourself to a bit of what is all around you,

Emadd9
Silly girl.

A3
Bm7　　　*E7*
Take a good look around you,

Bm7　　　*E7*
Take a good look you're bound to see

Gmaj7/A　　　*Gmaj7*　　　　　　*Bm7*
That you and me were meant to be for each other,

Emadd9　　*C*
Silly girl.

Inst. | *C* *B7* | *Em Em7 A* | *D* | |
| *G Fadd9* | *G7 Fmaj7* | *G7 Fmaj7* | *G* *G7* ||

A4
Bm7   *Emadd9*
Hold your hand out you silly girl,

D
See what you've done.

        Asus4   *A*
When you find yourself in the thick of it,

Asus4   *A*   *F#7*   *Bm7*
Help yourself to a bit of what is all around you.

        Emadd9
Silly girl.

Inst. | *C G7 C* ||

A5
C
Martha my dear,

            B7   *Em*   *Em7 A*
You have always been my inspiration,

D   *G*
Please be good to me.

Fadd9   *G7*
Martha my love,

Fmaj7   *G7*
Don't forget me,

Fmaj7   *G7*
Martha my dear.

Inst. | *C C/B C/A C/G* | *C* ||

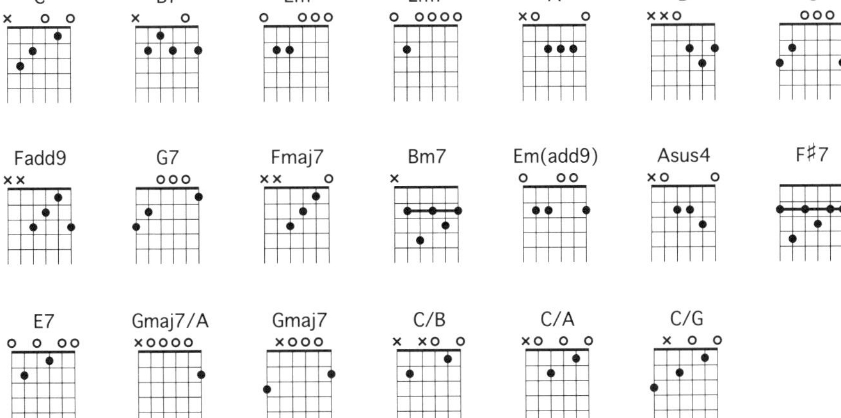

Mean Mr Mustard

Words & Music by
John Lennon & Paul McCartney

E7
A1 Mean Mister Mustard sleeps in the park,

Shaves in the dark trying to save paper.

B7   *B7 C7 C#7*
Sleeps in a hole in the road.

D7   *D7 C#7 C7*
Saving up to buy some clothes.

B7
Keeps a ten bob note up his nose,

      E7   *C7*   *B7*
Such a mean old man,

      E7   *C7*   *B7*
Such a mean old man.

E7
A2 His sister Pam works in a shop,

She never stops, she's a go getter.

B7   *B7 C7 C#7*
Takes him out to look at the Queen.

D7   *D7 C#7 C7*
Only place that he's ever been,

B7
Always shouts out something obscene,

      E7   *C7*   *B7*
Such a dirty old man,

E7   *C7*   *B7*
Dirty old man.

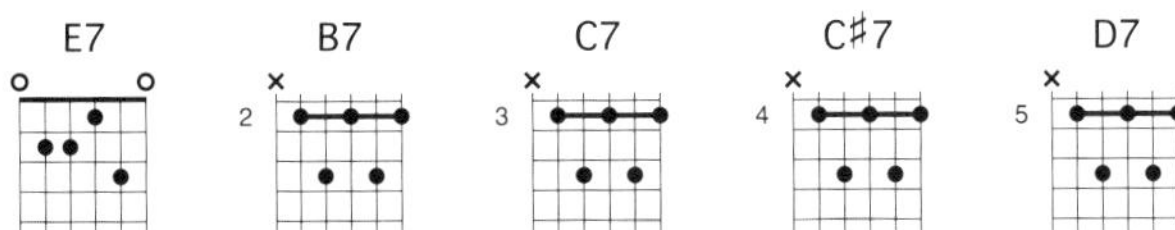

E7
B7
C7
C♯7
D7
2
3
4
5

Michelle

Words & Music by
John Lennon & Paul McCartney

** CAPO : 3 FRET.*

Inst. | *Dm Dm(maj7)* | *Dm7 Dm6* | *Gm Gmadd9 Gm Gm7* | *(A)* ‖

A1
D   (Gm7)
Michelle,   ma belle.

C   Bdim   A
These are words that go together well,

E7b9   A
My Michelle.

A2
D   (Gm7)
Michelle,   ma belle.

C   Bdim   A
Sont les mots qui vont très bien ensemble,

E7b9   A
Très bien ensemble.

B1
*   (Dm)*
I love you, I love you, I love you,

F7   Bb
That's all I want to say.

A7   (Dm)
Until I find a way,

*   Dm   Dm(maj7)   Dm7   Dm6*
I will say the only   words I know

*   Gm Gmadd9 Gm Gm7   (A)*
That you'll   un - der - stand.

A3
D   (Gm7)
Michelle,   ma belle.

C   Bdim   A
Sont les mots qui vont très bien ensemble,

E7b9   A
Très bien ensemble.

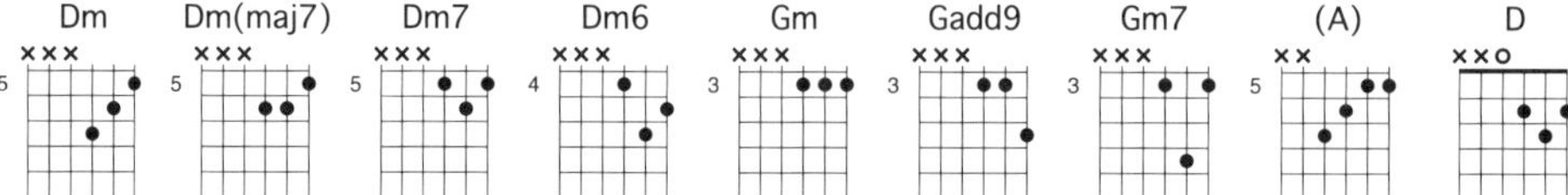

B2

(Dm)
I need to, I need to, I need to.

F7   Bb
I need to make you see,

A7   (Dm)
Oh, what you mean to me.

    Dm   Dm(maj7)   Dm7   Dm6
Until I do I'm   hoping you

     Gm   Gmadd9 Gm   Gm7   (A)
Will know   what I   mean.

(Dm)   (Gm7)
I love you.

Inst. | C | Bdim | A   E7b9 | A   ‖

B3

(Dm)
I want you, I want you, I want you.

F7   Bb
I think you know by now,

A7   (Dm)
I'll get to you somehow.

    Dm   Dm(maj7)   Dm7   Dm6
Until I do   I'm   telling you,

     Gm   Gmadd9   Gm   Gm7   (A)
So you'll   un - der - stand.

A4

D   (Gm7)
Michelle,   ma belle.

C   Bdim   A
Sont les mots qui vont très bien ensemble,

E7b9   A
Très bien ensemble.

         Dm   Dm(maj7)   Dm7   Dm6
And I will say the only   words I know

     Gm Gmadd9 Gm   Gm7   (A)   D
That you'll   un - der - stand, my Michelle.

Inst. | (Gm7) | C | Bdim | A   E7b9 ‖
          | (Gm7) | C | ... fade out

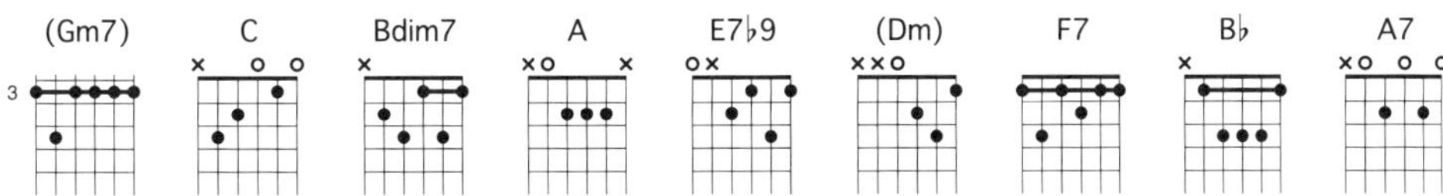

Misery

Words & Music by
John Lennon & Paul McCartney

[INTRO]
F   *G*
The world is treating me bad,

C   *Am*   *G*
Misery.

[A1]
C   *F*
I'm the kind of guy,

        C   *F*
Who never used to cry,

                          G
The world is treating me bad,

C   *Am*
Misery.

[A2]
       C   *F*
I've lost her now for sure,

      C   *F*
I won't see her no more,

              G
It's gonna be a drag,

C
Misery.

[B1]
Am   *C*
I'll remember all the little things we've done,

Am   *G*
Can't she see she'll always be the only one,

Only one.

<pre>
    C   F
A3 Send her back to me,

           C   F
    'Cause everyone can see,

                      G
    Without her I will be

        C
    In misery

    Am   C
B2 I'll remember all the little things we've done,

    Am   G
    She'll remember and she'll miss her only one,

    Lonely one.

    C   F
A4 Send her back to me,

           C   F
    'Cause everyone can see,

                      G
    Without her I will be

        C
    In misery,

    Am   C   Am
    Oh, In misery, ooh,

        C
    My misery,

    Am   C
    La, la, la, la, la, la, misery.
</pre>

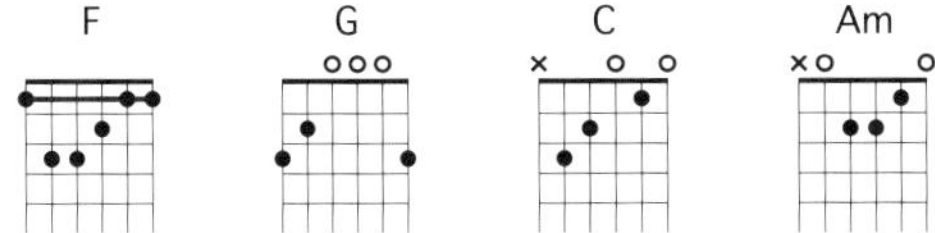

Mother Nature's Son

Words & Music by
John Lennon & Paul McCartney

* 음악과 함께 연주한다면, 조율기의 피치를 432 ~ 435Hz 사이로 조정합니다.

Inst. | Bm Bm7 | Bm6 E9 | D | D | D | D ||

A1
D   G/D   D
Born a poor young country boy,

Bm   Bm7   Bm6   E9
Mother Nature's son.

A   D/A   A
All day long

D/A   A   D/A   A   D/A   D   Dm7   G/D   D
I'm sitting singing songs for everyone.

Inst. | D Dm7 | G/D D ||

A2
D   G/D   D
Sit beside a mountain stream,

Bm   Bm7   Bm6   E9
See her waters rise.

A   D/A A D/A   A   D/A
Lis - ten to   the   pretty sound

       A   D/A   D   Dm7   G/D   D
Of music as she flies.

B1
           D   G/D   D
Do do, do do do do, do do do do, do.

                 G/D   D   Dmaj7
Do do do do, do do do do, do.

D7   G/D   Gm   D
Do do do.

|A3|
D   G/D   D
Find me in my field of grass,

Bm   Bm7   Bm6   E9
Mother Nature's son.

A   D/A   A   D/A
Sway-ing dais-ies

A   D/A   A   D/A   D   Dm7   G/D   D
Sing a lazy song beneath the sun.

|B2|
D   G/D   D
Do do, do do do do, do do do do, do.

G/D   D   Dmaj7
Do do do do, do do do do, do.

D7   G/D   Gm
Do do do.

D
Yeah, yeah, yeah.

|Inst.| ‖ *D G/D* | *G/D D* | *Bm Bm7* | *Bm6 E9* |
| *A D/A A D/A* | *A D/A A D/A* | *D Dm7* | *G/D   D* ‖

|OUTRO|
D   Dm7   G/D   D7
Ah.   Mother Nature's son.

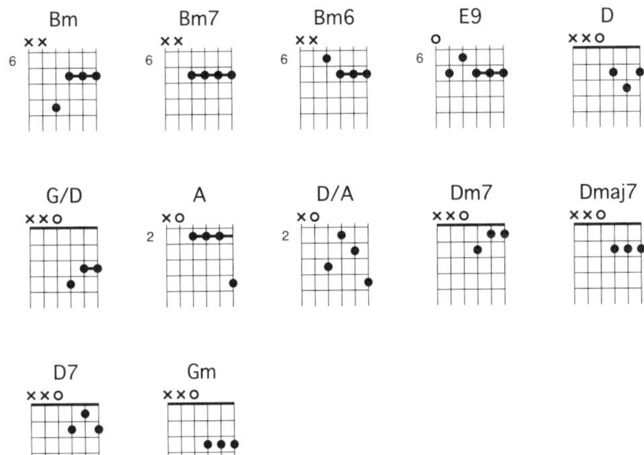

No Reply

Words & Music by
John Lennon & Paul McCartney

F6
A1 This happened once before,

G6   C
When I came to your door, no reply.

F6
They said it wasn't you,

G6   C
But I saw you peep through your window.

Am   Em   Fmaj7   Em
I saw the light,   I saw the light,

F6
I know that you saw me,

G6   C
'Cause I looked up to see your face.

F6
A2 I tried to telephone,

G6   C
They said you were not home, that's a lie.

F6
'Cause I know where you've been,

G6   C
I saw you walk in your door.

Am   Em   Fmaj7   Em
I nearly died,   I nearly died,

F6
'Cause you walked hand in hand

G6   C
With another man in my place.

$\boxed{\text{B1}}$
       C   *E*   *A*
If I were you, I'd realise that I

        Dm   *F*   *C*
Love you more than any other guy.

          E   *A*
And I'll forgive the lies that I

        Dm   *F*   *C*
Heard before, when you gave me no reply.

          F6
$\boxed{\text{A3}}$ I've tried to telephone,

          G6   *C*
They said you were not home, that's a lie,

          F6
'Cause I know where you've been,

      G6   *C*
And I saw you walk in your door.

   Am *Em*   *Fmaj7*   *Em*
I nearly died, I nearly died,

          F6
'Cause you walked hand in hand

     G6   *C*
With another man in my place.

   Am *Em*   *Fmaj7* *C6/9*
No reply,   no reply.

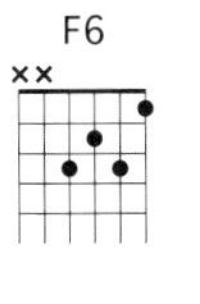
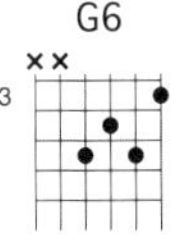
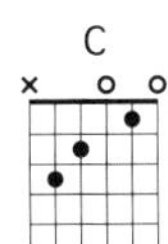
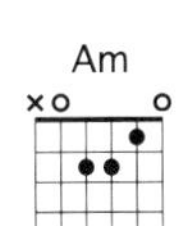
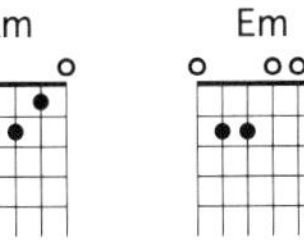
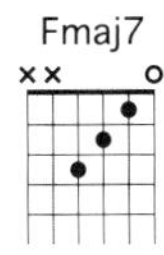
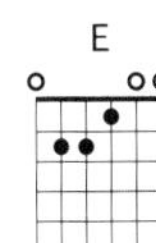
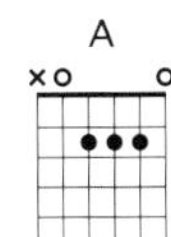
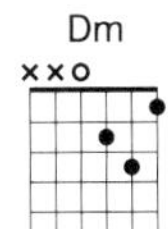
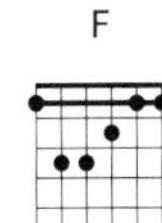

Norwegian Wood

Words & Music by
John Lennon & Paul McCartney

** CAPO : 2 FRET.*

Inst. ‖: *D* | *D* | *D Cadd9 G/B* | *D* :‖

A1
D
I once had a girl,

Or should I say,

Cadd9   G/B   D
She once had me.

D
She showed me her room,

Isn't it good,

Cadd9   G/B   D
Norwegian wood?

B1
    Dm   *G*
She asked me to stay and she told me to sit anywhere,

    Dm   *Em7*   *A*
So I looked around and I noticed there wasn't a chair.

A2
D
I sat on a rug,

Biding my time,

Cadd9   G/B D
Drinking her wine.

D
We talked until two,

And then she said,

Cadd9   G/B   D
"It's time for bed."

Inst. ‖: *D* | *D* | *D Cadd9 G/B* | *D* :‖

Dm
B2 She told me she worked in the morning and started to laugh. *G*

Dm
I told her I didn't and crawled off to sleep in the bath. *Em7* *A*

D
A3 And when I awoke,

I was alone,

Cadd9 *G/B* *D*
This bird had flown.

D
So I lit a fire,

Isn't it good,

Cadd9 *G/B* *D*
Norwegian wood.

Inst. | *D* | *D* | *D Cadd9 G/B* | *D* ‖

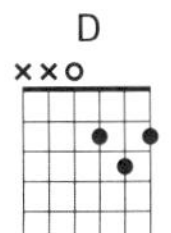

D

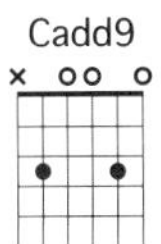

Cadd9

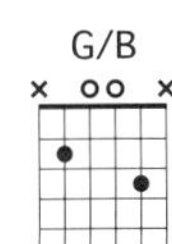

G/B

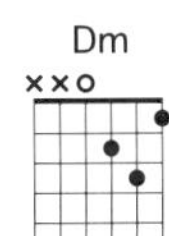

Dm

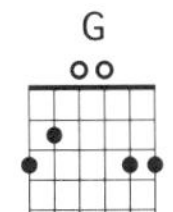

G

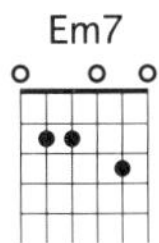

Em7

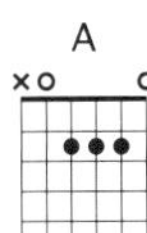

A

Not A Second Time

Words & Music by
John Lennon & Paul McCartney

A1
```
G                        Em
You know you made me cry,

G                              E
I see no use in wondering why,

   D      G      D7
I cried for you.
```

A2
```
G                              Em
And now you've changed your mind,

G                          E
I see no reason to change mine,

   D        Am        D
My crying is through, oh.
```

B1
```
Am                      Bm
You're giving me the same old line,

G            Em
I'm wondering why.

Am
You hurt me then, you're back again,

Bm       D7              Em
No, no, no, not a second time.
```

Inst. | Am | Bm | G | Em |
| Am | Am | Bm | D7 |
| Em | Em ||

A3

G   Em
You know you made me cry,

G   E
I see no use in wondering why,

   D   G   D
I cried for you,   yeah.

A4

G   Em
And now you've changed your mind,

G   E
I see no reason to change mine,

   D   Am   D
My crying is through, oh.

B2

Am   Bm
You're giving me the same old line,

G   Em
I'm wondering why.

Am
You hurt me then, you're back again,

Bm   D7   Em
No, no, no, not a second time.

OUTRO

                 G   Em
Not a second time,

                 G   Em
Not a second time.

               G   Em
No, no, no, no, no,   *... fade out*

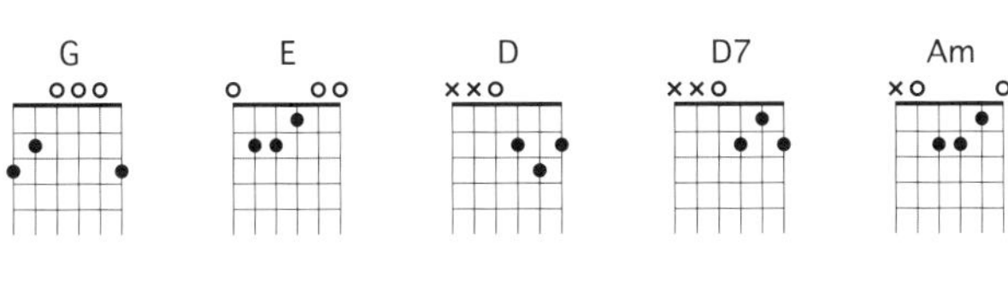

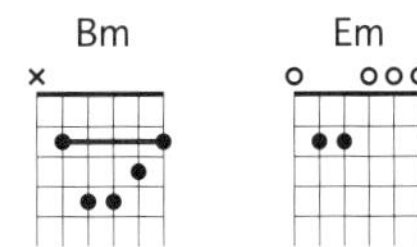

Nowhere Man

CAPO : 2 FRET.

Words & Music by
John Lennon & Paul McCartney

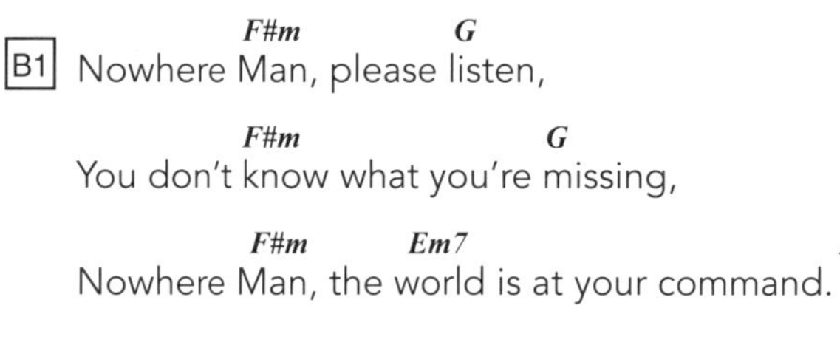

Inst. | D | A | G | D |
       | Em | Gm | D | D ‖

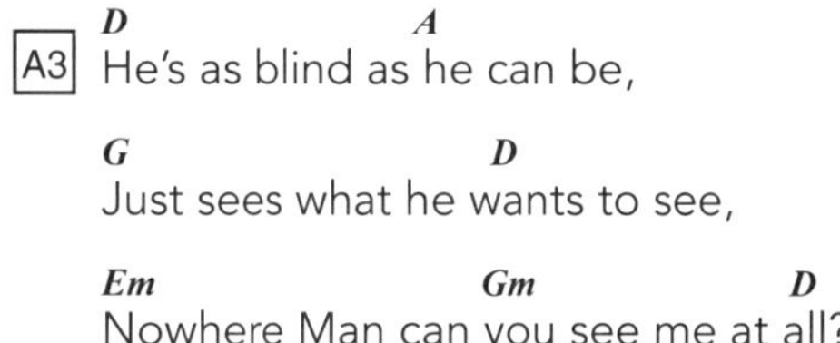

       F#m   *G*
B2 Nowhere Man, don't worry,

       F#m   *G*
Take your time, don't hurry,

       F#m   *Em7*   *A7*
Leave it all till somebody else lends you a hand.

D   *A*
A4 Doesn't have a point of view,

G   *D*
Knows not where he's going to,

Em   *Gm*   *D*
Isn't he a bit like you and me?

       F#m   *G*
B3 Nowhere Man, please listen,

       F#m   *G*
You don't know what you're missing,

       F#m   *Em7*   *A7*
Nowhere Man, the world is at your command.

D   *A*
A5 He's a real Nowhere Man,

G   *D*
Sitting in his Nowhere Land,

Em   *Gm*   *D*
Making all his nowhere plans for nobody.

Em   *Gm*   *D*
Making all his nowhere plans for nobody.

Em   *Gm*   *D*
Making all his nowhere plans for nobody.

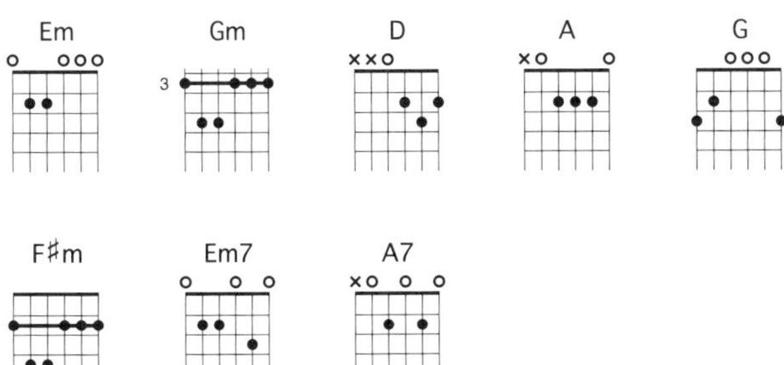

Ob-La-Di, Ob-La-Da

Words & Music by
John Lennon & Paul McCartney

** CAPO : 1 FRET.*

Inst. | E | A | A | A | A ||

A1
```
  A                                E
Desmond has a barrow in the market place,

  E7                       A
Molly is the singer in a band.

                                 D
Desmond says to Molly-girl I like your face,

          A              E            A
And Molly says this as she takes him by the hand.
```

B1
```
           A                      E    F#m7
:Ob La Di, Ob La Da, life goes on, bra,

  A           E        A
La La how their life goes on. :
```

A2
```
  A                              E
Desmond takes a trolly to the jeweller's store,

  E7                        A
Buys a twenty carat golden ring.

                           D
Takes it back to Molly waiting at the door,

          A              E            A
And as he gives it to her she begins to sing.
```

B2
```
           A                      E    F#m7
:Ob La Di, Ob La Da, life goes on, bra,

  A           E        A
La La how their life goes on. :
```

C1
```
  D                                               A  Asus2  A  A7
In a couple of years, they have built a home sweet home.

  D                                      A/E                E
With a couple of kids running in the yard of Desmond and Molly Jones.
```

|A3| *A*   *E*   *E7*   *A*
Happy ever after in the market place, Desmond lets the children lend a hand.

                                       D
Molly stays at home and does his pretty face

           A   *E*   *A*
And in the evening she still sings it with the band.

|B3| ‖:   *A*   *E*   *F#m7*
Ob La Di, Ob La Da, life goes on, bra,

A   *E*   *A*
La La how their life goes on. :‖

|C2| *D*   *A* *Asus2* *A* *A7*
In a couple of years, they have built a home sweet home.

 D   *A/E*   *E*
With a couple of kids running in the yard of Desmond and Molly Jones.

|A4| *A*   *E*   *E7*   *A*
Happy ever after in the market place, Molly lets the children lend a hand.

                                       D
Desmond stays at home and does his pretty face

           A   *E*   *A*
And in the evening she's singer with the band.

|B3| *A*   *E*   *F#m7*
Ob La Di, Ob La Da, life goes on, bra,

A   *E*   *A*
La La how their life goes on.

   A   *E*   *F#m7*
Ob La Di, Ob La Da, life goes on, bra,

A   *E*   *F#m7*
La La how their life goes on.

                                E   *A*
And if you want some fun, take Ob La Di Bla Da.

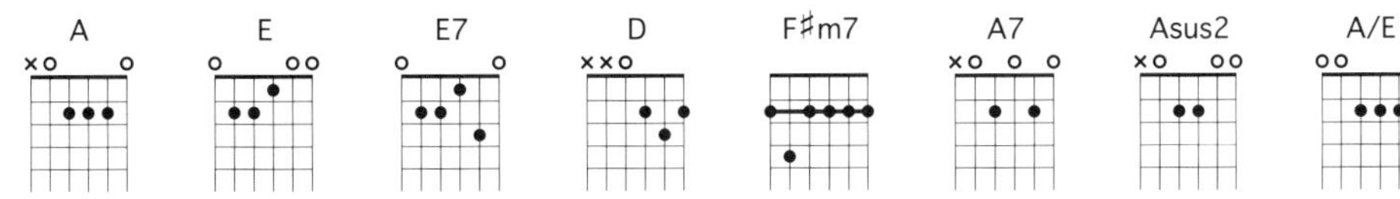

Octopus's Garden

Words & Music by
Ringo Starr

** CAPO : 4 FRET.*

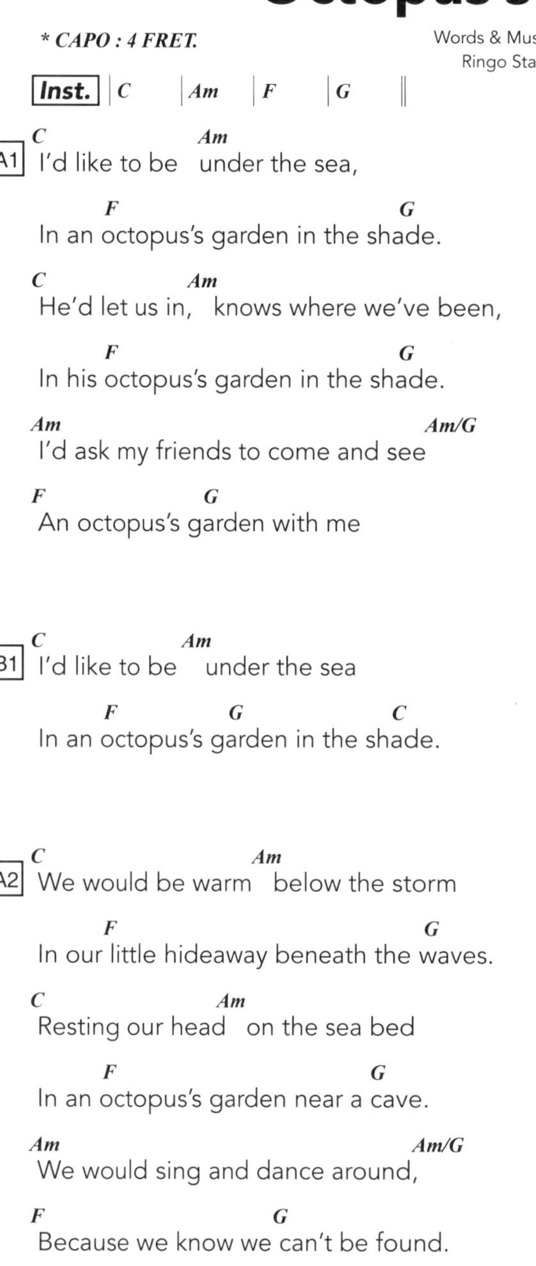

C   *Am*
B2 I'd like to be   under the sea

        F   *G*   *C*
In an octopus's garden in the shade

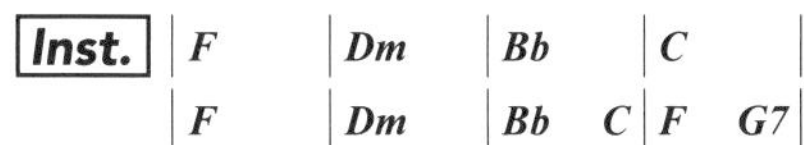

C   *Am*
A3 We would shout   and swim about

       F   *G*
The coral that lies beneath the waves.

C   *Am*
 Oh what joy for every girl and boy,

F   *G*
 Knowing they're happy and they're safe.

Am   *Am/G*
 We would be so happy, you and me,

F   *G*
 No one there to tell us what to do.

C   *Am*
B3 I'd like to be   under the sea

        F   *G*   *C* *Am* *G*
In an octopus's garden with you,

        F   *G*   *Am* *Am/G*
In an octopus's garden with you,

        F   *G*   *C* *B5* *C5*
In an octopus's garden with you.

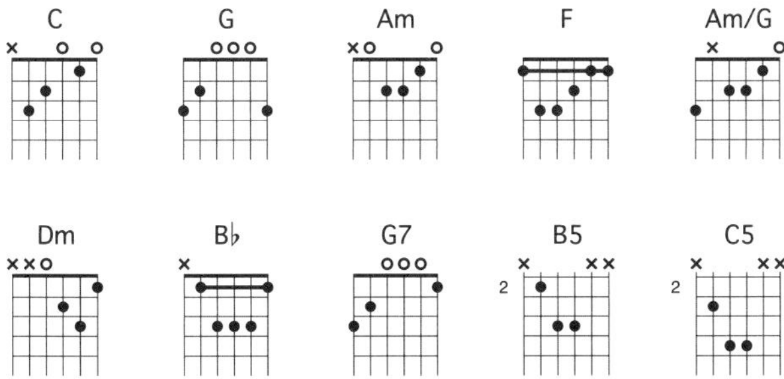

Oh! Darling

Words & Music by
John Lennon & Paul McCartney

Inst. | *Eaug* ‖

A   *E*
A1 Oh! darling, please believe me,

F#m7   *D*
I'll never do you no harm.

   Bm7   *E7*
Believe me when I tell you,

Bm7   *E7*   *A*   *D*   *A*   *E7*
I'll never do you no harm.

       A   *E*
A2 Oh! darling, if you leave me,

F#m7   *D*
I'll never make it alone.

   Bm7   *E7*
Believe me when I beg you,

Bm7   *E7*   *A*   *D*   *A*   *A7*
Don't ever leave me alone.

       D   *F*
B1 When you told me you didn't need me anymore,

       A   *A7*
Well you know I nearly broke down and cried.

       B
When you told me you didn't need me anymore

       E   *F*   *E*   *Eaug*
Well you know I nearly broke down and died.

A3
     A   *E*
Oh! darling, if you leave me,

F#m7   *D*
I'll never make it alone.

  Bm7   *E7*
Believe me when I tell you,

Bm7   *E7*   *A*   *D*
I'll never do you no harm.

A   *A7*
Believe me, darling.

B2
         D   *F*
When you told me you didn't need me anymore,

         A   *A7*
Well you know I nearly broke down and cried.

        B
When you told me you didn't need me anymore,

       E   *F*   *E*   *Eaug*
Well you know I nearly broke down and died.

A4
     A   *E*
Oh! darling, please believe me,

F#m7   *D*
I'll never let you down.

Oh, believe me darling.

  Bm7   *E7*
Believe me when I tell you,

Bm7   *E7*   *A*   *D*   *A*   *Bb7*   *A7*
I'll never do you no harm.

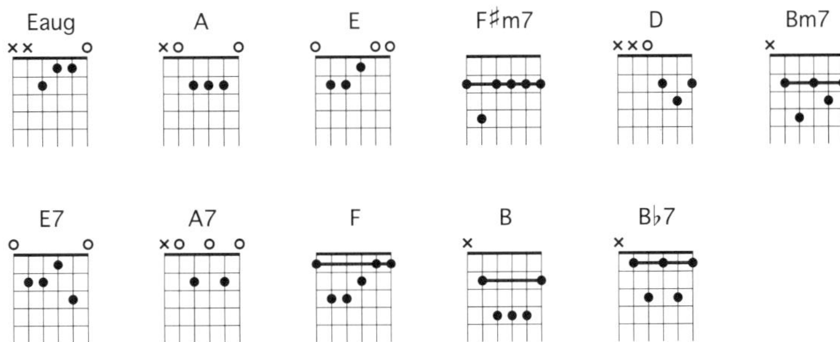

One After 909

Words & Music by
John Lennon & Paul McCartney

Inst. | *B7* | *B7* | *B7* | *B7* | *B7* | *B7* ‖

B7
A1 My baby says she's travelling on the one after nine o nine.

I said move over honey, I'm travelling on that line.

B7
B1 I said move over once, move over twice,

E7
Come on baby, don't be cold as ice.

B7   *F#7*   *B7*
Said she's travelling on the one after nine o nine.

B7
A2 I begged her not to go, and I begged her on my bended knee.

You're only fooling around, only fooling around with me.

B7
B2 I said move over once, move over twice,

E7
Come on baby, don't be cold as ice.

B7   *F#7*   *B7*
Said she's travelling on the one after nine o nine.

E7   *B7*
C1 Pick up my bags, run to the station.

C#7   *F#7*
Railman says, you've got the the wrong location.

E7   *B7*
Pick up my bag, run right home,

C#7   *F#7*
Then I find I've got the number wrong.

A3   *B7*
Well said she's travelling on the one after nine o nine.

I said move over honey, I'm travelling on that line.

B3   *B7*
I said move over once, move over twice,

E7
Come on baby, don't be cold as ice.

B7   *F#7*   *B7*
Said she's travelling on the one after nine o nine.

Inst. ‖: *B7* | *B7* | *B7* | *B7* :‖ *B7* | *B7* |
        | *E7* | *E7* | *B7* | *F#7* | *B7* | *B7* ‖

C2 *E7*   *B7*
Pick up my bags, run to the station.

C#7   *F#7*
Railman says, you've got the the wrong location.

E7   *B7*
Pick up my bag, run right home,

C#7   *F#7*
Then I find I've got the number wrong.

A4   *B7*
Well   she says she's travelling on the one after nine o nine.

I said move over honey, I'm travelling on that line.

B4   *B7*
I said move over once, move over twice,

E7
Come on baby, don't be cold as ice.

B7   *F#7*
Said she's travelling on the one after nine o nine.

B7   *F#7*
She said she's travelling on the one after nine o,

B7   *F#7*   *B7*
Said she's travelling on the one after nine o nine.

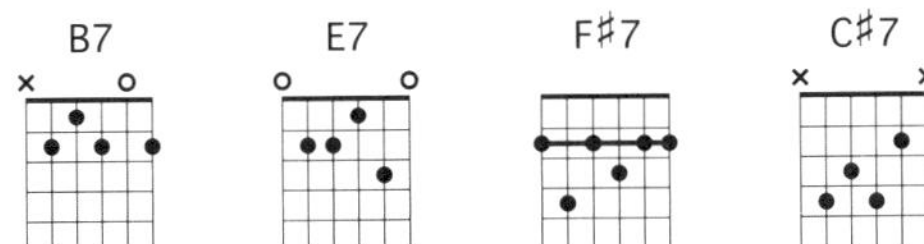

Only A Northern Song

Words & Music by
George Harrison

A1
A
If you're listening to this song,

Bm7
You may think the chords are going wrong.

E7
But they're not,

D
He just wrote it like that.

A2
A
When you're listening late at night,

Bm7
You may think the band are not quite right.

E7
But they are,

D
They just play it like that.

B1
E   *Bm7*   *G*   *C#7*
It doesn't really matter what chords I play,

F#7   *Bm*   *F#7*
What words I say or time of day it is,

D *A*   *E*
'Cause it's only a Northern Song

B2   *E*   *Bm7*   *G*   *C#7*
It doesn't really matter what clothes I wear,

    F#7   *Bm*   *F#7*
Or how I fare or if my hair is brown,

          D   *A*   *E*
When it's only a Northern Song.

A3 *A*
If you think the harmony

               Bm7
Is a little dark and out of key

    E7   *D*
You're correct, there's nobody there.

Inst. | *E Bm7* | *G C#7* | *F#7* | *Bm7* | *F#7* |

    D   *A*   *E*
And I told you there's no one there.

Inst. | *A* | *A* | *A* | *A* | *Bm7* | *Bm7* |
       | *E7* | *E7* | *D* | *D* | *E Bm7* | *G C#7* |
       | *F#7* | *Bm* | *F#7* | *D* | *A* | *E* ||

... fade out

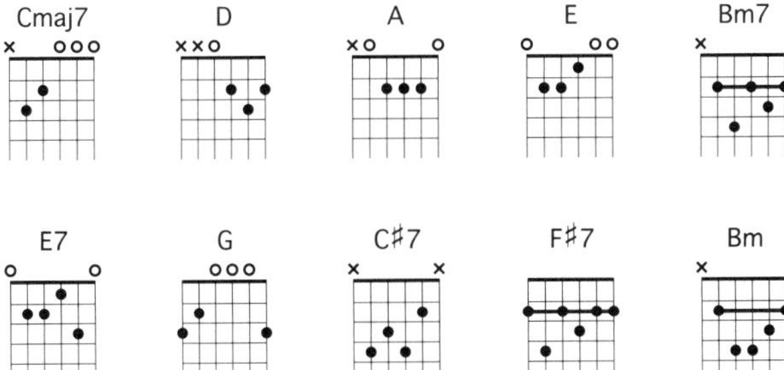

P.S. I Love You

Words & Music by
John Lennon & Paul McCartney

|INTRO|
```
G     C#      D
As I write this letter,

G       C#      D
Send my love to you,

   G       C#        D
Remember that I'll always,

        A          D
Be in love with you.
```

|A1|
```
D                    Em              D
Treasure these few words 'till we're together,

        A          Bm
Keep all my love forever,

A          Bb
P.S. I love you,

Bb    C    D
You, you, you.
```

|A2|
```
D               Em            D
I'll be coming home again to you love,

    A          Bm
Until the day I do love,

A          Bb
P.S. I love you,

Bb    C    D
You, you, you.
```

|B1|
```
G           D
As I write this letter,

G               D
Send my love to you,

    G             D
Remember that I'll always,

D    A       D
Be in love with you.
```


D   *Em*   *D*
A3 Treasure these few words till we're together,

           A   *Bm*
Keep all my love forever,

A   *Bb*
P.S. I love you.

Bb   *C*   *D*
You, you, you.

G   *D*
B2 As I write this letter, (oh,)

G   *D*
Send my love to you, (you know I want you to)

    G   *D*
Remember that I'll always, (yeah,)

D   *A*   *D*
Be in love with you.

D   *Em*   *D*
A4 I'll be coming home again to you, love,

      A   *Bm*
Until the day I do, love,

A   *Bb*
P.S. I love you.

Bb   *C*   *D*
You, you, you.

Bb   *C*   *D*
You, you, you.

Bb *C*   *D*
I love you.

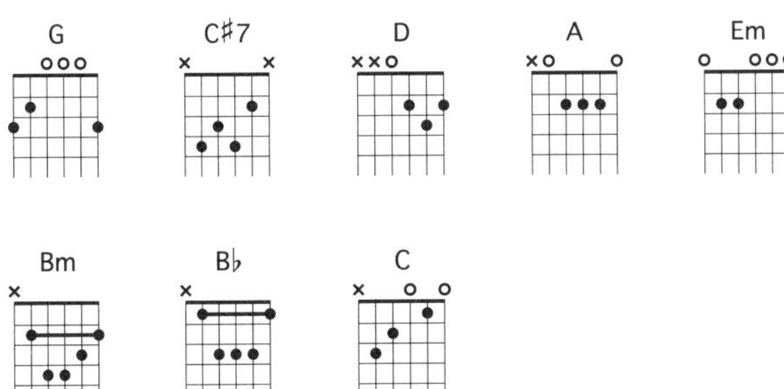

Paperback Writer

Words & Music by
John Lennon & Paul McCartney

INTRO Paperback writer, paperback writer.

Inst. | G7 | G7 | G7 | G7 ‖

A1
      G
Dear Sir or Madam, will you read my book?

It took me years to write, will you take a look?

Based on a novel by a man named Lear,

                                        C
And I need a job, so I want to be a paperback writer,

      G
Paperback writer.

A2
      G
It's the dirty story of a dirty man

And his clinging wife doesn't understand.

His son is working for the Daily Mail,

                                        C
It's a steady job, but he wants to be a paperback writer,

      G
Paperback writer.

Paperback writer, paperback writer.

Inst. | G7 | G7 | G7 | G7 ‖

G
|A3| It's a thousand pages, give or take a few,

I'll be writing more in a week or two.

I can make it longer if you like the style,

                                                           C
I can change it round, and I want to be a paperback writer,

          G   *G7*
Paperback writer.

G
|A4| If you really like it you can have the rights,

It could make a million for you overnight,

If you must return it, you can send it here,

                                                C
But I need a break and I want to be a paperback writer,

       G
Paperback writer.

Paperback writer, paperback writer.

Inst. | *G7* | *G7* | *G7* | *G7* ‖

G
|OUTRO| Paperback writer, paperback writer.

Paperback writer, paperback writer.

Paperback writer, paperback writer.   *... fade out*

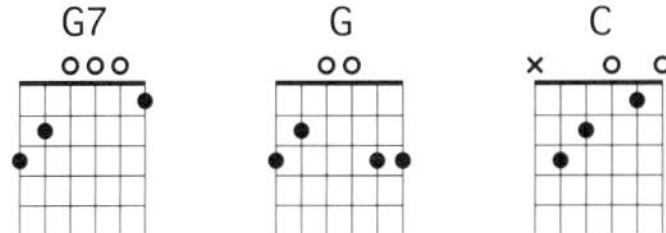

259

Penny Lane

Words & Music by
John Lennon & Paul McCartney

|A1|
        B   **C#m7**   **F#7**

In Penny Lane there is a barber showing photographs

     B   **Bm7**

Of every head he's had the pleasure to know,

        G#m7b5   **Gmaj7**

And all the people that come and go,

        F#sus4   **F#7**   **F#7sus4**   **F#7**

Stop and say hello.

|A2|
      B   **C#m7**   **F#7**

On the corner is a banker with a motorcar,

        B   **Bm7**

The little children laugh at him behind his back.

      G#m7b5   **Gmaj7**

And the banker never wears a mac

  F#7sus4   **F#7** **E**

In the pouring rain,   very strange.

|B1|
      A   **A/C#**   **D**

Penny Lane is in my ears and in my eyes.

A   **A/C#**   **D**

There beneath the blue suburban skies

   F#7

I sit, and meanwhile back.

|A3|
      B   **C#m7**   **F#7**

In Penny Lane there is a fireman with an hourglass

      B   **Bm7**

And in his pocket is a portrait of the Queen.

    G#m7b5   **Gmaj7**

He likes to keep his fire engine clean,

  F#sus4   **F#7**   **F#7sus4**   **F#7**

It's a clean machine.

Inst. | B | C#m7 F#7 | B | Bm7 |
| G#m7b5 | Gmaj7 | F#7sus4 F#7 | E ||

B2
       A   A/C#   D
Penny Lane is in my ears and in my eyes,

A   A/C#   D
Full of fish and finger pies

              F#7
In summer, meanwhile back.

A4
             B   C#m7   F#7
Behind the shelter in the middle of a roundabout

             B   Bm7
The pretty nurse is selling poppies from a tray,

             G#m7b5   Gmaj7   F#7sus4   F#7   F#7sus4   F#7
And though she feels as if she's in a play, she is anyway.

A5
             B   C#m7   F#7
In Penny Lane the barber shaves another customer,

             B   Bm7
We see the banker sitting waiting for a trim.

             G#m7b5   Gmaj7
And then the fireman rushes in

        F#7sus4   F#7 E
From the pouring rain,   very strange.

B3
            A   A/C#   D
Penny Lane is in my ears and in my eyes.

A   A/C#   D
There beneath the blue suburban skies

             F#7
I sit, and meanwhile back.

            B   B/D#   E
Penny Lane is in my ears and in my eyes.

B   B/D#   E   B
There beneath the blue suburban skies, Penny Lane.

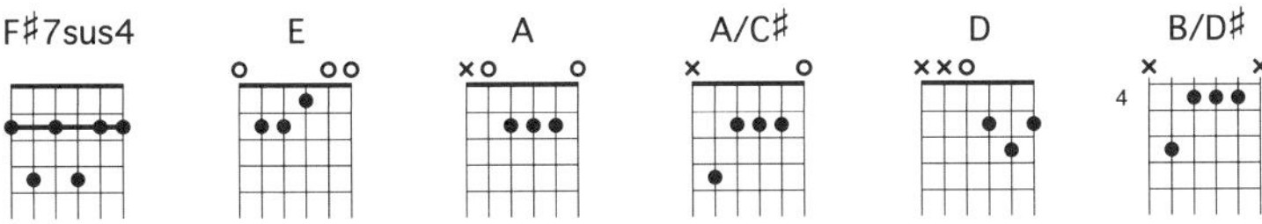

Piggies

Words & Music by
George Harrison

** CAPO : 6 FRET.*

Inst. ‖ D A │ D A ‖

A1
D   A
Have you seen the little piggies

D   A
Crawling in the dirt?

D   A
And for all the little piggies

Bm   E7
Life is getting worse,

Bm   E7   A
Always having dirt to play around in.

Inst. ‖ D A │ D A ‖

A2
D   A
Have you seen the bigger piggies

D   A
In their starched white shirts?

D   A
You will find the bigger piggies

Bm   E7
Stirring up the dirt

Bm   E7   A
Always have clean shirts to play around in.

Inst. ‖ D A │ D F#7 ‖

B1
Em   F#7
In their sties with all their backing.

G   D   A
They don't care what goes on around.

Em   F#7
In their eyes there's something lacking

G   A
What they need's a damn good whacking!

Inst. || D A | D A | D A | Bm E7 |
| Bm E7 | A | D A | D A ||

[A1]
D   A
Everywhere there's lots of piggies

D   A
Living piggy lives,

D   A
You can see them out for dinner

Bm   E7
With their piggy wives.

Bm   E7   A
Clutching forks and knives to eat their bacon.

Inst. || D A | Dm A | Dm A | E7 A |
| —— | Eb5 | Bb ||

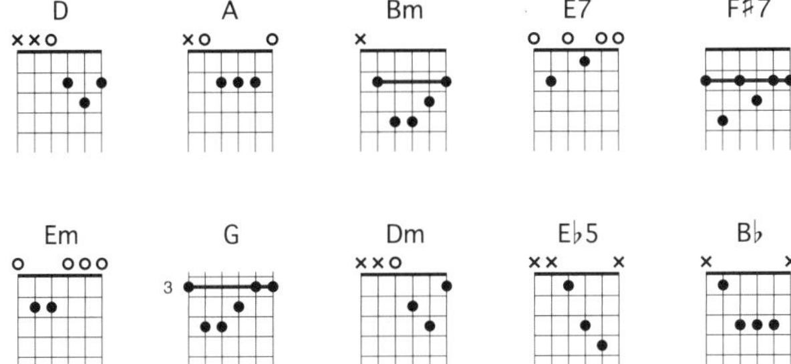

Please Please Me

Words & Music by
John Lennon & Paul McCartney

Inst. | E | E | E | E ‖

A1
E   A   E   G   A   B
Last night I said these words to my girl,

E   A   E
I know you never even try, girl.

B1
          A   F#m
Come on, come on,

          C#m   A
Come on, come on,

          E   A   B   E   A   B
Please please me, oh yeah, like I please you.

A2
E   A   E   G   A   B
You don't need me to show the way, love.

E   A   E
Why do I always have to say love.

B2
          A   F#m
Come on, come on,

          C#m   A
Come on, come on,

          E   A   B   E
Please please me, oh yeah, like I please you.

C1
A
I don't want to sound complaining,

B   E
But you know there's always rain in my heart. (in my heart)

A   B   E
I do all the pleasing with you, it's so hard to reason with you.

A   B   E   A   B
Oh yeah, why do you make me blue?

<pre>
 E   A   E   G   A   B
A3 Last night I said these words to my girl,

 E   A   E
    I know you never even try, girl.

           A   F#m
B3 Come on, come on,

           C#m   A
    Come on, come on,

            E   A
    Please please me, oh yeah,

       B
    Like I please you.

            E   A
    Please please me, oh yeah,

       B
    Like I please you.

            E   A
    Please please me, oh yeah,

        B   E   G   C   B   E
    Like I please you.
</pre>

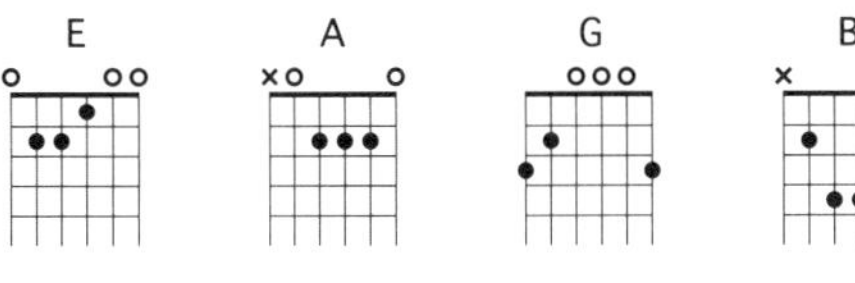

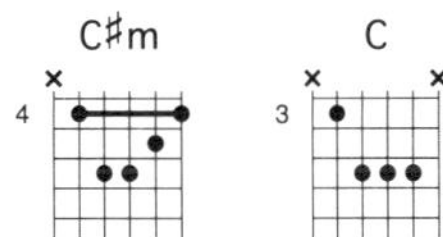

Polythene Pam

Words & Music by
John Lennon & Paul McCartney

Inst. ‖ D A | E | D A | E   ‖

```
              D       A          E
```
A1 Well you should see Polythene Pam,

```
              D               A          E
```
She's so good-looking but she looks like a man.

```
              G                       B7
```
Well you should see her in drag dressed in her polythene bag.

```
              C    D      E
```
Yes you should see Polythene Pam.

```
C        D       E
```
Yeah, yeah, yeah.

Inst. ‖ D   A | E | D   A | E   ‖

```
            D             A              E
```
A2 Get a dose of her in jackboots and kilt,

```
            D               A              E
```
She's killer-diller when she's dressed to the hilt.

```
            G                       B7
```
She's the kind of a girl that makes the News of the World,

```
              C                   D        E
```
Yes you could say she was attractively built.

```
C        D       E
```
Yeah, yeah, yeah.

Inst. ‖ D   A | E | D   A | E |
D A	E	D A	E
D A	E	D A	E
D A	E	D A	E
D A	E	D A	E
E	E	E	D	C#m	E7/B ‖

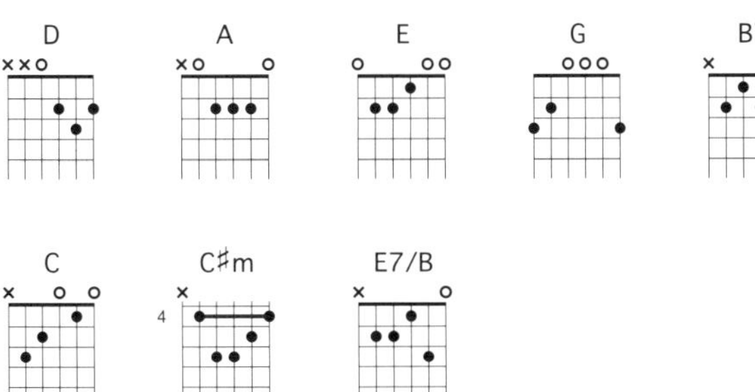
D
A
E
G
B7
C
C♯m
E7/B

Rain

Words & Music by
John Lennon & Paul McCartney

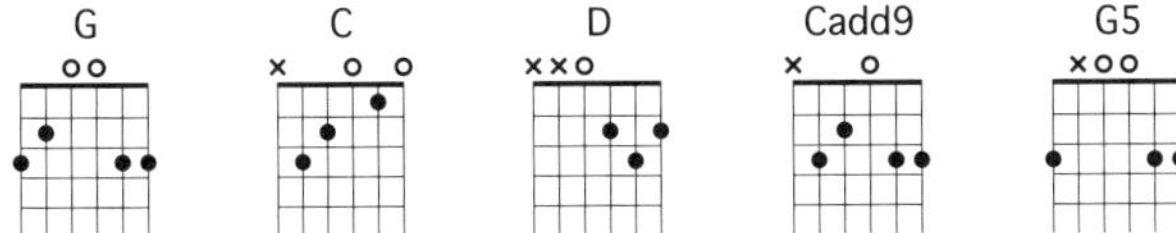

       G   *C*   *D*   *G*

A4 Can you hear me, that when it rains and shines,

    C   *D*   *G*

It's just a state of mind?

        Cadd9

Can you hear me,

      G

Can you hear me?

Inst. ‖: *G* | *G* | *G* | *G*   :‖   *... fade out*

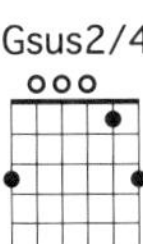

Revolution

(Single Version)

Words & Music by
John Lennon & Paul McCartney

** CAPO : 1 FRET.*

Inst. | *A* | *A* | *A* | *E7* ‖

A1
    A
You say you want a revolution,

              D   *A*
Well, you know, we all want to change the world.

You tell me that it's evolution,

              D   *E7*
Well, you know, we all want to change the world.

Bm/F#   *E7*
But when you talk about destruction,

Bm/F#   *G*   *A*   *F#*
Don't you know you can count me out.

B1
E7   *A*   *D*
Don't you know it's gonna be alright?

A   *D*   *A*   *D*
Alright,   alright.

Inst. | *E7* | *E7* ‖

A2
    A
You say you got a real solution,

              D   *A*
Well, you know, we'd all love to see the plan.

You ask me for a contribution,

              D   *E7*
Well you know, we're doing what we can.

Bm/F#   *E7*
But if you want money for people with minds that hate,

Bm/F#   *G*   *A*   *F#*
All I can tell you is, brother, you have to   wait.

B2
E7   *A*   *D*
Don't you know it's gonna be alright?

A   *D*   *A*   *D*
Alright,   alright.

Inst. | *E7* | *E7*   ‖
| *A* | *A* | *A* | *D* | *D* |
| *E7* | *E7* | *E7* | *E7*   ‖

A3
A
You say you'll change the constitution,

              D   *A*
Well you know, we all want to change your head

You tell me it's the institution,

            D   *E7*
Well you know, you better free your mind instead

Bm/F#   *E7*
But if you go carrying pictures of Chairman Mao,

Bm/F#   *G*   *A*   *F#*
You ain't gonna make it with anyone any - how.

B3
E7   *A*   *D*
Don't you know it's gonna be alright?

A   *D*   *A*   *D*
Alright,   alright.

Inst. | *E7* | *E7*   ‖

OUTRO
    A   *D*
Alright, alright.

    A   *D*
Alright, alright.

    A   *D*
Alright, alright.

    E7   *Bb6*   *A6*
Alright, alright.

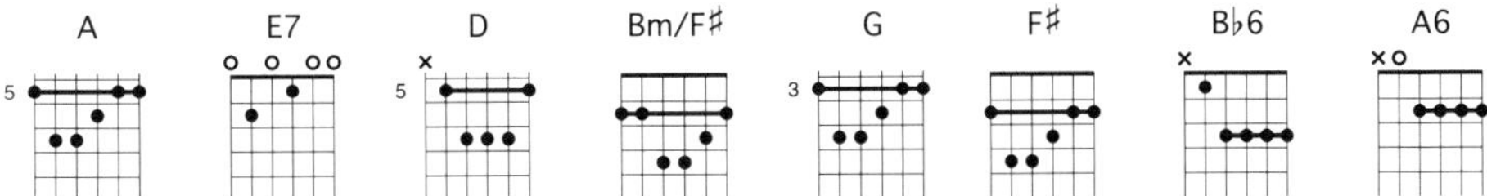

Rocky Raccoon

Words & Music by
John Lennon & Paul McCartney

Inst. | *Am7* | *Am7* ‖

A1
Am7
Now somewhere in the black mountain hills of Dakota

        D7sus4   *D7*
There lived a young boy named Rocky Raccoon-na.

G7   *C*
And one day his woman ran off with another guy,

C/B   *Am7*
Hit young Rocky in the eye, Rocky didn't like that

         D7sus4   *D7*
He said, "I'm gonna get that boy."

      G7
So one day he walked into town,

                       C   *C/B*
Booked himself a room in the local saloon.

A2
Am7   *D7sus4*   *D7*
Rocky Raccoon checked into his room,

G7   *C*   *C/B*
Only to find Gideon's Bible.

Am7   *D7sus4*   *D7*
Rocky had come equipped with a gun,

  G7   *C*   *C/B*
To shoot off the legs of his rival.

   Am7   *D7sus4*   *D7*
His rival it seems had broken his dreams

  G7   *C*   *C/B*
By stealing the girl of his fancy.

   Am7   *D7sus4*   *D7*
Her name was Magill and she called herself Lil

  G7   *C*   *C/B*
But everyone knew her as Nancy.

A3

| | Am7 | | D7sus4 | D7 |

Now she and her man, who called himself Dan,

| | G7 | | C | C/B |

Were in the next room at the hoe down.

| Am7 | | D7sus4 | D7 |

Rocky burst in, and grinning a grin,

| | G7 | | C | C/B |

He said, "Danny boy this is a showdown."

| | Am7 | | D7sus4 | D7 |

But Daniel was hot, he drew first and shot,

| | G7 | | C | C/B |

And Rocky collapsed in the corner.

Inst. ‖: Am7 | D7sus4 D7 | G7 | C C/B :‖

A4

| | Am7 | | D7sus4 | D7 |

Now the doctor came in stinking of gin,

| | G7 | | C | C/B |

And proceeded to lie on the table.

| | Am7 |

He said, "Rocky you met your match."

| | D7sus4 | D7 |

And Rocky said, "Doc it's only a scratch,

| | G7 | | C | C/B |

And I'll be better I'll be better Doc, as soon as I am able."

A5

| | Am7 | | D7sus4 | D7 |

Now Rocky Raccoon he fell back in his room,

| G7 | | C | C/B |

Only to find Gideon's bible.

| Am7 | | D7sus4 | D7 |

Gideon checked out and he left in no doubt

| | G7 | | C | C/B |

To help with good Rocky's revival.

Inst. | Am7 | D7sus4 D7 | G7 | C C/B |
| Am7 | D7sus4 D7 | G7 | C G7 | C ‖

Am7   D7sus4   D7   G7   C   C/B

Run For Your Life

Words & Music by
John Lennon & Paul McCartney

Inst. | D | D | D   ‖

           D   *Bm*
A1 Well I'd rather see you dead, little girl than to be with another man.

         D   *Bm*
You better keep your head, little girl, or I won't know where I am.

                Bm   *E*
B1 You'd better run for your life if you can, little girl,

Bm   *E*
Hide your head in the sand little girl,

Bm   *G*   *F#*   *Bm*
Catch you with another man, that's the end, little girl.

Inst. | D | D   ‖

         D   *Bm*
A2 Well I know that I'm a wicked guy and I was born with a jealous mind.

         D   *Bm*
And I can't spend my whole life trying just to make you toe the line.

                Bm   *E*
B2 You'd better run for your life if you can, little girl,

Bm   *E*
Hide your head in the sand little girl,

Bm   *G*   *F#*   *Bm*
Catch you with another man, that's the end, little girl.

Inst. | D | D | G | D | A7 | D   ‖

|A3|
   D   *Bm*
A3 Let this be a sermon, I mean everything I've said,

   D   *Bm*
Baby, I'm determined, and I'd rather see you dead.

                     Bm   *E*
B3 You'd better run for your life if you can, little girl,

Bm   *E*
Hide your head in the sand little girl,

Bm   *G*   *F#*   *Bm*
Catch you with another man, that's the end, little girl.

Inst. | *D* | *D* ||

     D   *Bm*
A4 I'd rather see you dead, little girl, than to be with another man.

     D   *Bm*
You better keep your head, little girl, or you won't know where I am.

                     Bm   *E*
B4 You'd better run for your life if you can, little girl,

Bm   *E*
Hide your head in the sand little girl,

Bm   *G*   *F#*   *Bm*
Catch you with another man, that's the end, little girl.

   D
OUTRO Na, na, na.

Na, na, na.

Na, na, na.

Na, na, na.   *... fade out*

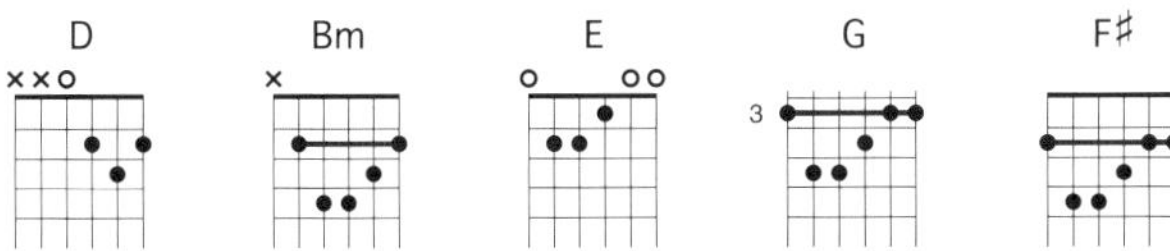

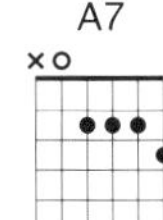

Savoy Truffle

Words & Music by
George Harrison

Inst. | *E7* | *E7* ‖

                   E7
A1 Cream tangerine and montelimar,

  F#   *A*
  A ginger sling with a pineapple heart,

  G   *B*
  A coffee dessert, yes you know it's good news.

          Em   *Emaug*   *Em6*
B1 But you'll have to have them all pulled out

        Emaug   *C*   *G*
  After the Savoy truffle.

Inst. | *E7* | *E7* ‖

                   E7
A2 Cool cherry cream, and nice apple tart.

  F#   *A*
  I feel your taste all the time we're apart,

  G   *B*
  Coconut fudge really blows down those blues.

          Em   *Emaug*   *Em6*
B2 But you'll have to have them all pulled out

        Emaug   *C*   *G*
  After the Savoy truffle.

  Em   *A*   *Asus4*   *A*
C1 You might not feel it now, but when the pain cuts through,

                  G   *B*   *Em*   *A*
  You're going to know and how the sweat is going to fill your head,

      Asus4   *A*   *G*   *B*
  When it becomes too much, you're going to shout aloud.

Inst. | *E7* | *E7* | *E7* | *E7* | *F#* | *F#* |
      | *A* | *A* | *G* | *G* | *B* | *B* ||

             Em   *Emaug*   *Em6*

B3 But you'll have to have them all pulled out

            Emaug   *C*   *G*

After the Savoy truffle.

            Em   *A*

C2 You know that what you eat you are,

             Asus4   *A*   *G*   *B*

But what is sweet now, turns so sour.

          Em   *A*

We all know Ob-La-Di-Bla-Da,

            Asus4   *A*   *G*   *B*

But can you show me, where you are?

    E7

A3 Cream tangerine and montelimar,

F#   *A*

A ginger sling with a pineapple heart,

G   *B*

A coffee dessert, yes you know it's good news.

            Em   *Emaug*   *Em6*

B4 But you'll have to have them all pulled out

            Emaug   *C*   *G*

After the Savoy Truffle.

            Em   *Emaug*   *Em6*

But you'll have to have them all pulled out

            Emaug   *C*   *G*

After the Savoy Truffle.

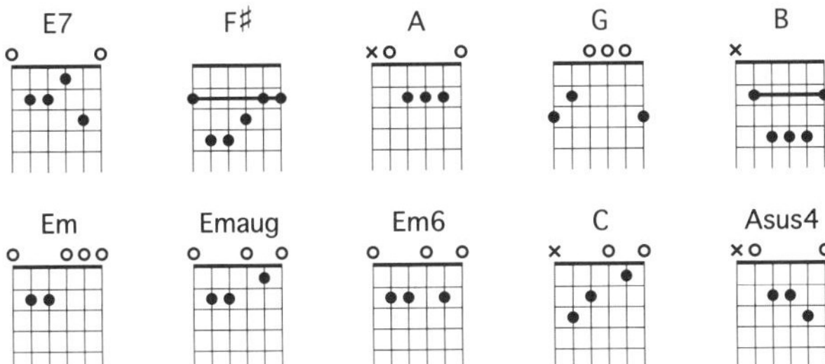

Sexy Sadie

Words & Music by
John Lennon & Paul McCartney

Inst. || C D | G F#7 | F D7 ||

A1
```
G          F#7   Bm
Sexy Sadie,    what have you done?

C              D           G    F#7
You made a fool of everyone,

C              D           G    F#7
You made a fool of everyone.

      F       D7
Sexy Sadie, oh, what have you done?
```

A2
```
G          F#7   Bm
Sexy Sadie,    you broke the rules

C              D           G    F#7
You laid it down for all to see,

C              D           G    F#7
You laid it down for all to see.

      F       D7
Sexy Sadie, oh, you broke the rules.
```

B1
```
G                     Am7              Bm7       Cmaj7
One sunny day the world was waiting for a lover,

G                     Am7          Bm7    C
She came along to turn on everyone.

        A7        Ab7
Sexy Sadie, the greatest of them all.
```

A3
```
G          F#7   Bm
Sexy Sadie,    how did you know?

C              D           G    F#7
The world was waiting just for you,

C              D           G    F#7
The world was waiting just for you,

      F       D7
Sexy Sadie, oh, how did you know?
```


|A4|
```
       G         F#7   Bm
```
Sexy Sadie,   you'll get yours yet,

```
C                        D     G   F#7
```
However big you think you are,

```
C           D              G   F#7
```
However big you think you are.

```
        F       D7
```
Sexy Sadie, oh, you'll get yours yet.

|B5|
```
G                             Am7              Bm7     Cmaj7
```
We gave her everything we owned just to sit at her table.

```
G                  Am7          Bm7    C
```
Just a smile would lighten everything.

```
        A7                    Ab7            G    F#7
```
Sexy Sadie she's the latest and the greatest of them all.

|OUTRO|
```
|Bm7      | C    D | G   F#7 |
```
Oh,

```
C           D              G    F#7
```
She made a fool of everyone,

```
F         D7    G    F#7
```
Sexy Sadie.

```
|Bm7      | C    D | G   F#7 |
```
Oh,

```
C           D              G    F#7
```
However big you think you are,

```
F         D7    G    F#7
```
Sexy Sadie.   *... fade out*

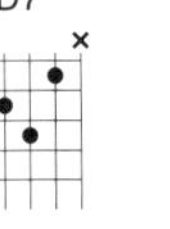

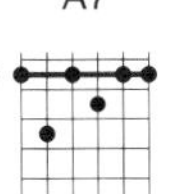

Sgt. Pepper's Lonely Hearts Club Band

Words & Music by
John Lennon & Paul McCartney

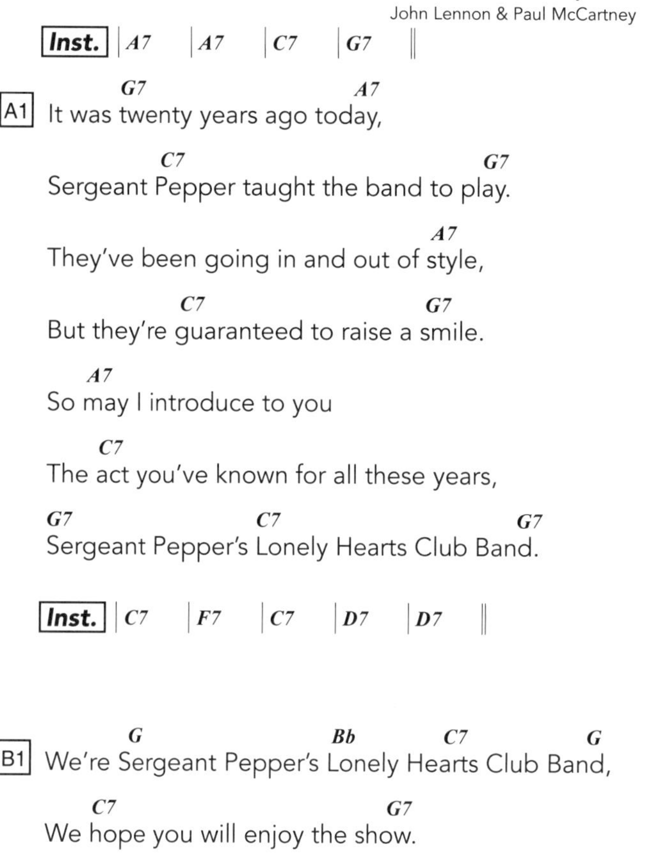

C1 It's wonderful to be here, *(C7)*

It's certainly a thrill. *(F7)*

You're such a lovely audience, *(C7)*

We'd like to take you home with us, *(D7)*

We'd love to take you home.

A2 I don't really want to stop the show, *(G7 ... A7)*

But I thought that you might like to know, *(C7 ... G7)*

That the singer's going to sing a song, *(A7)*

And he wants you all to sing along. *(C7 ... G7)*

So let me introduce to you *(A7)*

The one and only Billy Shears *(C7)*

And Sergeant Pepper's Lonely Hearts Club Band. *(G7 ... C7 ... G7)*

Inst. | C | C ‖

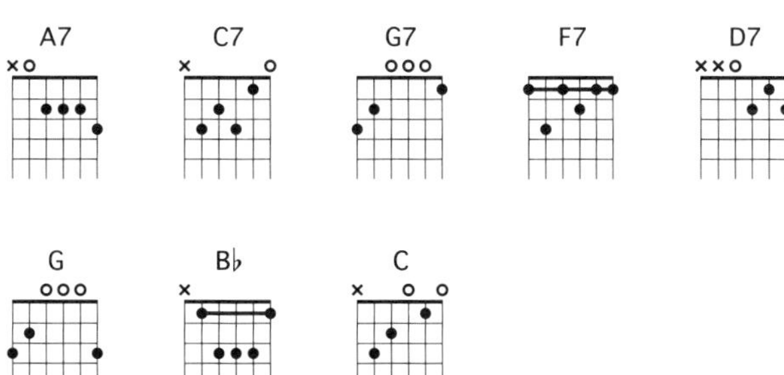

She Came In Through The Bathroom Window

Words & Music by
John Lennon & Paul McCartney

```
      A                                    D      Dsus4   D
A1  She came in through the bathroom window,

      A          F#m           D    Dsus4    D
    Protected by a silver spoon.

      A          F#m                 D         Dsus4
    But now she sucks her thumb and wonders

            D
    By the banks of her own lagoon.


      A                Dm
B1  Didn't anybody tell her?

      A                Dm
    Didn't anybody see?

    G7                        C        G/B    Am7
    Sunday's on the phone to Monday,

    G7                   C       A
    Tuesday's on the phone to me.


      A                         D    Dsus4    D
A2  She said she'd always been a dancer,

      A          F#m             D    Dsus4    D
    She worked at fifteen clubs a day,

      A          F#m                 D       Dsus4
    And though she thought I knew the answer,

            D
    Well, I knew what I could not say.
```


|A3|

A   *D*   *Dsus4*   *D*
And so I quit the police department,

A   *F#m*   *D*   *Dsus4*   *D*
And got myself a steady job.

A   *F#m*   *D*   *Dsus4*
And though she tried her best to help me,

              D
She could steal, but she could not rob.

|B2|

A   *Dm*
Didn't anybody tell her?

A   *Dm*
Didn't anybody see?

G7   *C*   *G/B*   *Am7*
Sunday's on the phone to Monday,

G7   *C*
Tuesday's on the phone to me,

          A
Oh yeah.

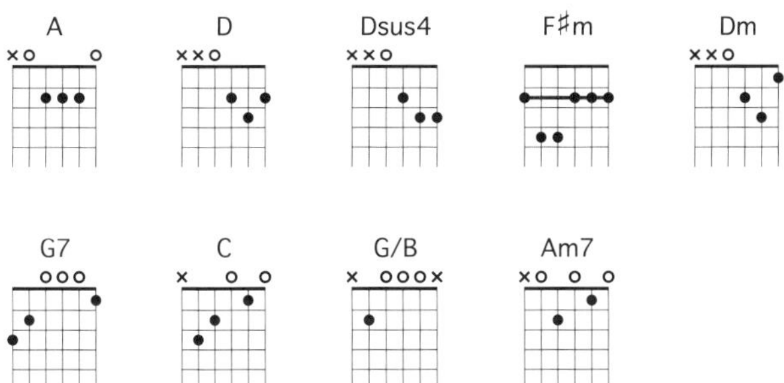

She Loves You

Words & Music by
John Lennon & Paul McCartney

INTRO
Em
She loves you, yeah, yeah, yeah,

A7
She loves you, yeah, yeah, yeah,

C   *G*
She loves you, yeah, yeah, yeah, yeah.

A1
G   *Em7*
You think you lost your love,

Bm   *D*
When I saw her yesterday.

G   *Em7*
It's you she's thinking of,

Bm   *D*
And she told me what to say.

G   *Em*
She says she loves you, and you know that can't be bad.

Cm   *D*
Yes, she loves you, and you know you should be glad.

A2
G   *Em7*
She said you hurt her so,

Bm   *D*
She almost lost her mind.

G   *Em7*
But now she says to let you knows,

Bm   *D*
You're not the hurting kind.

G   *Em*
She says she loves you, and you know that can't be bad.

Cm   *D*
Yes, she loves you, and you know you should be glad. Ooh!

       Em
B1 She loves you, yeah, yeah, yeah,

       A7
She loves you, yeah, yeah, yeah.

          Cm
And with a love like that,

      D7   *G*
You know you should be glad.

      G   *Em7*
A3 You know it's up to you,

    Bm   *D*
I think it's only fair.

G   *Em7*
Pride can hurt you too,

    Bm   *D*
Apologise to her.

           G   *Em*
Because she loves you, and you know that can't be bad.

       Cm   *D*
Yes, she loves you, and you know you should be glad. Ooh!

       Em
B2 She loves you, yeah, yeah, yeah,

       A7   *Cm*
She loves you, yeah, yeah, yeah, and with a love like that,

    D7   *G*   *Em*
You know you should be glad.

      Cm
With a love like that

     D   *G*   *Em*
You know you should be glad.

      Cm
With a love like that,

    D7   *G*
You know you should be glad.

Em   *C*   *G6*
Yeah, yeah, yeah, yeah, yeah, yeah, yeah.

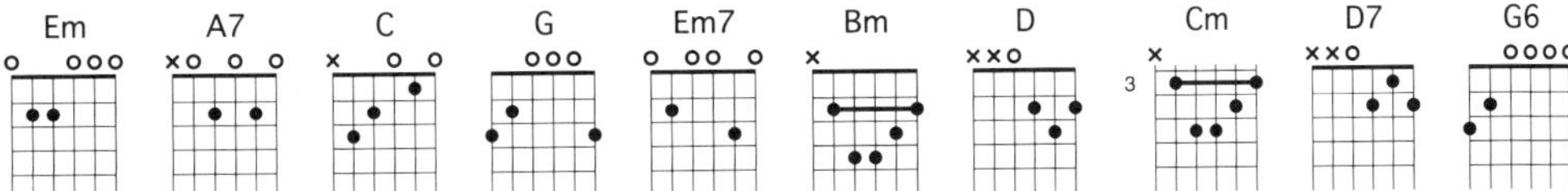

She Said She Said

Words & Music by
John Lennon & Paul McCartney

** CAPO : 1 FRET.*

Inst. ‖ A7 | A7 ‖

A1
<pre>
A7   G   D
She said,

             A7   G   D
"I know what it's like to be dead.

             A7   G   D
I know what it is to be sad."

             A7   G   D   A7
And she's making me feel like I've never been born.
</pre>

Inst. ‖ A7 G | D A7 ‖

A2
<pre>
A7   G   D
I said,

             A7   G   D
"Who put all those things in your head?

                  A7   G   D
Things that make me feel that I'm mad,

             A7   G   D   A7
And you're making me feel like I've never been born."
</pre>

Inst. ‖ A7 G | D A7 ‖

B1
<pre>
A7   G   A7
She said, "you don't understand what I said."

       G   A7
I said, "No, no, no, you're wrong.

                  Em   A7
When I was a boy

                 D
Everything was right,

A7   D
Everything was right."
</pre>

A3
A7   *G*   *D*
I said,

        A7   *G*   *D*
"Even though you know what you know,

    A7   *G*   *D*
I know that I'm ready to leave,

    A7   *G*   *D*   *A7*
'Cause you're making me feel like I've never been born."

Inst. ‖ *A7* *G* | *D* *A7* ‖

B2
A7   *G*   *A7*
She said, "you don't understand what I said."

   G   *A7*
I said, "No, no, no, you're wrong.

     Em   *A7*
When I was a boy

   D
Everything was right,

A7   *D*
Everything was right."

A4
A7   *G*   *D*
I said,

       A7   *G*   *D*
"Even though you know what you know,

   A7   *G*   *D*
I know that I'm ready to leave,

    A7   *G*   *D*   *A7*
'Cause you're making me feel like I've never been born."

Inst. ‖ *A7* *G* | *D* *A7* ‖

OUTRO
A7
She said,

"I know what it's like to be dead,"

"I know what it is to be sad,"

"I know what it's like to be dead."

She's A Woman

Inst. | (E7) | (E7) | (D7) | (D7) | A7 | A7 | A7 | A7 ‖

A1
```
A7                    D7              A7
My love don't give me presents,

              D7              A7
I know that she's no peasant,

D7
Only ever has to give me love forever and forever.,

     A7        D7              A7
My love don't give me presents,

E7
Turn me on when I get lonely,

D7                          A7      D7      A7    E7
People tell me that she's only fooling, I know she isn't.
```

A2
```
     A7          D7          A7
She don't give the boys the eye,

          D7        A7
She hate to see me cry,

D7
She is happy just to hear me say

That I will never leave her.

A7              D7          A7
She don't give the boys the eye,

E7
She will never make me jealous,

D7                          A7        D7          A7
Gives me all her time as well as loving, don't ask me why.
```

B1
```
C#m                     F#
She's a woman who understands,

C#m                 D       E
She's a woman who loves her man.
```

A3
A7   *D7*   *A7*
My love don't give me presents,

        D7   *A7*
I know that she's no peasant,

D7
Only ever has to give me love forever and forever.

    A7   *D7*   *A7*
My love don't give me presents,

E7
Turn me on when I get lonely,

D7   *A7*
People tell me that she's only fooling,

   D7   *A7*   *E7*
I know she isn't.

Inst. | *A7* | *A7* | *A7* | *A7* | *D7* | *D7* |
       | *A7* | *A7* | *E7* | *D7* | *A7* | *E7* |

B2
C#m   *F#*
She's a woman who understands,

C#m   *D*   *E*
She's a woman who loves her man.

A4
A7   *D7*   *A7*
My love don't give me presents,

        D7   *A7*
I know that she's no peasant,

D7
Only ever has to give me love forever and forever.

    A7   *D7*   *A7*
My love don't give me presents,

E7
Turn me on when I get lonely,

D7   *A7*
People tell me that she's only fooling,

   D7   *A7*
I know she isn't.

OUTRO
      A7
She's a woman, she's a woman,

      D7   *A7*
She's a woman, she's a woman.

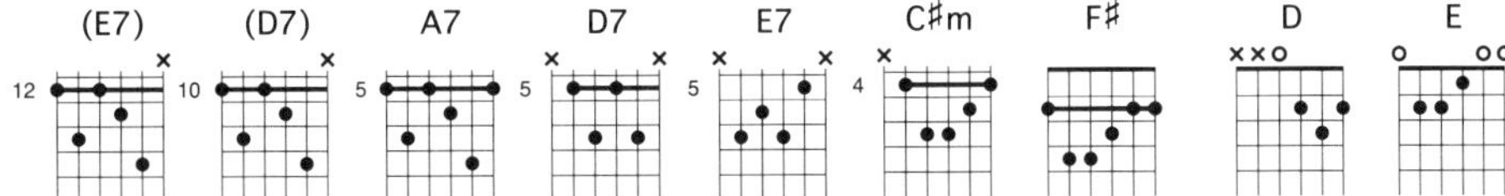

She's Leaving Home

Words & Music by
John Lennon & Paul McCartney

Inst. | *E* | *E* | *E* | *E* ‖

A1
E   *Bm*   *F#m7*   *C#m7*   *F#7*
Wednesday morning at five o'clock, as the day begins.

B7sus4   *B*
Silently closing her bedroom door,

B7sus4   *B*
Leaving the note that she hoped would say more.

A2
       E   *Bm*   *F#m7*   *C#m7*   *F#7*
She goes downstairs to the kitchen clutching her handkerchief.

B7sus4   *B*
Quietly turing the backdoor key,

B7sus4   *B*
Stepping outside she is free.

B1
E
She (We gave her most of our lives,)

Is leaving (Sacrificed most of our lives,)

                 Bm/D   *C#m7*
Home. (We gave her everything money could buy.)

             F#7
She's leaving home after living alone (Bye, bye)

      C#m7   *F#7*
For so many years.

A3
E   *Bm*   *F#m7*   *C#m7*   *F#7*
Father snores as his wife gets into her dressing gown.

B7sus4   *B*
Picks up the letter that's lying there.

B7sus4   *B*
Standing alone at the top of the stairs.

|A4| *E*   *Bm*   *F#m7*
She breaks down and cries to her husband,

        C#m7
"Daddy our baby's gone."

B7sus4   *B*
"Why would she treat us so thoughtlessly?"

B7sus4   *B*
"How could she do this to me?"

|B2| *E*
She (We never though of ourselves,)

Is leaving (Never a thought for ourselves,)

            Bm/D   *C#m7*
Home (We've struggled hard all our lives to get by.)

          F#7
She's leaving home after living alone (Bye, bye)

   C#m7   *F#7*
For so many years.

|A5| *E*   *Bm*   *F#m7*   *C#m7*   *F#7*
Friday morning at nine o'clock she is far away.

B7sus4   *B*   *B7sus4*   *B*
Waiting to keep the appointment she made, Meeting a man from the motor trade.

|B3| *E*
She (What did we do that was wrong?)

Is having (We didn't know it was wrong,)

       Bm/D   *C#m7*
Fun. (Fun is the one thing that money can't buy,)

         F#7
Something inside that was always denied (Bye, bye)

   C#m7   *F#7*
For so many years.

   C#m7   *F#7*   *A*   *E*
She's leaving home. bye, bye.

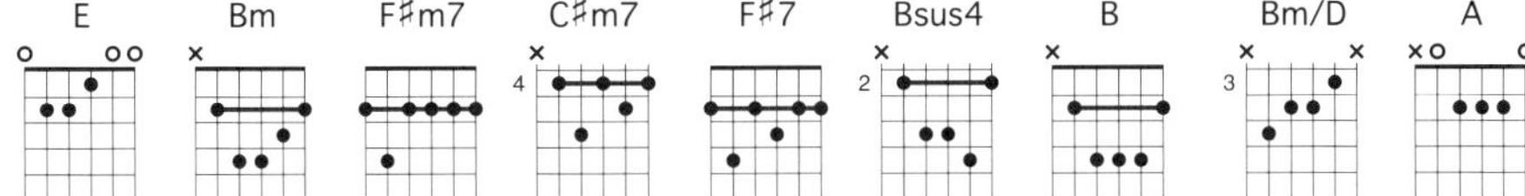

Something

Words & Music by
George Harrison

Inst. ‖ *F Eb G/D* ‖

A1
C   *Cmaj7*
Something in the way she moves,

C7   *F*   *F/E*
Attracts me like no other lover.

D7   *G*
Something in the way she woos me.

Am   *Am(maj7)*
I don't want to leave her now,

Am   *D7*
You know I believe, and how.

Inst. ‖ *F Eb G/D* ‖

A2
C   *Cmaj7*
Somewhere in her smile she knows

C7   *F*   *F/E*
That I don't need no other lover.

D7   *G*
Something in her style that shows me,

Am   *Am(maj7)*
I don't want to leave her now,

Am7   *D7*
You know I believe, and how.

Inst. ‖ *F Eb G/D* | *A* ‖

B1
A   *C#m/G#*   *F#m7*   *A/E*
You're asking me will my love grow,

D   *G*   *A*
I don't know, I don't know.

A   *C#m/G#*   *F#m7*   *A/E*
You stick around now it may show,

D   *G*   *C*
I don't know, I don't know.

Inst.	C	Cmaj7	C7	F F/E	D7	G	
	Am Am(maj7)	Am7	D7	F Eb G/D			

A3
C   Cmaj7
Something in the way she knows,

C7   F   F/E
And all I have to do is think of her.

D7   G
Something in the things she shows me.

Am   Am(maj7)
I don't want to leave her now,

Am7   D7
You know I believe her now.

Inst.	F Eb G/D	A	F Eb G/D	C	

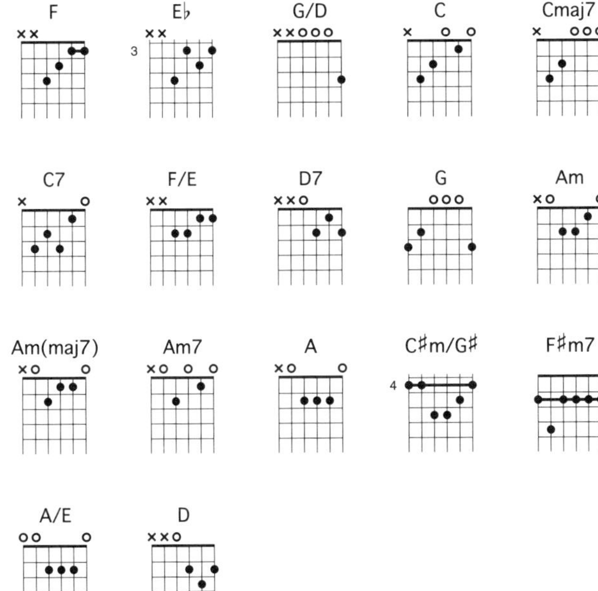

Strawberry Fields Forever

** CAPO : 1 FRET.*

Words & Music by
John Lennon & Paul McCartney

Inst. | (E) (Emaj7) | (E7) | (F#m) (E) | (D)   (A) |

A1
```
A                                                    Em7
Let me take you down, 'cause I'm going to Strawberry Fields.

F#7                      D              F#7
Nothing is real and nothing to get hung about.

D                    A
Strawberry Fields forever.
```

B1
```
E         Emaj7     E7          F#m        E                D
Living is easy with eyes closed, misunderstanding all you see.

                E           A                  F#m   D     E            D   A
It's getting hard to be someone but it all works out, it doesn't matter much to me.
```

A2
```
A                                                    Em7
Let me take you down, 'cause I'm going to Strawberry Fields.

F#7                      D              F#7
Nothing is real and nothing to get hung about.

D                    A
Strawberry Fields forever.
```

B2
```
E         Emaj7     E7      F#m        E                D
No one I think is in my tree, I mean it must be high or low.

                E              A              F#m   D     E          D       A
That is you can't you know tune in but it's all right, that is I think it's not too bad.
```

A3
```
A                                                    Em7
Let me take you down, 'cause I'm going to Strawberry Fields.

F#7                      D              F#7
Nothing is real and nothing to get hung about.

D                    A
Strawberry Fields forever.
```


E   *Emaj7*   *E7*   *F#m*   *E*   *D*

B3 Always know, sometimes think it's me, but you know I know when it's a dream.

         E   *A*   *F#m* *D*   *E*   *D*   *A*

I think a 'No' I mean a 'Yes' but it's all wrong, that is I think I disagree.

A   *Em7*

A4 Let me take you down, 'cause I'm going to Strawberry Fields.

F#7   *D*   *F#7*

Nothing is real and nothing to get hung about.

D   *A*   *F#m*

Strawberry Fields forever,

D   *A*

Strawberry Fields forever,

D   *E*   *D*

Strawberry Fields forever.

Inst. ‖: *A* |*A* |*A* |*A* :‖

... fade out

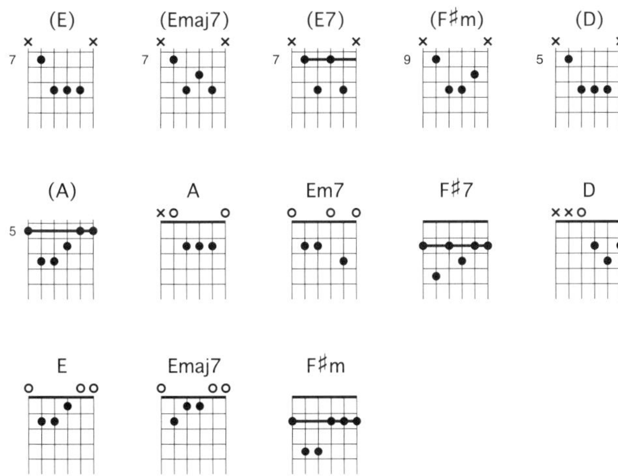

Sun King

Words & Music by
John Lennon & Paul McCartney

Inst. | E | E | E | E |
F#m7	F#m7 B6	E6	E
F#m7	F#m7 B6	E6	E
F#m7	F#m7 B6	E6	E	

A
F/G
Ah.

C   Cmaj7   Gm7   A7
Here comes the Sun King,

C   Cmaj7   Gm7   A7
Here comes the Sun King,

F   D7
Everybody's laughing,

F   D7
Everybody's happy,

C   Em7   C7   F
Here comes the Sun King.

B
F#m7   B6 E6   E
Quando paramucho mi amore de felice carafon,

F#m7   B6 E6   E
Mundo paparazzi mi amore chicka ferdy parasol,

F#m7   B6   E6 (E6)
Questo obrigado tanta mucho que canite carousel.

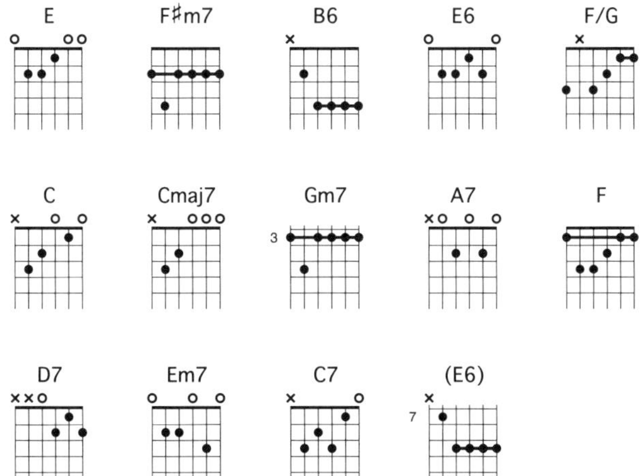

E
F♯m7
B6
E6
F/G
C
Cmaj7
Gm7
A7
F
D7
Em7
C7
(E6)

Taxman

Words & Music by
George Harrison

Inst. | *D7* | *D7* ‖

D7   *D7#9*

A1 Let me tell you how it will be,

D7   *D7#9*

There's one for you, nineteen for me,

D7   *C*   *G7*   *D7*

'Cause I'm the Taxman, yeah, I'm the Taxman.

D7   *D7#9*

A2 Should five per cent appear too small,

D7   *D7#9*

Be thankful I don't take it all.

D7   *C*   *G7*   *D7*

'Cause I'm the Taxman, yeah I'm the Taxman.

D7

B1 If you drive a car, I'll tax the street,

C7

If you try to sit, I'll tax your seat.

D7

If you get too cold I'll tax the heat,

C7

If you take a walk, I'll tax your feet.

D7

Taxman.

Inst. | *D7* | *D7#9* *D7* | *D7* |
         | *D7* | *D7* | *D7#9* *D7* ‖

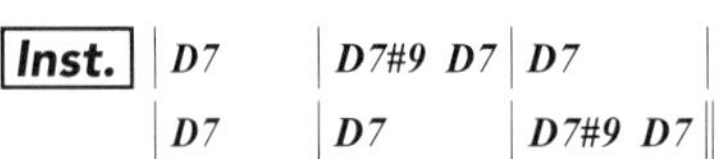

C   *G7#9*   *D7*

'Cause I'm the Taxman, yeah I'm the Taxman.

|A3|
D7
Don't ask me what I want it for.

D7#9   *D7*
(A-ah Mister Wilson.)

If you don't want to pay some more.

D7#9   *D7*
(A-ah Mister Heath.)

        C   *G7#9*   *D7*
'Cause I'm the Taxman, yeah, I'm the Taxman.

|A4|
D7
Now my advice for those who die,

D7#9   *D7*
Taxman,

Declare the pennies on your eyes.

D7#9   *D7*
Taxman,

        C   *G7#9*   *D7*
'Cause I'm the taxman, yeah, I'm the Taxman.

        F7
And you're working for no one but me.

Inst. | *D7* | *D7* | *D7#9* *D7* | *D7* |
| *D7* | *D7* | *D7#9* ||

... fade out

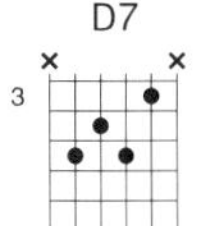

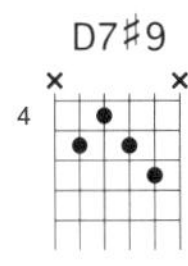

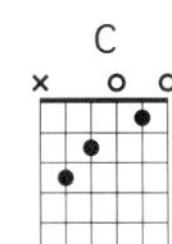

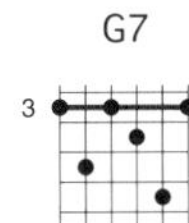

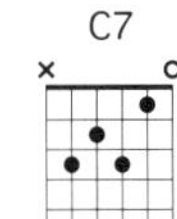

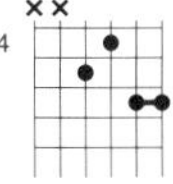

Tell Me What You See

Words & Music by
John Lennon & Paul McCartney

```
Inst. | G    | G        ‖
```

A1
```
       G      Cadd9    D        G          Cadd9     G
If you let me take your heart I will prove to you,

       G          Cadd9 D   G    Cadd9 D     G
We will never be apart if I'm part of you.
```

B1
```
       Cadd9            G           Cadd9            G
Open up your eyes now, tell me what you see.

       Cadd9        G          Cadd9        D     G
It is no surprise now, what you see is me.
```

A2
```
       G        Cadd9      D          G        Cadd9     G
Big and black the clouds may be, time will pass away.

       G      Cadd9      D        G    Cadd9      D         G
If you put your trust in me I'll make bright your day.
```

B2
```
       Cadd9            G           Cadd9               G
Look into these eyes now, tell me what you see.

       Cadd9        G          Cadd9        D     G
Don't you realise now, what you see is me.
```

C1
```
       G7                 C
Tell me what you see.
```

```
Inst. | G     | D7   | G    | G    ‖
```

A3
```
G       Cadd9   D         G             Cadd9   G
Listen to me one more time, how can I get through?

G           Cadd9   D     G  Cadd9    D      G
Can't you try to see that I'm trying to get to you?
```

B3
```
Cadd9           G         Cadd9             G
Open up your eyes now, tell me what you see.

Cadd9       G         Cadd9       D    G
It is no surprise now, what you see is me.
```

C2
```
G7                    C
Tell me what you see.
```

Inst. | G | D7 | G | G ‖

A4
```
G       Cadd9   D         G             Cadd9   G
Listen to me one more time, how can I get through?

            Cadd9   D    G    C      D      G
Can't you try to see that I'm trying to get to you?
```

B4
```
Cadd9           G         Cadd9               G
Open up your eyes now, tell me what you see.

Cadd9       G         Cadd9       D    G
It is no surprise now, what you see is me.

G7                               C        G
Mmm - mmm - mmm - mmm - mmm.
```

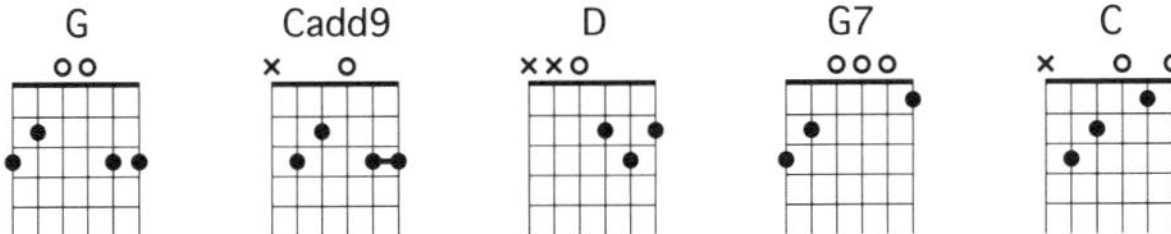

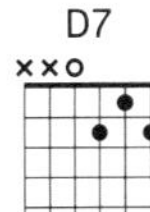

Tell Me Why

Words & Music by
John Lennon & Paul McCartney

Inst. ‖ Em7 A | Em7 A | Em7 A ‖

A1
Em7   A   D   Em7   A   D Em7 A
Tell me why you cried,   and why you lied to me,

      D   Em7   A   D Em7 A
Tell me why you cried,   and why you lied to me.

B1
    D   Bm
Well I gave you everything I had,

        Em   A7
But you left me sitting on my own,

        D   Bm
Did you have to treat me oh so bad?

      Em   A7
All I do is hang my head and moan.

A2
    D   Em7   A   D Em7 A
Tell me why you cried,   and why you lied to me,

    D   Em7   A   D Em7 A
Tell me why you cried,   and why you lied to me.

B2
    D   Bm
If it's something I have said or done,

      Em   A7
Tell me what and I'll apologise,

      D   Bm
If you don't, I really can't go on,

       Em   A7
Holding back these tears in my eyes.

<pre>
       D   Em7   A   D Em7 A
A3 Tell me why you cried,   and why you lied to me,

              D   Em7   A   D   D7
    Tell me why you cried,   and why you lied to me.

           G7
C1 Well I beg you on my bended knees,

            A7
    If you'll only listen to my pleas,

             Bm
    Is there anything I can do,

          Em7   A7   D
    'Cause I really can't stand it, I'm so in love with you.

       D   Em7   A   D Em7 A
A4 Tell me why you cried,   and why you lied to me,

              D   Em7   A   Bm   Bb7 Asus4 A6 D
    Tell me why you cried,   and why you lied to me.
</pre>

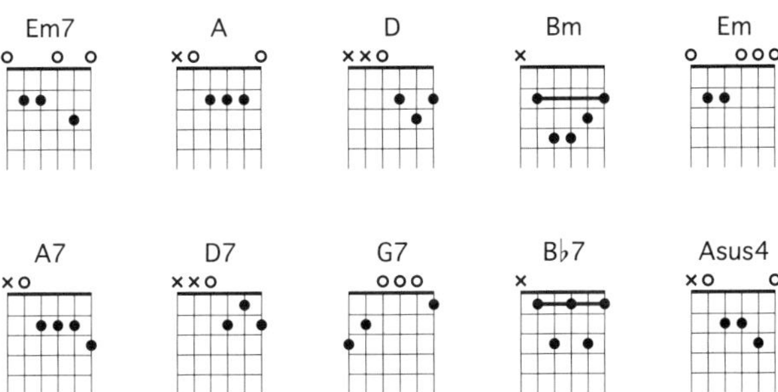

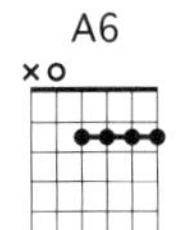

Thank You Girl

Words & Music by
John Lennon & Paul McCartney

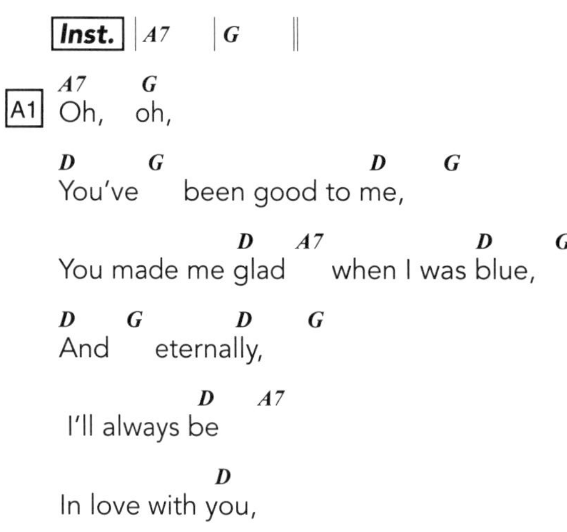

|C1| *Bm*   *D*   *A7*
Thank you girl for loving me the way that you do, (way that you do,)

Em   *A7*   *D*
That's the kind of love that is too good to be true,

|B3| *G*   *A7*   *G*   *A7*
And all I gotta do is thank you girl, thank you girl.

Inst. ‖ *A7* | *G*   ‖

|A3| *A7*   *G*
Oh,   oh,

D   *G*   *D*   *G*
You've   been good to me,

                 D   *A7*   *D*   *G*
You made me glad   when I was blue,

D   *G*   *D*   *G*
And   eternally,

              D   *A7*
I'll always be

               D
In love with you,

|B4| *G*   *A7*   *G*   *A7*
And all I gotta do is thank you girl, thank you girl.

Inst. ‖ *A7* | *G*   ‖

|OUTRO| *A7*   *G*   *D*   *G*   *D*   *G*
Oh,   oh,   oh.

A7   *G*   *D*   *G*   *D*   *G*
Oh,   oh,   oh.

A7   *G*   *D*
Oh,   oh.

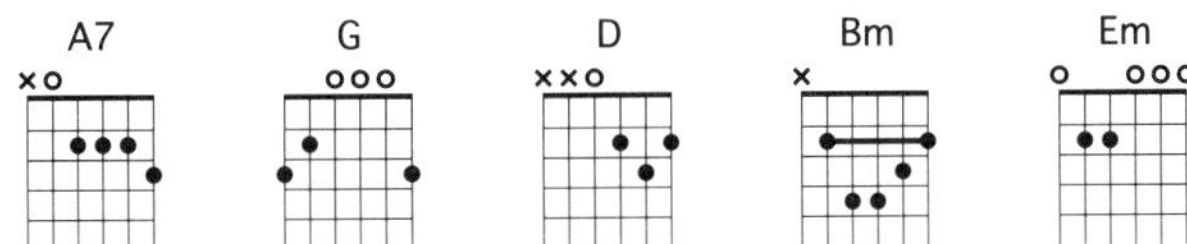

The Ballad Of John And Yoko

Words & Music by
John Lennon & Paul McCartney

Inst. | *E* | *E* ‖

    E
A1 Standing in the dock at Southampton,

Trying to get to Holland or France.

    E7
The man in the mac said, "You've got to turn back".

You know they didn't even give us a chance.

                   A
B1 Christ you know it ain't easy,

                   E
You know how hard it can be.

               B7
The way things are going

                 E
They're going to crucify me.

    E
A2 Finally made the plane into Paris,

Honey mooning down by the Seine.

    E7
Peter Brown called to say,

"You can make it O.K.,

You can get married in Gibraltar, near Spain".

A
|B2| Christ you know it ain't easy,

E
You know how hard it can be.

B7
The way things are going

E
They're going to crucify me.

E
|A3| Drove from Paris to the Amsterdam Hilton,

Talking in our beds for a week.

E7
The newspeople said, "Say what you doing in bed?"

I said, "We're only trying to get us some peace."

|B3| B 반복

A
|C1| Saving up your money for a rainy day,

Giving all your clothes to charity.

Last night the wife said,

"Oh boy, when you're dead,

B7
You don't take nothing with you but your soul - think!"

E
|A4| Made a lightning trip to Vienna,

Eating chocolate cake in a bag.

E7
The newspapers said, "She's gone to his head,

They look just like two gurus in drag."

|B4| Christ you know it ain't easy, *A*

You know how hard it can be. *E*

The way things are going *B7*

They're going to crucify me. *E*

E
|A5| Caught the early plane back to London.

Fifty acorns tied in a sack.

E7
The men from the press said, "We wish you success,

It's good to have the both of you back".

|B5| Christ you know it ain't easy, *A*

You know how hard it can be. *E*

The way things are going *B7*

They're going to crucify me. *E*

B7
|OUTRO| The way things are going.

They're going to crucify me. *E*

Inst. | *B7* | *B7* | *E* | *E6*   ‖

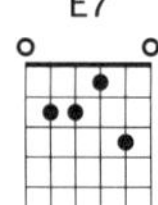
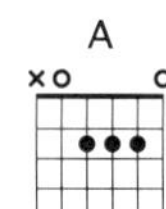
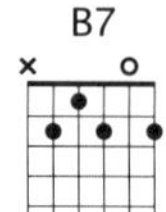
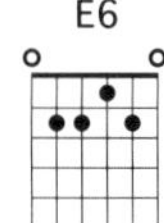

The End

Words & Music by
John Lennon & Paul McCartney

Inst. |A |D B E A |A B7 |
| B A |—— —— | 1 DRUMS |

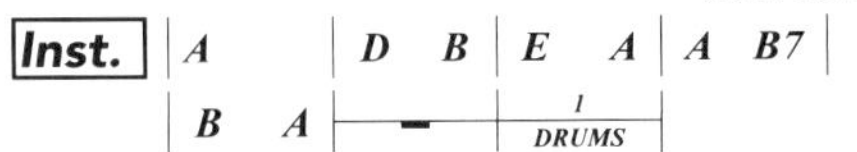

INTRO Oh yeah, all right.

A   *B7*   *A*
Are you going to be in my dreams tonight?

Inst. |—— 8 DRUMS——|
|A7 |D7 |A7 |D7 ||

A7   *D7*   *A7*   *D7*   *A7*   *D7*
Love you, love you, love you, love you, love you, love you.

A
A7   *D7*   *A7*   *D7*   *A7*   *D7*
Love you, love you, love you, love you, love you, love you.

A7   *D7*   *A7*   *D7*   *A7*   *D7*
Love you, love you, love you, love you, love you, love you.

A7   *D7*   *A7*   *D7*   *A7*   *D7*
Love you, love you, love you, love you, love you, love you.

Inst. |A |A ||

B
A
And in the end,

    G/D
The love you take

   F   *Dm7*
Is equal to the love

G7   *C*
You make.

       D/C   *Cm7*   *F/C*   *C*
Ah.

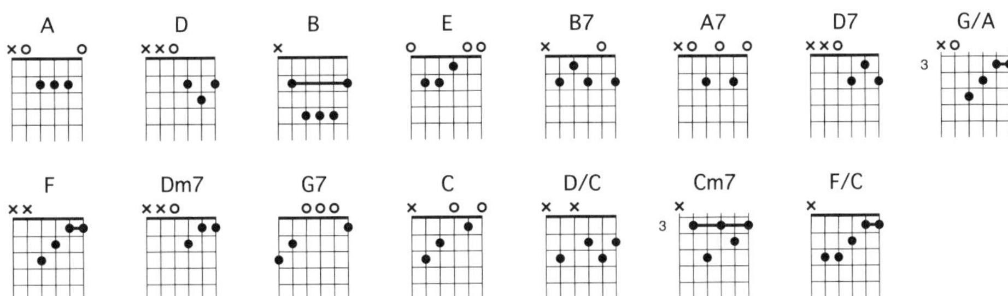

The Continuing Story Of Bungalow Bill

Words & Music by
John Lennon & Paul McCartney

Inst. | Emadd9 | Emadd9 | Emadd9 | Emadd9 ||

A1
```
C       G        C    Fm        C
```
Hey, Bungalow Bill, what did you kill,

```
Fm         G
```
Bungalow Bill?

```
A    E        A    Dm         A
```
Hey, Bungalow Bill, what did you kill,

```
Dm         E
```
Bungalow Bill?

B1
```
Am            Am/C          F            G
```
He went out tiger hunting with his elephant and gun.

```
Am         Am/C         F                G
```
In case of accidents, he always took his mom.

```
            E          G          Am        Fm
```
He's the all American bullet-headed saxon mother's son.

All the children sing.

A2
```
C       G        C    Fm        C
```
Hey, Bungalow Bill, what did you kill,

```
Fm         G
```
Bungalow Bill?

```
A    E        A    Dm         A
```
Hey, Bungalow Bill, what did you kill,

```
Dm         E
```
Bungalow Bill?

Am   *Am/C*   *F*   *G*
|B2| Deep in the jungle where the mighty tiger lies,

Am   *Am/C*   *F*   *G*
Bill and his elephants were taken by surprise.

E   *G*   *Am*   *Fm*
So Captain Marvel zapped in right between the eyes.

All the children sing.

C   *G*   *C* *Fm*   *C*
|A3| Hey, Bungalow Bill, what did you kill,

Fm   *G*
Bungalow Bill?

A   *E*   *A*   *Dm*   *A*
Hey, Bungalow Bill, what did you kill,

Dm   *E*
Bungalow Bill?

Am   *Am/C*   *F*   *G*
|B3| The children asked him if to kill was not a sin,

Am   *Am/C*   *F*   *G*
Not when he looks so fierce, his mommy butted in.

E   *G*   *Am*   *Fm*
If looks could kill, it would have been us instead of him.

All the children sing.

C   *G*   *C* *Fm*   *C*
|A4| ‖:Hey, Bungalow Bill, what did you kill,

Fm   *G*
Bungalow Bill?

A   *E*   *A*   *Dm*   *A*
Hey, Bungalow Bill, what did you kill,

Dm   *E*
Bungalow Bill? :‖ 3회 반복

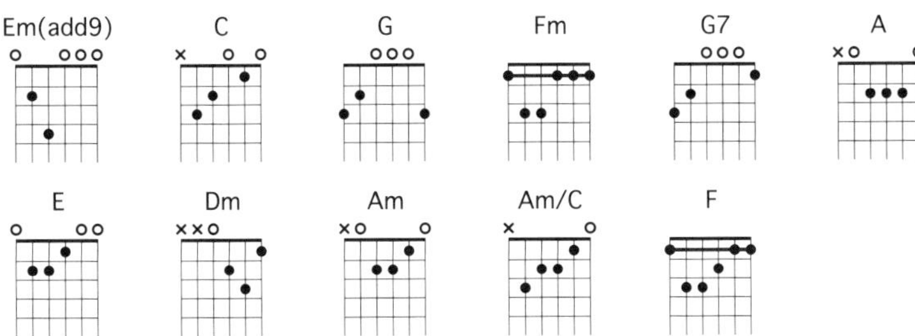

The Fool On The Hill

Words & Music by
John Lennon & Paul McCartney

Inst. | *D6* | *D6* ‖

A1
D6   *Em/D*
Day after day, alone on the hill,

D6   *Em/D*
The man with the foolish grin is keeping perfectly still,

Em7   *A7*
But nobody wants to know him,

      D6   *Bm7*
They can see that he's just a fool,

Em7   *A7*
And he never gives an answer,

B1
         Dm   *Dmaug*   *Dm*   *Dmaug*
But the fool   on   the   hill, sees the sun going down,

         C7   *Dm*   *Dm7*
And the eyes in his head, see the world spinning round.

| *D6* ‖

A2
D6   *Em/D*
Well on the way his head in a cloud,

     D6   *Em/D*
The man of a thousand voices talking perfectly loud.

Em7   *A7*
But nobody ever hears him,

      D6   *Bm7*
Or the sound he appears to make,

Em7   *A7*
And he never seems to notice,

B2
         Dm   *Dmaug*   *Dm*   *Dmaug*
But the fool   on   the   hill, sees the sun going down,

         C7   *Dm*   *Dm7*
And the eyes in his head, see the world spinning round.

Inst. ‖: *D6* | *D6* | *Em/D* | *Em/D* :‖

A3
Em7   *A7*   *D6*   *Bm7*
And nobody seems to like him, they can tell what he wants to do.

       Em7   *A7*
And he never shows his feelings,

B3
           Dm *Dmaug*   *Dm*   *Dmaug*
But the fool   on   the   hill, sees the sun going down,

          C7   *Dm*   *Dm7*
And the eyes in his head, see the world spinning round.

C1
D6   *Em/D*
Oh,   oh.

D6   *Em/D*
'Round, 'round, 'round, 'round, 'round.

A4
      Em7   *A7*   *D6*   *Bm7*
And he never listens to them, he knows that they're the fool.

Em7   *A7*
They don't like him.

B4
           Dm *Dmaug*   *Dm*   *Dmaug*
But the fool   on   the   hill, sees the sun going down,

          C7   *Dm*   *Dm7*
And the eyes in his head, see the world spinning round.

C2
D6
Oh,

Em7/D
'Round, 'round, 'round, 'round, 'round.   *... fade out*

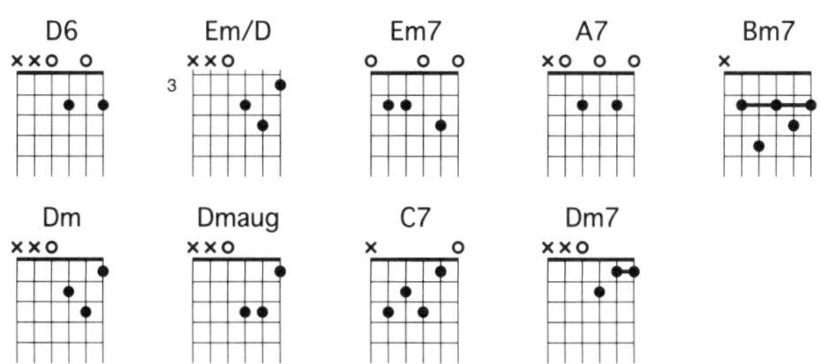

The Inner Light

** CAPO : 1 FRET.*

Words & Music by
George Harrison

Inst. ‖: D5 | D5 | D5 | D5 | D5 :‖

D   D7   G/D   D   D7   Em/D
Without going out of my door, I can know all things of earth.

D   D7   Em   D   D7   G/D
Without looking out of my window, I could know the ways of heaven

G/D   D   D7
The farther one travels, the less one knows,

D   G/D   D
The less one really knows.

Inst. ‖: D5 | D5 | D5 | D5 | D5 :‖

D   D7   Em/D   D   D7   G/D
Without going out of my door, you can know all things of earth,

D   D7   Em   D   D7   G/D
Without looking out of my window, you can know the ways of heaven.

G/D   D   D7
The farther one travels, the less one knows,

D   G/D   D
The less one really knows.

D
Arrive without travelling,

See all without looking,

Do all without doing.

Inst. | D | D | D5 | D5 | D5 | D5 |

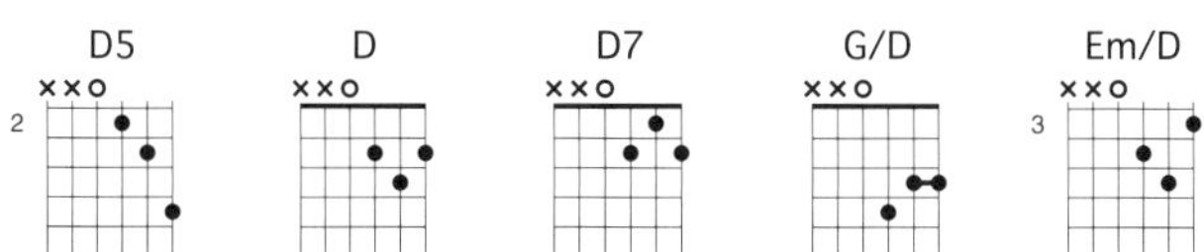
D5
D
D7
G/D
Em/D

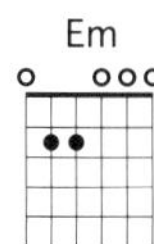
Em

The Long And Winding Road

** CAPO : 1 FRET.*

Words & Music by
John Lennon & Paul McCartney

|A1|
```
     Bm                G/A       D    D7      G
The long and winding road that leads to your door,

      F#m          Bm
Will never disappear,

Em             A7      C/D
I've seen that road before

G  F#m      Bm         Em           A7   A7sus4     D
It always leads me here, leads me to   your   door.
```

|A2|
```
     Bm                G/A       D    D7      G
The wild and windy night the rain washed away,

   F#m  Bm         Em     A7       C/D
Has left a pool of tears crying for the day.

G    F#m           Bm         Em      A7    A7sus4   D
Why leave me standing here, let me know   the     way.
```

|B1|
```
D/A             G            D/F#          Em    A7
Many times I've been alone and many times I've cried.

D/A         G            D/F#          Em    A7
Anyway you'll never know the many ways I've tried,
```

|A3|
```
     Bm                G/A       D    D7         G
And still they lead me back to the long and winding road.

    F#m         Bm
You left me standing here

Em      A7       C/D
A long, long time ago.

G    F#m           Bm         Em      A7   A7sus4   D
Don't leave me waiting here, lead me to   your   door.
```

|Inst.| ‖: D/A G | D/F# Em A7 :‖

Bm		*G/A*	*D*	*D7*	*G*

A4 But still they lead me back to the long and winding road.

F#m   *Bm*
You left me standing here

Em   *A7*   *C/D*
A long, long time ago.

G   *F#m*   *Bm*   *Em*   *A7*   *D*
Don't keep me waiting here, lead me to you door.

G/A   *D*
Yeah, yeah, yeah, yeah.

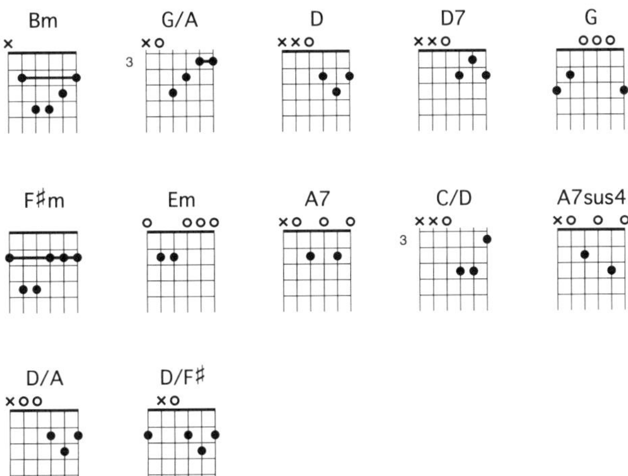

The Night Before

Words & Music by
John Lennon & Paul McCartney

Inst. ‖ *D* | *D* | *F* | *F* | *G7* | *G7* | *A7* | *A7* ‖

A1
  D   *C* *G*   *A*
We said our goodbyes, ah, the night before.

  D   *C* *G*   *A*
Love was in your eyes, ah, the night before.

  Bm   *Gm6* *Bm*   *Gm6*
Now today I find you have changed your mind.

  D   *G7*   *D* *F* *G*
Treat me like you did the night before.

A2
  D   *C* *G*   *A*
Were you telling lies, ah, the night before?

  D   *C*   *G*   *A*
Was I so unwise, ah, the night before?

  Bm   *Gm6* *Bm*   *Gm6*
When I held you near you were so sincere,

  D   *G7*   *D*
Treat me like you did the night before.

B1
  Am   *D7*   *G*   *C/G* *G*
Last night is a night I will remember you by.

  Bm   *E7*   *A7*
When I think of things we did it makes me wanna cry.

A3
  D   *C* *G*   *A*
We said our goodbye, ah, the night before.

  D   *C* *G*   *A*
Love was in your eyes, ah, the night before.

  Bm   *Gm6* *Bm*   *Gm6*
Now today I find you have changed your mind.

  D   *G7*   *D* *F* *G*
Treat me like you did the night before.

Inst.	D	C	G	A	
	D	C	G	A	‖

A4

Bm   *Gm6*   *Bm*   *Gm6*
When I held you near you were so sincere.

D   *G7*   *D*
Treat me like you did the night before.

B2

Am   *D7*   *G*   *C/G*   *G*
Last night is a night I will remember you by.

Bm   *E7*   *A7*
When I think of things we did it makes me wanna cry.

A5

D   *C*   *G*   *A*
Were you telling lies, ah, the night before?

D   *C*   *G*   *A*
Was I so unwise, ah, the night before?

Bm   *Gm6*   *Bm*   *Gm6*
When I held you near you were so sincere.

D   *G7*   *D*
Treat me like you did the night before,

F   *D*
Like the night before.

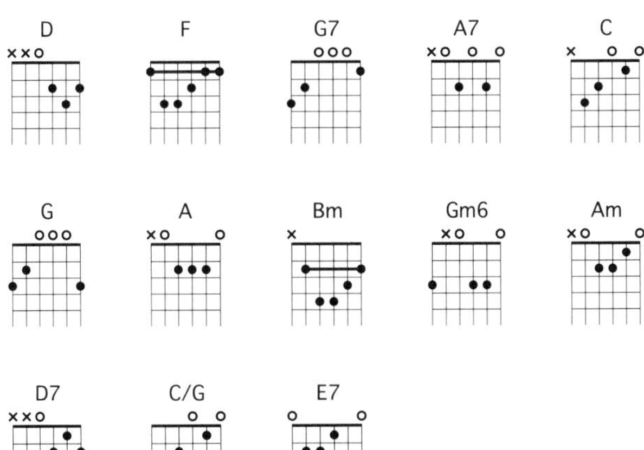

The Word

Words & Music by
John Lennon & Paul McCartney

Inst. | *D7#9* | *D7#9* ‖

D7#9
A1 Say the word and you'll be free, say the word and be like me,

G7   *D7#9*
Say the word I'm thinking of, have you heard the word is love?

Asus4 A *Gsus4* *G*
It's so   fine, It's sun - shine,

D7#9
It's the word, love.

D   *Cadd9*
B1 In the beginning I misunderstood,

F   *G*
But now I've got it, the word is good.

D7#9
A2 Spread the word and you'll be free, spread the word and be like me,

G7   *D7#9*
Spread the word I'm thinking of, have you heard the word is love?

Asus4 A *Gsus4* *G*
It's so   fine, It's sun - shine,

D7#9
It's the word, love.

D   *Cadd9*
B2 Everywhere I go I hear it said,

F   *G*
In the good and bad books that I have read.

A3
D7#9
Say the word and you'll be free, say the word and be like me,

G7   *D7#9*
Say the word I'm thinking of, have you heard the word is love?

Asus4 A   *Gsus4   G*
It's so   fine, It's sun - shine,

D7#9
It's the word, love.

B3
D   *Cadd9*
Now that I know what I feel must be right,

F   *G*
I'm here to show everybody the light.

A4
D7#9
Give the word a chance to say, that the word is just the way.

G7   *D7#9*
It's the word I'm thinking of, and the only word is love.

Asus4 A   *Gsus4   G*
It's so   fine, It's sun - shine,

D7#9
It's the word, love.

Inst. | *D* | *Cadd9* | *F* | *G* | *D7#9* | *D7#9* ||

OUTRO
D7#9
Say the word, love,

G7
Say the word, love,

D7#9
Say the word, love,

Asus4   A   Gsus4   G
Say the word,

D7#9
love

Inst. | *D* | *Cadd9* | *F* || *... fade out*

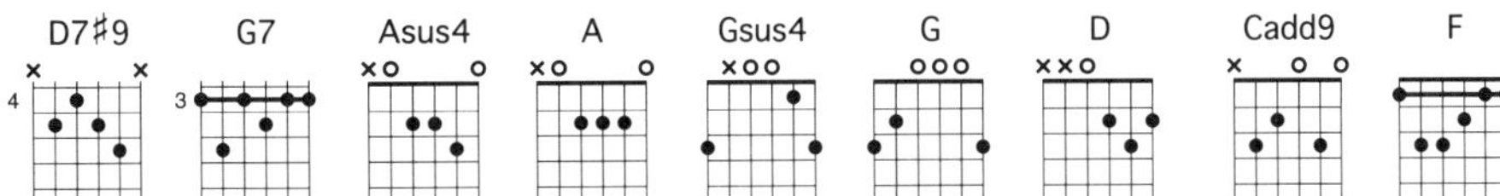

There's A Place

Words & Music by
John Lennon & Paul McCartney

Inst. | E | A | E | A ||

A1
                  E
There is a place,

A   E
Where I can go,

A   E
When I feel low,

C#m   B7
When I feel blue.

               C#m   A
And it's my mind,

                 E   A
And there's no time

          F#m   C#m/G#
When I'm alone.

A2
           E
I think of you,

A   E
And things you do,

A   E
Go 'round my head,

C#m   B7
The things you've said,

     A   B7
Like I love only you.

B1
C#m   F#
In my mind there's no sorrow,

E   G#7
Don't you know that it's so?

C#m   F#
There'll be no sad tomorrow,

E   G#7   C#m
Don't you know that it's so.

E
[A3] There is a place,

A   *E*
Where I can go,

A   *E*
When I feel low,

C#m   .   *B7*
When I feel blue,

       G#m   *A*
And it's my mind,

        E   *A*
And there's no time

     F#m   *C#m/G#*
When I'm alone.

      E   *A*
[OUTRO] There's a place,

      E   *A*
There's a place,

      E   *A*
‖: There's a place, :‖ *... fade out*

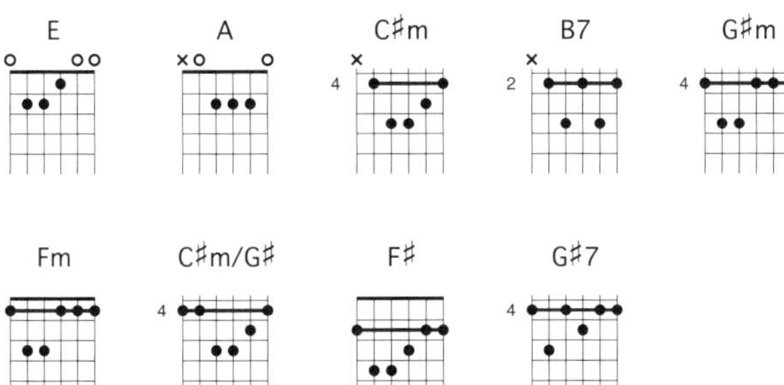

Things We Said Today

Words & Music by
John Lennon & Paul McCartney

Inst. | *Am* | *Am* ‖

A1
Am   *Em*   *Am*   *Em*   *Am*
You say you will love me if I have to go,

Am   *Em*   *Am*   *Em*   *Am*
You'll be thinking of me, somehow I will know.

C   *C7*
Someday when I'm lonely,

F   *Bb*
Wishing you weren't so far away,

Am   *Em*   *Am*   *Em*   *Am*
Then I will remember the things we said today.

A2
Am   *Em*   *Am*   *Em*   *Am*
You say you'll be mine, girl, until the end of time.

Am   *Em*   *Am*   *Em*   *Am*
These days such a kind girl seems so hard to find.

C   *C7*
Someday when we're dreaming

F   *Bb*
Deep in love, not a lot to say.

Am   *Em*   *Am*   *Em*   *Am*
Then we will remember the things we said today.

B1
A   *D*
Me, I'm just the lucky kind.

B7   *E7*   *A*
Love to hear you say that love is love.

D
And, though we may be blind,

B7   *Bb*
Love is here to stay. and that's

<pre>
      Am   Em   Am   Em   Am
A3 Enough to make you mine, girl, be the only one.

    Am   Em   Am   Em   Am
    Love me all the time, girl. we'll go on and on.

    C   C7
    Someday when we're dreaming

    F   Bb
    Deep in love, not a lot to say.

    Am   Em   Am   Em   A
    Then we will remember the things we said today.
</pre>

<pre>
    A   D
B2 Me, I'm just the lucky kind.

    B7   E7   A
    Love to hear you say that love is love.

                      D
    And, though we may be blind,

    B7   Bb
    Love is here to stay. and that's
</pre>

<pre>
      Am   Em   Am   Em   Am
A4 Enough to make you mine, girl, be the only one.

    Am   Em   Am   Em   Am
    Love me all the time, girl. we'll go on and on.

    C   C7
    Someday when we're dreaming

    F   Bb
    Deep in love, not a lot to say.

    Am   Em   Am   Em   Am
    Then we will remember the things we said today.
</pre>

<pre>
Inst.   ‖: Am | Am | Am | Am :‖   ... fade out
</pre>

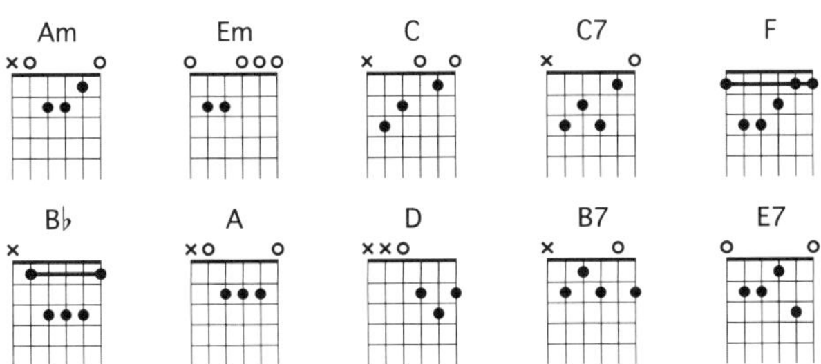

Think For Yourself

Words & Music by
George Harrison

Inst. | G7 | G7 ‖

A1
Am   *Dm*
I've got a word or two

Bb   *C*   *G7*
To say about the things that you do.

Am   *Dm*
You're telling all those lies

Bb   *C*   *G7*
About the good things that we can have

      Am
If we close our eyes.

B1
C7
Do what you want to do,

   G7
And go where you're going to,

Eb/Bb
Think for yourself,

     D7   *G7*
'Cause I won't be there with you.

A2
Am   *Dm*
I left you far behind

Bb   *C*   *G7*
The ruins of the life that you had in mind.

Am   *Dm*
And though you still can't see,

Bb   *C*
I know your mind's made up,

    G7   *Am*
You're gonna cause more misery,

B2

C7
Do what you want to do,

G7
And go where you're going to,

Eb/Bb   *D7*   *G7*
Think for yourself 'cause I won't be there with you.

A3

Am   *Dm*
Although your mind's opaque,

Bb   *C*   *G7*
Try thinking more if just for your own sake.

Am   *Dm*
The future still looks good,

Bb   *C*   *G7*
And you've got time to rectify

                        Am
All the things that you should.

B3

C7
Do what you want to do,

G7
And go where you're going to,

Eb/Bb   *D7*   *G7*
Think for yourself 'cause I won't be there with you.

B4

C7
Do what you want to do,

G7
And go where you're going to,

Eb/Bb
Think for yourself,

            D7   *C7*   *G7*
'Cause I won't be there with you.

Eb/Bb
Think for yourself,

            D7   *C7*   *G7*
'Cause I won't be there with you.

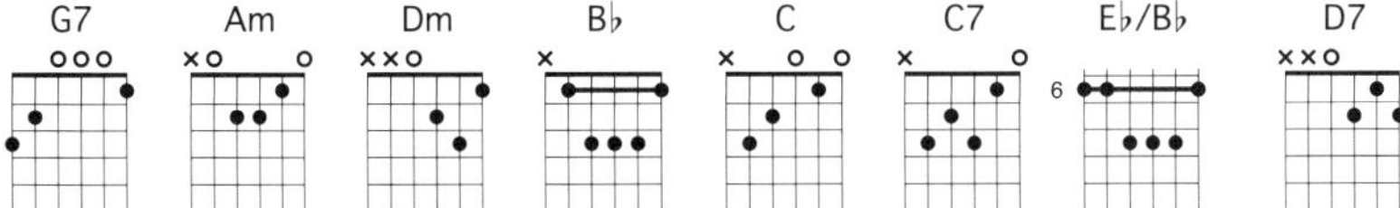

This Boy

Words & Music by
John Lennon & Paul McCartney

Inst. | D/F# D/E D/F# ‖ D Bm7 | Em7 A ‖

A1
Dmaj7   Bm7   Em7
That boy

        A   Dmaj7   Bm7
Took my love away,

Em7   A   Dmaj7   Bm7
Tough he'll regret it someday,

    Em7   A   D   Bm7 Em7   A
But this boy wants you back again.

A2
Dmaj7   Bm7   Em7
That boy

     A   Dmaj7   Bm7
Isn't good for you,

Em7   A   Dmaj7   Bm7
Though he may want you too,

Em7   A   D   D9
This boy wants you back again. ——

B1
      G   F#7
Oh, and this boy would be happy,

    Bm   D   D7
Just to love you, buy oh my - hi - hi - a,

G   E9
That boy won't be happy,

A
Till he's seen you cry.

> *Dmaj7*   *Bm7*   *Em7*

A3 This boy

>   *A*   *Dmaj7*   *Bm7*

Wouldn't mind the pain,

> *Em7*   *A*   *Dmaj7*   *Bm7*

Would always feel the same,

>   *Em7*   *A*   *D*   *Bm7*   *Em7*   *A*

If this boy gets you back again.

> *Dmaj7*   *Bm7*   *Em7*   *A*

OUTRO This boy.

> *Dmaj7*   *Bm7*   *Em7*   *A*

𝄆 This boy. 𝄇   *... fade out*

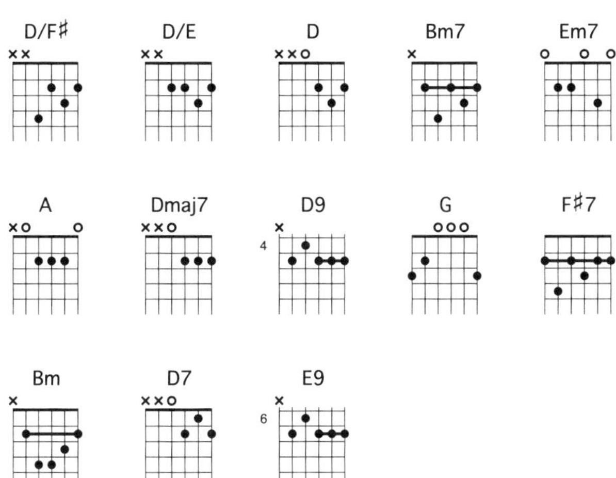

Ticket To Ride

Words & Music by
John Lennon & Paul McCartney

Inst. | A | A | A | A ||

     A
A1 I think I'm gonna be sad, I think it's today, yeah.

                         Bm   *E*
The girl that's driving me mad is going away.

F#m   *D7*
She's got a ticket to ride,

F#m   *Gmaj7*
She's got a ticket to ride,

F#m   *E*   *A*
She's got a ticket to ride, and she don't care.

     A
A2 She said that living with me was bringing her down, yeah.

                         Bm   *E*
For she would never be free when I was around.

F#m   *D7*
She's got a ticket to ride,

F#m   *Gmaj7*
She's got a ticket to ride,

F#m   *E*   *A*
She's got a ticket to ride, and she don't care.

     D7
B1 I don't know why she's riding so high,

                                    E   *E7*
She ought to think twice, she ought to do right by me.

     D7
Before she gets to saying goodbye,

                                    E
She ought to think twice, she ought to do right by me.

A3
    A
I think I'm gonna be sad, I think it's today, yeah.

                                        Bm   *E*
The girl that's driving me mad is going away, yeah.

   F#m   *D7*
Ah, she's got a ticket to ride,

F#m   *Gmaj7*
She's got a ticket to ride,

F#m   *E*   *A*
She's got a ticket to ride, and she don't care.

B2
  D7
I don't know why she's riding so high,

                             E   *E7*
She ought to think twice, she ought to do right by me.

 D7
Before she gets to saying goodbye,

                            E
She ought to think twice, she ought to do right by me.

A3
  A
She said that living with me was bringing her down, yeah.

                       Bm   *E*
For she would never be free when I was around.

F#m   *D7*
She's got a ticket to ride,

F#m   *Gmaj7*
She's got a ticket to ride,

F#m   *E*   *A*
She's got a ticket to ride, and she don't care.

OUTRO
  A
My baby don't care, my baby don't care.

My baby don't care, my baby don't care.

My baby don't care, my baby don't care.   *... fade out*

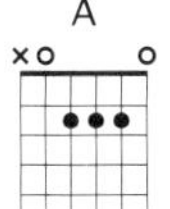

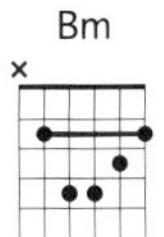

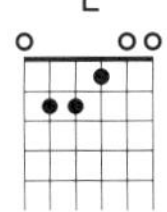

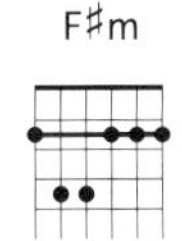

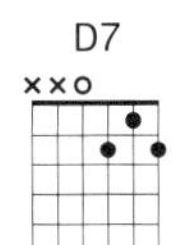

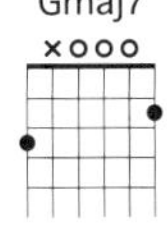

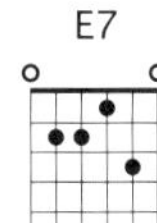

Tomorrow Never Knows

Words & Music by
John Lennon & Paul McCartney

Inst. | C | C | C | C ‖

A1
   C
Turn off your mind, relax and float down stream,
      C11   C
It is not dying, it is not dying.

A2
   C
Lay down al thoughts, surrender to the void,
     C11   C
It is shining, it is shining.

A3
   C
Yet you may see the meaning of within,
     C11   C
It is being, it is being.

Inst. | C | C | C | C |
| C | C | C | C ‖

A4
   C
That Love is all and love is everyone,
     C11   C
It is knowing, it is knowing.

A5
   C
That ignorance and hate may mourn the dead,
     C11   C
It is believing, it is believing.

C
A6 But listen to the colour of your dreams,

       C11   *C*
It is not living, it is not living.

C
A7 Or play the game existence to the end

       C11   *C*
Of the beginning, of the beginning,

       C11   *C*
Of the beginning, of the beginning,

       C11   *C*
Of the beginning, of the beginning,

       C11   *C*
Of the beginning.

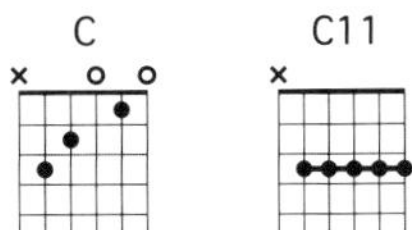

Two Of Us

Words & Music by
John Lennon & Paul McCartney

Inst. | *(G)* | *(G)* | *(G)* | *(G)* ‖

    G   *C*   *G/B*   *Am7*

A1 Two of us riding nowhere, spending someone's hard earned pay.

    G   *C*   *G/B*   *Am7*   *G*

You and me Sunday driving, not arriving on   our   way back home

    D   *C*   *G*

B1 We're on our way home,

    D   *C*   *G*

We're on our way home,

    C   *G*

We're going home.

Inst. | *G* | *G* | *G* | *G* ‖

    G   *C*   *G/B*   *Am7*

A2 Two of us sending postcards, writing letters on my   wall.

    G   *C*   *G/B*   *Am7*   *G*

You and me burning matches, lifting latches, on   our   way back home

    D   *C*   *G*

B2 We're on our way home,

    D   *C*   *G*

We're on our way home,

    C   *G*

We're going home.

    Bb   *Dm*

C1 You and I have memories,

    Gm7   *Am*   *D7*

longer than the road that stretches out ahead.

A3

     G   *C G/B Am7*
Two of us wearing raincoats, standing solo in the sun.

 G   *C G/B Am7   G*
You and me chasing paper, getting nowhere on our way back home.

B3

 D   *C G*
We're on our way home,

 D   *C G*
We're on our way home,

 C   *G*
We're going home.

C2

 Bb   *Dm*
You and I have memories,

 Gm7   *Am*   *D7*
Longer than the road that stretches out ahead.

A4

 G   *C G/B Am7*
Two of us wearing raincoats, standing solo in the sun.

 G   *C G/B Am7   G*
You and me chasing paper, getting nowhere on our way back home.

B4

 D   *C G*
We're on our way home,

 D   *C G*
We're on our way home,

 C   *G*
We're going home.

Inst. | *(G)* | *(G)* | *(G)* | *(G)* |
     | *(G)* | *(G)* | *(G)* | *(G)* | *... fade out*

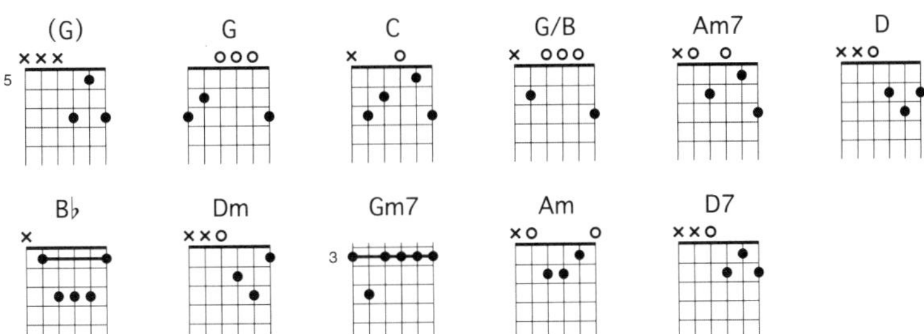

Wait

Words & Music by
John Lennon & Paul McCartney

** CAPO : 2 FRET.*

|A1|
                  Em7 A/E Am/E Em   B7   Em
It's been a long time, now I'm coming back home,

                  Em7 A/E Am/E Em   B7   Em
I've been away   now, oh   how I've been alone.

|B1|
    G6   G6/C G6   G6/C   G6   G6/C
Wait   till I come back to your side,

           G6   B7   Em
We'll forget the tears we've cried.

|A2|
                  Em7   A/E   Am/E Em   B7   Em
But if your heart breaks, don't wait, turn me away,

                  Em7   A/E Am/E Em B7   Em
And if your heart's strong, hold   on,   I won't delay.

|B2|
    G6   G6/C G6   G6/C   G6   G6/C
Wait   till I come back to your side,

           G6   B7   Em
We'll forget the tears we've cried.

|C1|
        A   D
I feel as though you ought to know

               G   Em
That I've been good as good as I can be.

        A   D
And if you do, I'll trust in you,

             G   B7sus4 (B7)
And know that you will wait for me.

A3   *Em7 A/E Am/E Em   B7   Em*
It's been a long time, now   I'm   coming back home,

            Em7   A/E Am/E Em B7   Em
I've been away   now, oh   how I've been alone.

B3 *G6   G6/C G6   G6/C   G6   G6/C*
Wait   till I come back to your side,

               G6   B7   Em
We'll forget the tears we've cried.

C2   *A*   *D*
I feel as though you ought to know

            G   *Em*
That I've been good as good as I can be.

        A   *D*
And if you do, I'll trust in you,

            G   *B7sus4 (B7)*
And know that you will wait for me.

A4   *Em7   A/E Am/E Em B7   Em*
But if your heart breaks, don't wait, turn me away,

             Em7   A/E   Am/E   Em B7   Em
And if your heart's strong, hold   on,   I won't delay.

B4 *G6   G6/C G6   G6/C   G6   G6/C*
Wait   till I come back to your side,

               G6   B7   Em
We'll forget the tears we've cried.

A5   *Em7 A/E Am/E Em   B7   Em*
It's been a long time, now   I'm   coming back home,

            Em7   A/E Am/E Em B7   Em
I've been away   now, oh   how I've been alone.

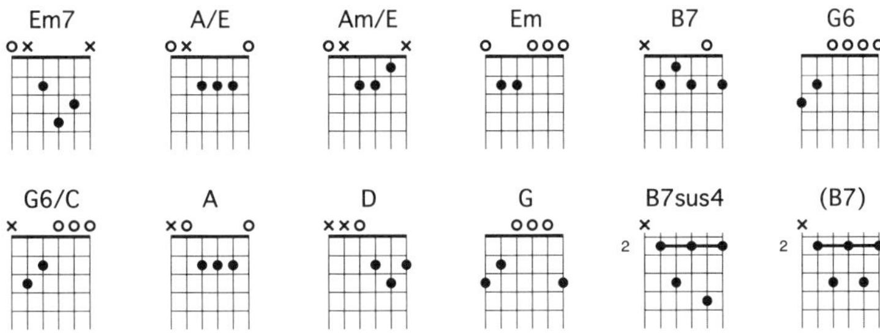

We Can Work It Out

Words & Music by
John Lennon & Paul McCartney

|A1|
```
 D            Dsus4    D
Try to see it my     way,
                   Dsus4          C          D
Do I have to keep on talking till I can't go on?
                 Dsus4     D
While you see it your     way,
                 Dsus4           C            D
Run the risk of knowing that our love may soon be gone.
```

|B1|
```
 G            D    G              A
We can work it out, we can work it out.
```

|A2|
```
 D                   Dsus4    D
Think of what you're say  -  ing.
                 Dsus4           C            D
You can get it wrong and still you think that it's alright.
             Dsus4    D
Think of what I'm say  -  ing,
                 Dsus4       C              D
We can work it out and get it straight, or say good night.
```

|B2|
```
 G            D    G              A
We can work it out, we can work it out.
```

|C1|
```
 Bm                   Bm/A      G      F#7sus4
Life is very short, and there's no time
       F#7         Bm          Bm/A   Bm/G    Bm/F#
For fussing and fighting, my friend.
 Bm                       Bm/A    G      F#7sus4
I have always thought that it's a     crime,
     F#7  Bm     Bm/A      Bm/G    Bm/F#
So I will ask you once a  -  gain.
```

A3
D   *Dsus4*   *D*
Try to see it my   way,

          Dsus4   *C*   *D*
Only time will tell if I am right or I am wrong.

            Dsus4   *D*
While you see it your   way,

               Dsus4   *C*   *D*
There's a chance that we may fall apart before too long.

B3
G   *D*   *G*   *A*
We can work it out, we can work it out.

C2
Bm   *Bm/A*   *G*   *F#7sus4*
Life is very short, and there's no time

    F#7   *Bm*   *Bm/A* *Bm/G* *Bm/F#*
For fussing and fighting, my friend.

Bm   *Bm/A*   *G*   *F#7sus4*
I have always thought that it's a   crime,

    F#7 *Bm*   *Bm/A*   *Bm/G*   *Bm/F#*
So I will ask you once a - gain.

A4
D   *Dsus4*   *D*
Try to see it my   way,

           Dsus4   *C*   *D*
Only time will tell if I am right or I am wrong.

            Dsus4   *D*
While you see it your   way

               Dsus4   *C*   *D*
There's a chance that we may fall apart before too long.

B4
G   *D*   *G*   *A*
We can work it out, we can work it out.

Inst. | *D* | *D* |

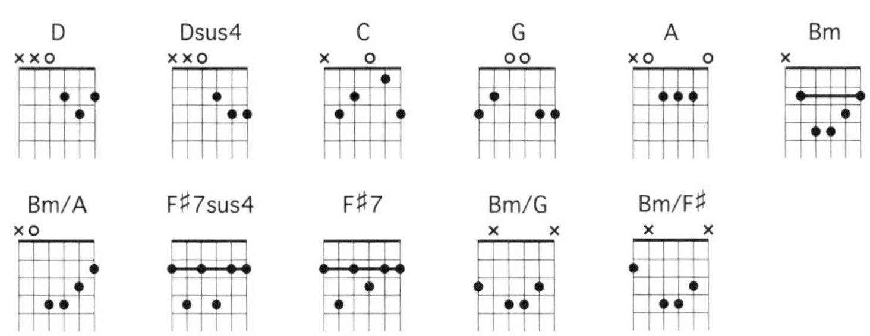

What Goes On

Words & Music by
John Lennon & Paul McCartney & Richard Starkey

Inst. | E7 B7 | E7 ‖

A1
E7
What goes on — in your heart?

A7
What goes on — in your mind?

E7
You are tearing me apart,

A7
When you treat — me so unkind.

B7sus4 (B7)   *E*
What goes on — in your mind?

B1
E7
The other day I saw you

Am
As I walked along the road.

E7
But when I saw him with you

Am
I could feel my future fold.

B7   *E7*
It's so easy for a girl like you to lie

B7
Tell me why.

A2
E7
What goes on — in your heart?

A7
What goes on — in your mind?

E7
You are tearing me apart,

A7
When you treat — me so unkind.

B7sus4 (B7)   *E*
What goes on — in your mind?

|B2| E7
I met you in the morning,

Am
waiting for the tides of time.

E7
But now the tide is turning.

Am
I can see that I was blind.

B7　　　　　E7
It's so easy for a girl like you to lie

B7　　　　　E7
Tell me why, what goes on — in your heart?

Inst. | E7 | A7 | E7 | E7 |
　　　　| E7 | A7 | B7 | E7 ‖

|B3| E7
I used to think of no on else,

Am
But you were just the same,

E7
You didn't even think of me

Am
As someone with a name.

B7　　　　　　　E7
Did you mean to break my heart and watch me die?

B7
Tell me why.

|A2| E7
What goes on — in your heart?

A7
What goes on — in your mind?

E7
You are tearing me apart,

A7
When you treat — me so unkind.

B7sus4 (B7)　　E
What goes on — in your mind?

Inst. | E7 | E7 | E ‖

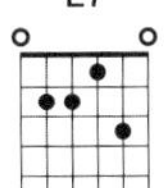

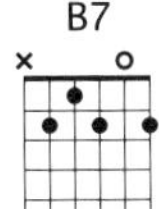

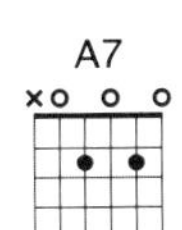

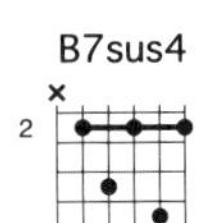

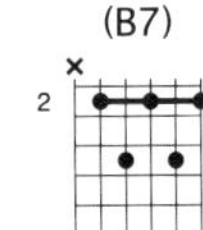

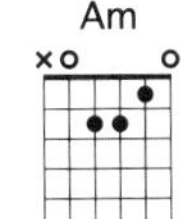

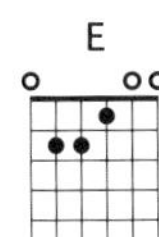

What You're Doing

Words & Music by
John Lennon & Paul McCartney

Inst. | 4 DRUMS | D | G | D | G ||

A1
```
D                    G
```
Look what you're doing,

```
D          G
```
I'm feeling blue and lonely,

```
       Bm            G
```
Would it be too much to ask you,

```
                 D   G
```
What you're doing to me?

A2
```
D            G
```
You got me running

```
D              G
```
And there's no fun in it,

```
           Bm            G
```
Why should it be so much to ask of you,

```
                 D
```
What you're doing to me?

B1
```
G                 Bm
```
I've been waiting here for you,

```
G                    Bm
```
Wondering what you're gonna do,

```
Em
```
And should you need a love that's true,

```
      A
```
It's me.

D   *G*
[A3] Please stop your lying,

D   *G*
You've got me crying, girl,

        Bm   *G*
Why should it be so much to ask of you,

              D   *G*
What you're doing to me?

| **Inst.** | D | G7 | D | G7 | |
| Bm | G7 | G7 | D | |

G   *Bm*
[B2] I've been waiting here for you,

G   *Bm*
Wondering what you're gonna do,

Em
And should you need a love that's true,

     A
It's me.

D   *G*
[A4] Please stop your lying,

D   *G*
You've got me crying, girl,

        Bm   *G*
Why should it be so much to ask of you,

            D
What you're doing to me?

         G   *D*
What you're doing to me?

         G   *D*   *G*
What you're doing to me?

| **Inst.** | D | D | A | A | |
| :D | G7 | D | G7 :| | *... fade out* |

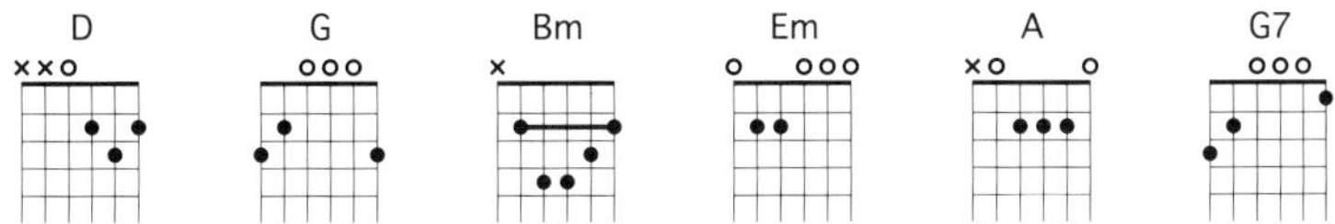

When I Get Home

Words & Music by
John Lennon & Paul McCartney

A1
    A7   *A7*
Woh-ah, woh-ah,

    D7   *G7*
I got a whole lot of things to tell her,

    Am   *G*
When I get home.

B1
    C7   *F7*
Come on, out of my way,

    C7   *F7*
'Cause I'm gonna see my baby today,

    C7   *F7*   *G7*
I've got a whole lot of things I've gotta say to her.

A2
    A7   *A7*
Woh-ah, woh-ah,

    D7   *G7*
I got a whole lot of things to tell her,

    Am   *G*
When I get home.

B2
    C7   *F7*
Come on if you please,

    C7   *F7*
I've got no time for trivialities,

    C7   *F7*   *G7*
I've got a girl who's waiting home for me tonight.

A3
    A7   *A7*
Whoa-ho, whoa-ho,

    D7   *G7*
I got a whole lot of things to tell her,

    Am
When I get home.

                  C7
C1 When I'm getting home tonight,

          Am
I'm gonna hold her tight.

         C7   *Am*
I'm gonna love her till the cows come home,

      F   *G*
I bet I'll love her more,

      F   *G*   *Am*   *G*
Till I walk out that door again.

         C7   *F7*
B3 Come on, let me through,

         C7   *F7*
I've got so many things, I've got to do,

         C7   *F7*   *G7*
I've got no business being here with you this way.

         A7   *A7*
A4 Whoa-ho, whoa-ho,

         D7   *G7*
I got a whole lot of things to tell her,

         Am
When I get home.

         D7   *G7*
I got a whole lot of things to tell her,

         C
When I get home.

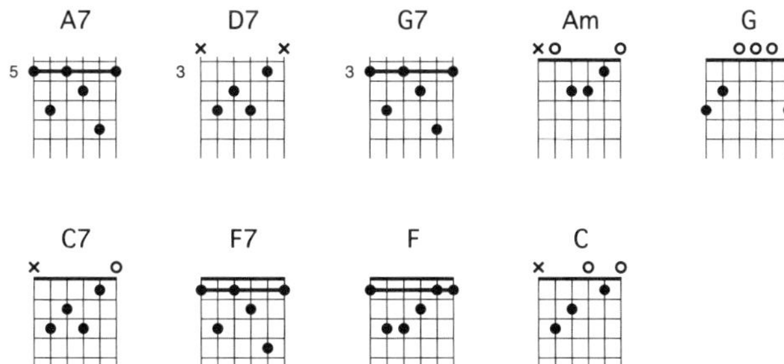

When I'm Sixty Four

Words & Music by
John Lennon & Paul McCartney

** CAPO : 1 FRET.*

Inst. | *C* | *C* | *F G* | *C* | *C* | *C* ‖

A1
C
When I get older losing my hair,

             G
Many years from now,

G7
Will you still be sending me a valentine,

              C
Birthday greetings, bottle of wine.

C
If I'd been out till quarter to three,

C7   *F*
Would you lock the door,

F   *Fm*   *C*   *A*
Will you still need me, will you still feed me,

D7   *G7*   *C* *G*   *C*
When I'm sixty-four.

Inst. | *Am* | *Am* | *G* | *C Am* ‖

B1
Am   *E7*
You'll be older too,

Am   *D7*
And if you say the word,

F   *G*   *C*
I could stay with you.

Inst. | *G* | *G* ‖

A1
C
I could be handy, mending a fuse

             G
When your lights have gone.

G7
You can knit a sweater by the fireside,

          C
Sunday mornings go for a ride,

C
Doing the garden, digging the weeds,

C7   *F*
Who could ask for more.

F   *Fm*   *C*   *A*
Will you still need me, will you still feed me,

D7   *G7* *C* *G* *C*
When I'm sixty-four.

Am
B2 Every summer we can rent a cottage,

      G   *Am*
In the Isle of Wight, if it's not too dear.

        E7
We shall scrimp and save.

Am   *Dm*
Grandchildren on your knee,

F *G*   *C* *G*
Vera Chuck & Dave

Inst. | *G* | *G* | ‖

C
A3 Send me a postcard, drop me a line,

      G
Stating point of view

G7
Indicate precisely what you mean to say

      C
Yours sincerely, wasting away

C
Give me your answer, fill in a form

C7   *F*
Mine for evermore.

F   *Fm*   *C*   *A*
Will you still need me, will you still feed me,

D7   *G7* *C* *G* *C*
When I'm sixty-four.

Inst. | *C* | *C* | *F* *G* | *C* *G* *C* ‖

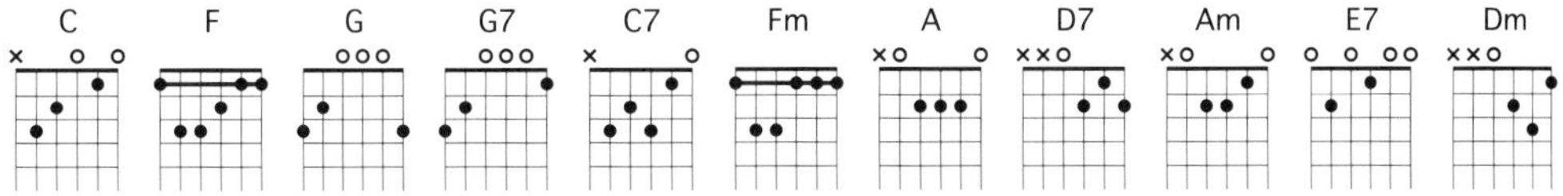

While My Guitar Gently Weeps

Words & Music by
George Harrison

Inst. |Am |Am/G |D/F# |Fmaj7 |
|Am |G |D |E ||

A1
Am   Am/G   D/F#   Fmaj7
I look at you all see the love there that's sleeping,

Am   G   D   E
While my guitar gently weeps.

Am   Am/G   D/F#   Fmaj7
I look at the floor and I see it needs sweeping,

Am   G   C   E
Still my guitar gently weeps.

B1
A   C#m   F#m   C#m   Bm   E
I don't know why — nobody told you how to unfold your love

A   C#m   F#m   C#m
I don't know how — someone controlled you,

Bm   E
They bought and sold you.

A2
Am   Am/G   D/F#   Fmaj7
I look at the world and I notice it's turning,

Am   G   D   E
While my guitar gently weeps.

Am   Am/G   D/F#   Fmaj7
With every mistake, we must surely be learning,

Am   G   C   E
Still my guitar gently weeps.

Inst. |Am |Am/G |D/F# |Fmaj7 |
Am	G	D	E
Am	Am/G	D/F#	Fmaj7
Am	G	C	E	

	A	*C#m*	*F#m*	*C#m*

B2 I don't know how — you were diverted,

Bm   *E*
You were perverted too,

A   *C#m*   *F#m*   *C#m*
I don't know how — you were inverted,

Bm   *E*
No one alerted you.

Am   *Am/G*   *D/F#*   *Fmaj7*

A3 I look at you all see the love there that's sleeping

Am   *G*   *D*   *E*
While my guitar gently weeps

Am   *Am/G*   *D/F#*   *Fmaj7*
I Look at you all.

Am   *G*   *C*   *E*
Still my guitar gently weeps.

Inst.
```
| Am      | Am/G  | D/F#  | Fmaj7  |
| Am      | G     | D     | E      |
| Am      | Am/G  | D/F#  | Fmaj7  |
| Am      | G     | C     | E      |
| Am      | Am/G  | D/F#  | Fmaj7  |
|: Am     | G     | C     | E    :|     ... fade out
```

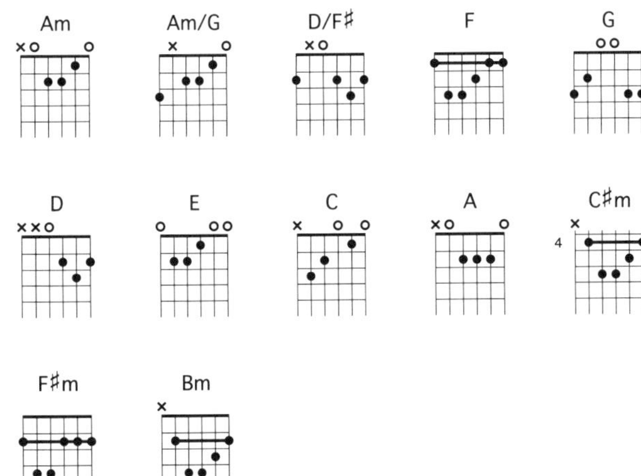

Why Don't We Do It In The Road

Words & Music by
John Lennon & Paul McCartney

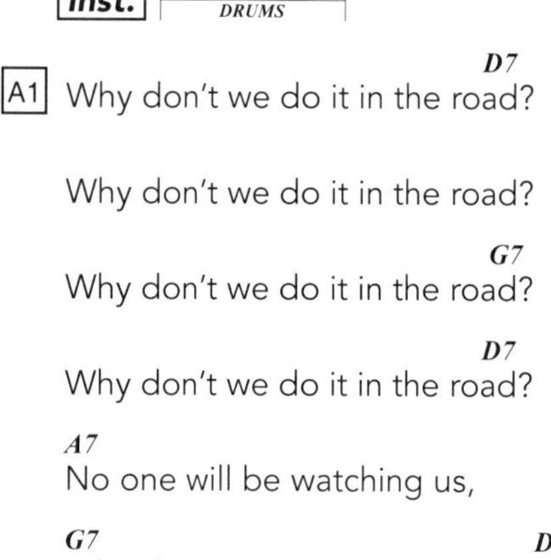

|A1|
D7
Why don't we do it in the road?

Why don't we do it in the road?

G7
Why don't we do it in the road?

D7
Why don't we do it in the road?

A7
No one will be watching us,

G7 *D7*
Why don't we do it in the road?

|A2|
D7
Why don't we do it in the road?

Why don't we do it in the road?

G7
Why don't we do it in the road?

D7
Why don't we do it in the road?

A7
No one will be watching us,

G7 *D7*
Why don't we do it in the road?

D7

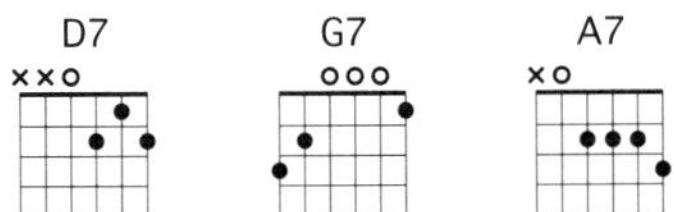

A3 Why don't we do it in the road?

Why don't we do it in the road?

G7

Why don't we do it in the road?

D7

Why don't we do it in the road?

A7
No one will be watching us,

G7   *D7*
Why don't we do it in the road?

D7   G7   A7

Wild Honey Pie

Words & Music by
John Lennon & Paul McCartney

* 반음 낮추어 튜닝합니다.

Inst. | *G7* | *F7* | *E7* *Eb7* | *D7* ||

A1
G7
Honey Pie,

Honey Pie,

Inst. | *G7* | *F7* | *E7* *Eb7* | *D7* ||

A2
G7
Honey Pie,

Honey Pie,

Inst. | *G7* | *F7* | *E7* *Eb7* | *D7* ||

A3
G7
Honey Pie,

F7
Honey Pie,

G7
Honey Pie,

F7
Honey Pie,

G7
I love you, Honey Pie

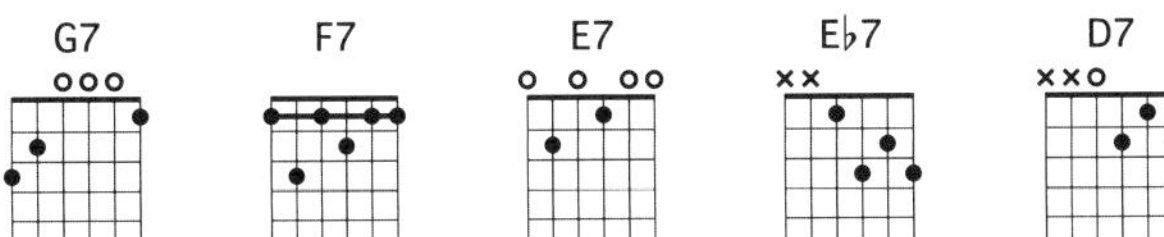

G7
F7
E7
E♭7
D7

With A Little Help From My Friends

Words & Music by
John Lennon & Paul McCartney

INTRO
    C   D   E
Bil - ly Shears.

A1
E   *B*   *F#m7*
What would you think if I sang out of tune,

                       B7   *E*
Would you stand up and walk out on me?

             B   *F#m7*
Lend me your ears and I'll sing you a song.

               B7   *E*
And I'll try not to sing out of key.

B1
         D   *A*   *E*
Oh, I get by with a little help from my friends,

         D   *A*   *E*
Mm, I get high with a little help from my friends,

            A   *E*   *B*
Mm, I'm gonna try with a little help from my friends.

A2
E   *B*   *F#m7*
What do I do when my love is away?

                 B7 *E*
(Does it worry you to be alone?)

E   *B*   *F#m7*
How do I feel by the end of the day?

                    B7   *E*
(Are you sad because you're on your own?)

B2
         D   *A*   *E*
No, I get by with a little help from my friends,

         D   *A*   *E*
Mm, I get high with a little help from my friends,

            A   *E*
Mm, I'm gonna try with a little help from my friends,

|C1|
       C#m   *F#*
Do you need anybody?

    E   *D*   *A*
I need somebody to love.

      C#m   *F#*
Could it be anybody?

    E   *D*   *A*
I want somebody to love.

|A3|
E   *B*   *F#m7*
Would you believe in a love at first sight?

        B7   *E*
Yes I'm certain that it happens all the time.

     B   *F#m7*
What do you see when you turn out the light?

      B7   *E*
I can't tell you, but I know it's mine.

|B3|
    D   *A*   *E*
Oh I get by with a little help from my friends

    D   *A*   *E*
Mm I get high with a little help from my friends

     A   *E*
Oh I'm gonna try with a little help from my friends

|C2| * |C1| 반복

|B4|
    D   *A*   *E*
Oh, I get by with a little help from my friends,

    D   *A*   *E*
Mm, gonna try with a little help from my friends,

   A   *E*
Oh, I get high with a little help from my friends,

    D   *A*
Yes, I get by with a little help from my friends,

    C *D* *E*
With a little help from my friends.

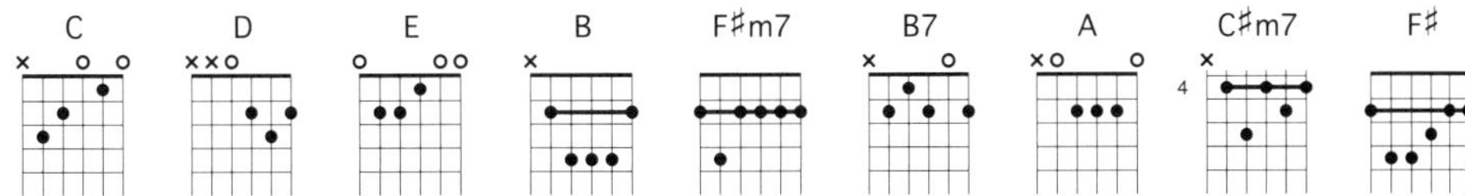

Within You Without You

** CAPO : 1 FRET.*

Words & Music by
George Harrison

Inst. | C5   *11* |

|A1|
C   Csus4   C5   C7
We were   talk-ing

C   Csus2   C   Csus4   C
About the space be — tween us   all,

Csus4   C5   C7
And the   people

C   Csus2   C   Csus4   C   Csus4   C
Who hide themselves be — hind a   wall of illu — sions,

Csus4   C   Csus4   C7   C   Csus4   C
Never   glimpse the truth then it's far too late when they pass away.

|A2|
C   Csus4   C5   C7
We were   talking

C   Csus2   C   Csus4   C
About the love we   all would share

Csus4   C5   C7
When we   find it

C   Csus2   C   Csus4   C
To try our best to   hold it   there

Csus4   C   Csus4   C7
With our   love, with our   love

C   Csus4   C   C7   C
We could save the world, if they only knew.

|B1|
C5
Try to realise it's all within yourself,

C   Csus4   C
No-one else can make you   change.

C5
And to see you're really only very small,

C   Csus4   C   Csus2
And life flows within you and with — out you.

Inst. | |C5——————35——————‖

                C   Csus4   C   C7
A3 We were   talking

                C   Csus2   C   Csus4 C
About the love that's   gone so   cold

                        Csus4 C   C7
And the   people,

                        C   Csus2 C   Csus4   C
Who gain the world and   lose their   soul.

                        Csus4   C
They don't   know,

                        Csus4   C
They can't   see,

                        Csus4   C   C7   C
Are you   one of them?

Inst. | |C5——————7——————‖

        C5
B2 When you've seen beyond yourself,

Then you may find, peace of mind,

        C   Csus4   C
Is waiting there,

C5
And the time will come when you see

we're all one, and life flows on within you

C   Csus4   C   Csus2
And with — out you.

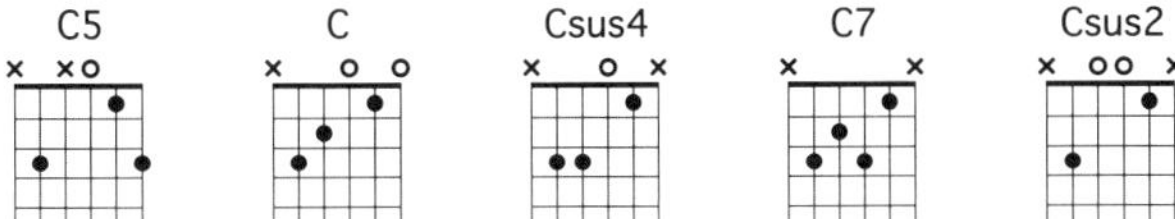

Yellow Submarine

Words & Music by
John Lennon & Paul McCartney

* 반음 낮추어 튜닝합니다.

A1
      D   *C*   *G*
In the town where I was born,

Em   *Am*   *C*   *D7*
Lived a man who sailed to sea,

G   *D*   *C*   *G*
And he told us of his life,

Em   *Am*   *C*   *D7*
In the land of submarines.

A2
G   *D*   *C*   *G*
So we sailed up to the sun,

Em   *Am*   *C*   *D7*
Till we found the sea of green,

G   *D*   *C*   *G*
And we lived beneath the waves,

Em   *Am*   *C*   *D7*
In our yellow submarine.

B1
G   *D*
We all live in our yellow submarine,

               G
Yellow submarine, yellow submarine.

              D
We all live in our yellow submarine,

               G
Yellow submarine, yellow submarine.

A3
        D   *C*   *G*
And our friends are all on board,

Em   *Am*   *C*   *D7*
Many more of them live next door,

G   *D*   *C*   *G*   *D*
And the band begins to play.

Inst. `‖ G    | D7  G ‖`

B2
G   D
We all live in our yellow submarine,

                          G
Yellow submarine, yellow submarine.

                          D
We all live in our yellow submarine,

                          G
Yellow submarine, yellow submarine.

Inst. `| D7    C | G    Em | Am    C | D7    G |`
`| D    C | G    Em | Am    C | D7    G ‖`

A3
G   D   C G
As we live a life of ease,

Em   Am   C   D7
Everyone of us has all we need,

G   D   C   G
Sky of blue and sea of green,

Em   Am   C   D7
In our yellow submarine.

B3
G   D
We all live in our yellow submarine,

                          G
Yellow submarine, yellow submarine.

G   D
We all live in our yellow submarine,

                          G
Yellow submarine, yellow submarine.

OUTRO
G   D
We all live in our yellow submarine,

                          G
Yellow submarine, yellow submarine.   *... fade out*

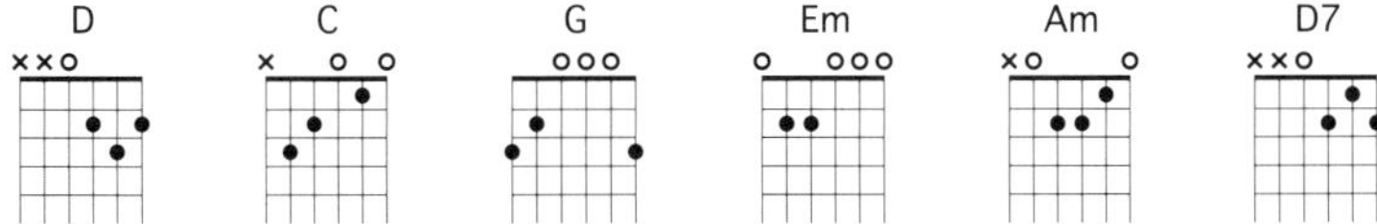

Yer Blues

Words & Music by
John Lennon & Paul McCartney

A1
E7
Yes I'm lonely, wanna die,

A7   *E7*
Yes I'm lonely, wanna die.

G
If I ain't dead already,

B7   *E*   *A*   *E*   *B7*
Oh, girl you know the reason why.

A2
E7
In the morning, wanna die,

A7   *E7*
In the evening, wanna die.

G
If I ain't dead already,

B7   *E*   *A*   *E*   *B7*
Oh, girl you know the reason why.

B1
E
My mother was of the sky,

D   *E*
My father was of the earth,

D   *E*
But I am of the universe,

E7
And you know what it's worth.

A3
A7   *E7*
I'm lonely wanna die

G
If I ain't dead already

B7   *E*   *A*   *E*   *B7*
Ooh girl you know the reason why.

<pre>
         E
[B2] The eagle picks my eye,

     D   E
       The worm, he licks my bone,

     D   E
       I feel so suicidal,

             E7
     Just like Dylan's Mr. Jones.

     A7   E7
[A4] Lonely, wanna die,

             G
     If I ain't dead already,

     B7   E   A   E   B7
     Oh, girl you know the reason why.

     E
[A5] Black cloud crossed my mind

     D E
       Blue mist round my soul,

     D E
       Feel so suicidal,

         E7
     Even hate my rock and roll,

           A7   E
     Wanna die, yeah, wanna die,

           G
     If I ain't dead already,

     B7   E   A   E   B7
     Oh, girl you know the reason why.
</pre>

<pre>
[Inst.] |E |E |E |E |A7 |A7 |
         |E |E |G |B7 |E A|E B7|
         |E |E |E |E |A7 |A7 |
         |E |E |G |B7 |E   ‖

[Inst.2] |E7 |E7 |A7 |E7 |
         |G B7|E7 |G |B7 | ... fade out
</pre>

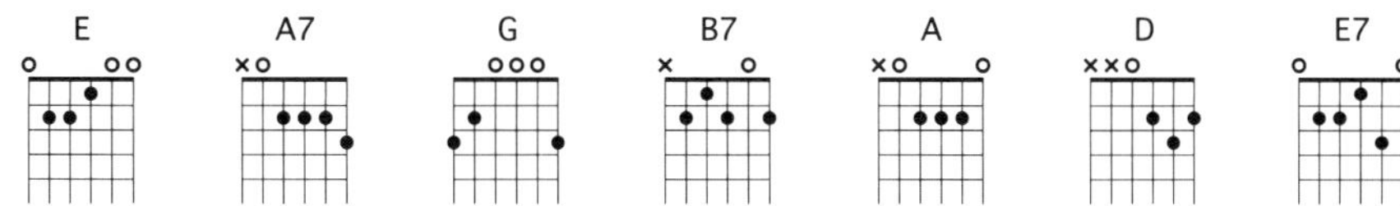

Yes It Is

Words & Music by
John Lennon & Paul McCartney

Inst. | *E* ‖

A1
E   *A*   *F#m7*   *B7*
If you wear red tonight,

E   *A*   *D6*   *B7*
Remember what I said tonight,

C#m/G#   *A*
For red is the colour that my baby wore,

D   *C#m*
And what is more, it's true,

E
Yes it is.

A2
E   *A*   *F#m7*   *B7*
Scarlet were the clothes she wore,

E   *A*   *D*   *B7*
Everybody knows I've sure.

C#m/G#   *A*
I would remember all the things we planned,

D   *C#m*
Understand, it's true,

E   *E7*
Yes it is, it's true.

E
Yes it is.

B1
Bm   *E*   *A*   *F#m*
I could be happy with you by my side

Bm   *E*   *C#m*
If I could forget her, but it's my pride.

E
Yes it is, yes it is.

F#   *B7*
Oh, yes it is, yeah.

E   *A*   *F#m7*   *B7*

A3 Please don't wear red tonight.

E   *A*   *D6*   *B7*

This is what I said tonight.

     C#m/G#   *A*

For red is the colour that will make me blue,

     D   *C#m*

In spite of you, it's true,

E   *E7*

Yes it is, it's true.

E

Yes it is.

Bm   *E*   *A*   *F#m*

B2 I could be happy with you by my side

Bm   *E*   *C#m*

If I could forget her, but it's my pride.

     E

Yes it is, yes it is.

     F#   *B7*

Oh, yes it is, yeah.

E   *A*   *F#m7*   *B7*

A4 Please don't wear red tonight.

E   *A*   *D6*   *B7*

This is what I said tonight.

     C#m/G#   *A*

For red is the colour that will make me blue,

     D   *C#m*

In spite of you, it's true,

E   *G#*

Yes it is, it's true.

A   *E*

Yes it is, it's true.

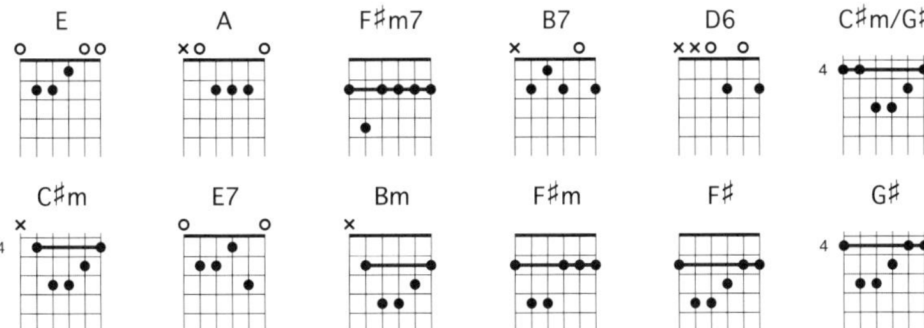

Yesterday

Words & Music by
John Lennon & Paul McCartney

* 6번줄 기준으로 'D'가 되도록
한음씩 낮추어 튜닝합니다.

Inst. | G | G ‖

A1
G   F#m7
Yesterday,

   B7   Em   Em/D
All my troubles seemed so far away,

C D7   G   G/F#
Now it looks as though they're here to stay,

  Em7 A   C G
Oh, I be - lieve in yes - terday.

A2
G   F#m7
Suddenly,

   B7   Em   Em/D
I'm not half to man I used to be,

C   D7   G   G/F#
There's a shadow hanging over me.

  Em7 A   C G
Oh, yesterday came suddenly.

B1
B7sus4 B7 Em D (C)
Why - she - had - to - go

Em/B Am6   D7   G
I don't know she wouldn't say.

B7sus4 B7 Em   D (C) Em/B
I - said - some - thing wrong, now I

Am6   D7   G
Long for yesterday.

A3

| G | F#m7 |
Yesterday,

| | B7 | Em | Em/D |
Love was such an easy game to play,

| C | D7 | G | G/F# |
Now I need a place to hide away,

| | Em7 | A | C | G |
Oh, I be - lieve in yesterday.

B2

| B7sus4 | B7 | Em | D | (C) |
Why - she - had - to - go

| Em/B | Am6 | D7 | G |
I don't know she wouldn't say.

| B7sus4 | B7 | Em | D | (C) | Em/B |
I - said - some - thing wrong, now I

| Am6 | D7 | G |
Long for yesterday.

A4

| G | F#m7 |
Yesterday,

| | B7 | Em | Em/D |
Love was such an easy game to play,

| C | D7 | G | G/F# |
Now I need a place to hide away,

| | Em7 | A | C | G |
Oh, I be - lieve in yesterday.

| G | A7 | (C) | G |
Mmm.

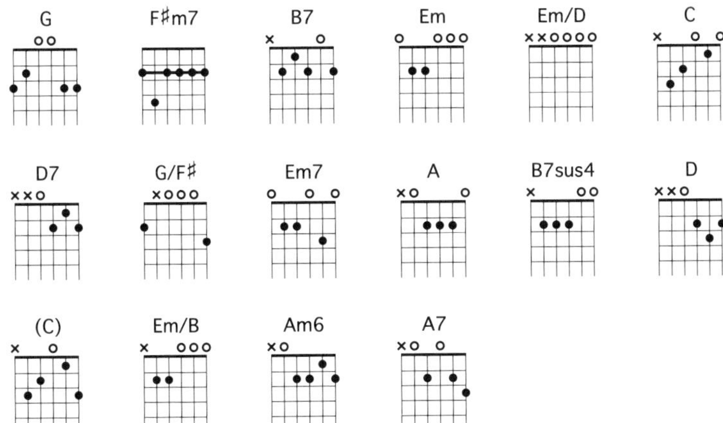

You Can't Do That

Words & Music by
John Lennon & Paul McCartney

Inst. | G7 | G7 | G7 | G7 ‖

A1
     G7
I got something to say that might cause you pain,

If I catch you talking to that boy again,

     C7
I'm gonna let you down,

     G7
And leave you flat.

     D7
Because I told you before,

C7   *G7*   *D7*
Oh, you can't do that.

A2
     G7
Well, it's the second time, I've caught you talking to him,

Do I have to tell you one more time, I think it's a sin.

     C7
I think I'll let you down. let you down

     G7
And leave you flat. gonna let you down and leave you flat,

     D7
Because I've told you before,

C7   *G7*
Oh, you can't do that.

B1
     B7   *Em*
Everybody's green,

     Am   *Bm*   *G7*
'Cause I'm the one, who won your love,

     B7   *Em*
But if they's seen,

     Am   *Bm*   *D*
You're talking that way they'd laugh in my face.

|A3|
G7
So please listen to me, if you wanna stay mine,

I can't help my feelings, I'll go out of my mind.

      C7
I'm gonna let you down, let you down,

        G7
And leave you flat, gonna let you down and leave you flat,

      D7
Because I've told you before,

C7   *G7*   *D7*
Oh, you can't do that.

Inst. | *G7* | *G7* | *G7* | *G7* | *C7* | *C7* |
| *G7* | *G7* | *D7* | *C7* | *G7* | *G7* ||

|B2|
      B7   *Em*
Everybody's green,

    Am   *Bm*   *G7*
'Cause I'm the one, who won your love,

      B7   *Em*
But if they's seen,

    Am   *Bm*   *D*
You're talking that way they'd laugh in my face.

|A4|
   G7
So please listen to me, if you wanna stay mine,

I can't help my feelings, I'll go out of my mind.

      C7
I'm gonna let you down, let you down,

        G7
And leave you flat, gonna let you down and leave you flat,

      D7
Because I've told you before,

C7   *G7*   *F7*   *F#7*   *G7*
Oh, you can't do that.

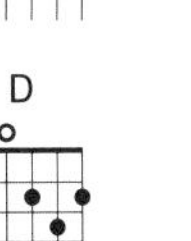
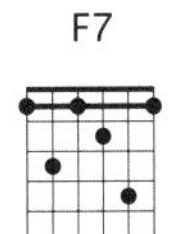
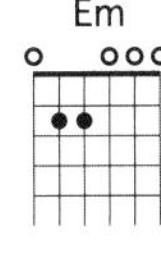
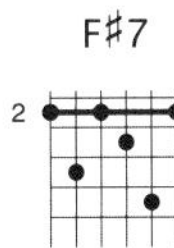

You Know My Name(Look Up The Number)

Words & Music by
John Lennon & Paul McCartney

`Inst.` | G/D | A/C# || D F#m | G A | D F#m | G A ||

G   F#aug/Bb Bm   E7

A1 You know my name,   look up the number.

G   D   Em7   A
You know my name,   look up the number.

D F#m   G   A
You, you know, you know my name,

D F#m   G   A   D
You, you know, you know my name.

B1 Good evening and welcome to Slaggers,

                        D
Featuring Denis O'Bell

Em7
And Ringo, Hey, Ringo.

D
Let's hear it for Denis. ha-hay!

Em7
Good evening.

G   F#aug/Bb Bm   E7

A2 You know my name,   better look up the number.

G   D   Em7   A
You know my name,   that's right look up the number.

D D/F#   G   A

A3 You, you know, you know my name,

D D/F#   G   A
You, you know, you know my name.

G   *F#aug/Bb*   *Bm*
You know my name, ba ba ba ba ba ba ba ba pum.

      E7
Look up my number.

G   *D*
You know my name,

Em7   *A*
That's right look up the number.

    D   *Em7*
A4 Oh, you know, you know, you know my name,

D   *Em7*
You know, you know, you know my name.

      G
Huh huh huh huh,

     F#aug/Bb   *Bm*
You know my name, ba ba ba pum.

      E7
Look up the number

G   *D* *Em7*   *A*
You know my name, look up the number.

D   *Em7*   *A*
You, you know, you know my name, baby,

D   *Em7*   *A*
You, you know, you know my name,

D   *A7*
You know, you know my name,

D   *A7*
You know, you know my name.

B2 Oh, let's hear it. go on Denis,

Let's hear it for Denis O'Bell.

```
      D     D/F#              G                 A
A5  You know, you know, you know my name,

      D     D/F#              G                 A
    You know, you know, you know my name,

      G                      F#aug/Bb
    You know my name,      look up the number,

    Bm                      E7                  G
    You know my name,      look up me number

    D         Em7                   A
    You know, you know my name,   look up me number
```

```
      D                 D/F#          G                 A
A6  You know my name, you know my number two,

          D                   D/F#          G                 A
    You know my number three, and you know my number four,

    D               D/F#          G             G#dim
    You know my name, you know number two,

          A
    You know my name, you know my number,

                              D
    What's up with you?
```

You know my name, that's right

Yeah.

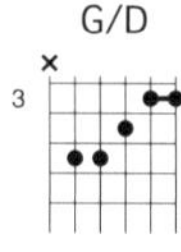

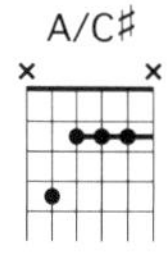

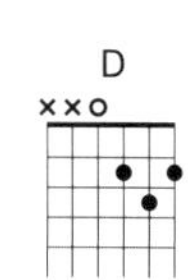

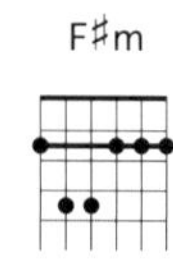

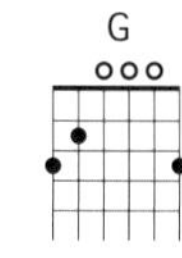

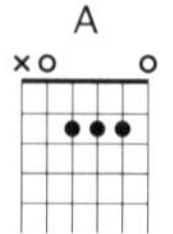

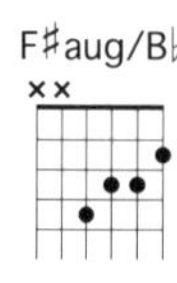

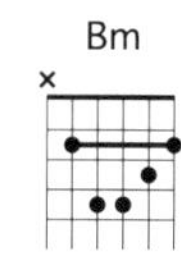

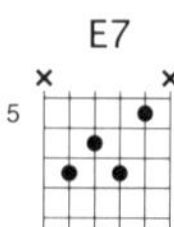

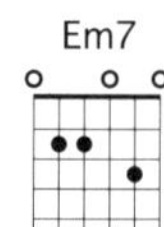

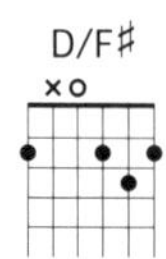

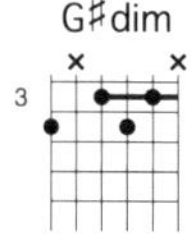

CAPO : 1 FRET.

You'll Be Mine

Words & Music by
John Lennon & Paul McCartney

Inst. ‖ A D7 | A E7 ‖

              A   *C#m*   *F#m*   *A*
A1 When the stars fall at night, you'll be mine, yes I know

        E7   *D7*
You'll be mine, until you die,

        A   *E7*
You'll be mine.

       A   *C#m*   *F#m*   *A*
A2 And so all the night, you'll be mine, you'll be mine.

        E7   *D7*   *A*
And the stars gonna shine, you'll be mine,

A7
Now.

   D7
B1 My darling, when you brought me that toast the other morning,

A   *A7*
I, I looked into your eyes and I could see

     D7
A National Health eyeball.

         B7
And I loved you like I have never done,

       E7
I have never done before.

     A   *C#m*
A3 Yes, the stars gonna shine

       F#m   *A*
And you'll be mine, and you'll be mine.

     E7   *D7*   *A*
You'll be mine, and the stars gonna shine.

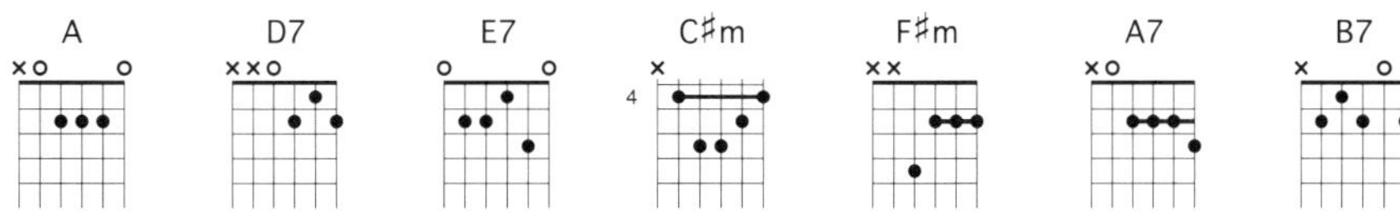

You Know What To Do

Words & Music by
George Harrison

Inst. | D | D ‖

A1
        A   *E*
When I see you, I just don't know what to say,

    A   *E*
I like to be with you every hour of the day.

B1
            A   *E*
So if you want me,

            A   *E*
Just like I need you,

      A   *D*
You know what to do.

A2
    A   *E*
I watched you walking by, and you looked all alone,

    A   *E*
I hope that you won't mind if I walk you back home.

B2
            A   *E*
And if you want me,

            A   *E*
Just like I need you,

      A   *D*
You know what to do.

C1
Bm
Just call on me when you are lonely,

Bm(maj7)
I'll keep my love for you only.

A   *D*
I'll call on you if I'm lonely too.

A3
A Understand, I'll stay with you everyday, *E*

A Make you love me more in every way. *E*

B3 So if you want me, *A* *E*

Just like I want you, *A* *E*

You know what to do. *A* *D*

C2 *Bm* Just call on me when you are lonely,

Bm(maj7) I'll keep my love for you only.

A I'll call on you if I'm lonely too. *D*

A4 *A* Understand, I'll stay with you everyday, *E*

A Make you love me more in every way. *E*

B4 So if you want me, *A* *E*

Just like I need you, *A* *E*

You know what to do. *A* *D*

Inst. | *D* | *D* | *D* | *D* ||

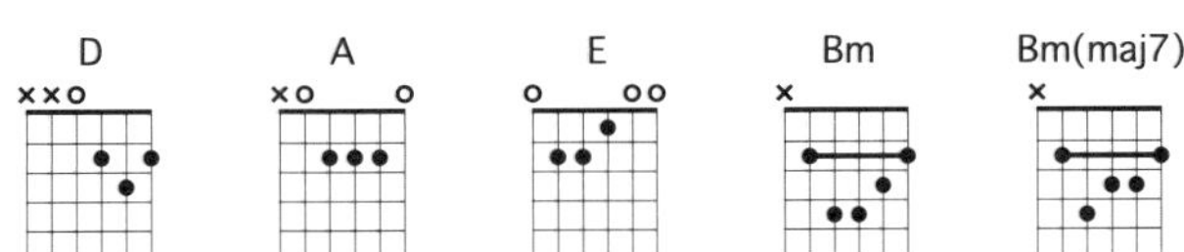

You Like Me Too Much

Words & Music by
John Lennon & Paul McCartney

Inst. | G | Bb D7 | G ‖

A1
G
Though you've gone away this morning,
              Am

           C   *G7*
You'll be back again tonight,

      Am
Telling me there'll be no next time

        C   *G7*
If I just don't treat you right,

B1
      Bm7   *D7*
You'll never leave me and you know it's true,

         G   *C*   *D*
'Cause you like me too much and I like you.

A2
         Am
You've tried before to leave me,

        C   *G7*
But you haven't got the nerve,

        Am
To walk out and make me lonely,

        C   *G7*
Which is all that I deserve.

B2
      Bm7   *D7*
You'll never leave me and you know it's true,

         G   *C*   *D*
'Cause you like me too much and I like you.

C1
Em7   *A7*   *Bm7*   *A7*
I really do, and it's nice when you believe me,

Em7 A7   *D7*
If you leave me.

A3 *Am*   *C*   *G7*
I will follow I will follow you and bring you back where you belong,

         Am   *C*   *G7*
'Cause I could't really stand it, I'd admit that I was wrong.

B3 *Bm7*   *D7*
I wouldn't let you leave me 'cause it's true,

          G   *C*   *D7*
'Cause you like me too much and I like you.

Inst. | *G* | *G* | *G* | *G* | *C* | *C* |
| *G* | *G* | *D7* | *D7* | *D7* | *D7* ‖

          G   *C*   *D*
'Cause you like me too much and I like you.

C2 *Em7*   *A7*   *Bm7*   *A7*
I really do, and it's nice when you believe me,

Em7 *A7*   *D7*
If   you leave me.

A4 *Am*   *C*   *G7*
I will follow you and bring you back where you belong

         Am   *C*   *G7*
'Cause I could't really stand it, I'd admit that I was wrong,

B4 *Bm7*   *D7*
I wouldn't let you leave me 'cause it's true,

          G   *C*   *D*
'cause you like me too much and I like you,

          G   *C*   *D*
'cause you like me too much and I like you.

Inst. | *G* | *G* | *Bb* *D7* | *G* ‖

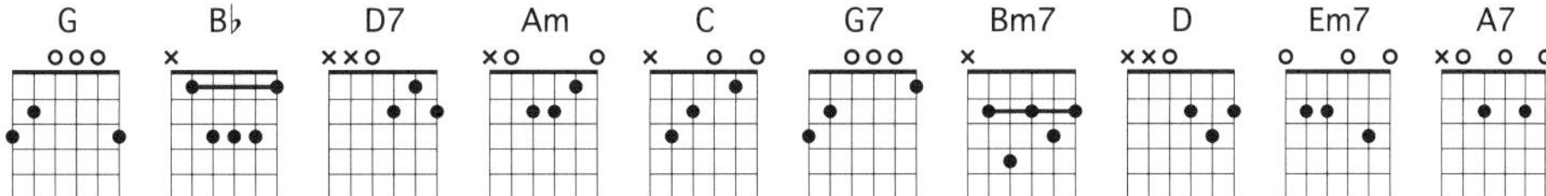

You Never Give Me Your Money

Words & Music by
John Lennon & Paul McCartney

Inst. |*Am7* |*Dm7* |*G7* |*C* |*Fmaj7* |*Bm7b5* *E7* |*Am* |*Am* ‖

A1
Am7   *Dm7*
You never give me your money,

G7   *C*
You only give me your funny paper,

Fmaj7   *Bm7b5*   *E7*
And in the middle of nego — tiations,

          Am
You break down.

A2
Am7   *Dm7*
I never give you my number,

G7   *C*
I only give you my situation,

Fmaj7   *Bm7b5*   *E7*
And in the middle of inves — tigation

          Am   *C/G*   *G*
I break down.

B1
C   *E7*
Out of college, money spent,

Am   *C7*
See no future, pay no rent,

F   *G*   *C*
All the money's gone, nowhere to go,

C   *E7*
Any jobber got the sack,

Am   *C7*
Monday morning, turning back,

F   *G*   *C*
Yellow lorry slow, nowhere to go.

          Bb   *F*   *C*
But oh, that magic feeling, nowhere to go,

          Bb   *F*   *C*
But oh, that magic feeling, nowhere to go,

Nowhere to go.

Inst. | *Bb* | *F* | *C* | *Bb* | *F* | *C* | *Bb* | *F* | *C* |
| *D7* | *Eb7* *G7* | *C7* *A7* | *Eb7* *G7* | *F#7* *Eb7* |
| *A7* *F#7* *G7* *G#7* ‖

A3

A   *B*
One sweet dream,

C   *E*   *A*
Pick up the bags and get in the limousine.

Dm   *G*
Soon we'll be away from here,

Am/D   *G*   *A*
Step on the gas and wipe that tear away,

      B   *C*   *G/B*   *A*
One sweet dream came true   today,

   C   *G/B*   *A*
Came true   today,

   C   *G/B*   *A*
Came true   today,

   C   *G/B*   *A*
Yes it did.

OUTRO

C   *G/B*
One two three four five six seven,

A
All good children go to Heaven.

C   *G/B*
One two three four five six seven,

A
All good children go to Heaven.   *... fade out*

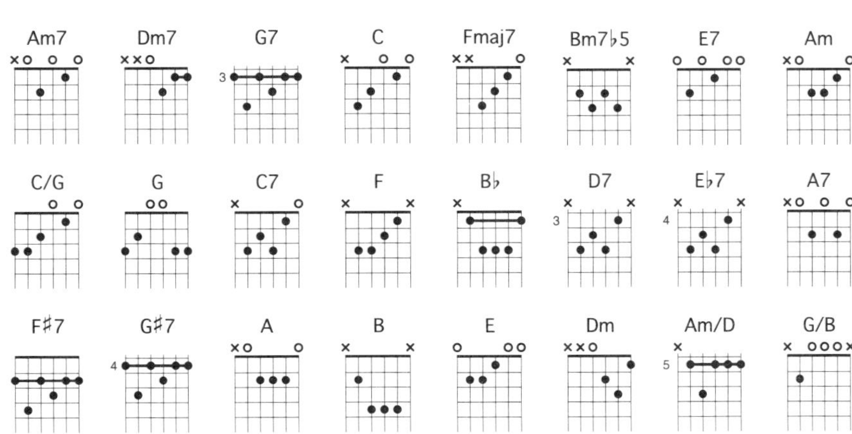

You Won't See Me

Words & Music by
John Lennon & Paul McCartney

Inst. | D A | A |

A1
```
     A         B7        D        A
When I call you up, your line's engaged,

A           B7        D        A
I have had enough, so act your age.

        A7    D      Dm          A
We have lost the time that was so hard to find,

        A       B7
And I will lose my mind

    D    A
If you won't see me, you won't see me,

D     A
You won't see me.
```

A2
```
     A       B7          D        A
I don't know why, you should want to hide,

     A       B7        D        A
But I can't get through, my hands are tied.

     A7    D     Dm              A
I won't want to stay, I don't have much to say,

       A      B7
But I can't turn away,

       D    A
And you won't see me, you won't see me,

D     A
You won't see me.
```

B1
```
Bm           Dm         Ddim7        A
Time after time, you refuse to even listen,

B7                    E7
I wouldn't mind if I knew what I was missing.
```


<pre>
                   A   B7   D   A
A3 Though the days are few, they're filled with tears,

                      B7   D   A
    And since I lost you, it feels like years,

              A7   D   Dm   A
    Yes, it seems so long, girl, since you've been gone,

              A   B7
    And I just can't go on,

        D   A
    If you won't see me, you won't see me,

      D   A
    You won't see me.

    Bm   Dm   Ddim7   A
B2 Time after time, you refuse to even listen,

    B7   E7
    I wouldn't mind if I knew what I was missing.

              A   B7   D   A
A4 Though the days are few, they're filled with tears,

              A   B7   D   A
    And since I lost you, it feels like years,

              A7   D   Dm   A
    Yes, it seems so long, girl, since you've been gone,

              A   B7
    And I just can't go on,

          D   A
    If you won't see me, you won't see me,

      D   A
    You won't see me, you won't see me.

    Inst. | A | B7 | D | A |
           | A | B7 | D | A || ... fade out
</pre>

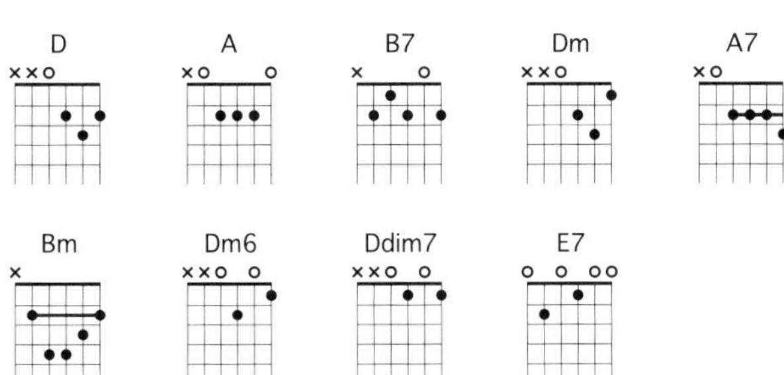

You're Going To Lose That Girl

Words & Music by
John Lennon & Paul McCartney

| A1 |

              E   *C#m*
You're gonna lose that girl, (yes, yes, you're gonna lose that girl.)

                   F#m   *B7*
You're gonna lose that girl.

| B1 |

E   *G#*
If you don't take her out tonight,

          F#m
She's gonna change her mind, (she's gonna change her mind.)

E   *G#*
And I will take her out tonight,

         F#m   *B7*
And I will treat her kind. (i'm gonna treat her kind.)

| A2 |

           E   *C#m*
You're gonna lose that girl, (yes, yes, you're gonna lose that girl.)

          F#m   *B7*
You're gonna lose that girl.

| B2 |

E   *G#*
If you don't treat her right, my friend,

          F#m   *B7*
You're gonna find her gone, (you're gonna find her gone,)

E   *G#*
'Cause I will treat her right, and then

         F#m   *B7*
You'll be the lonely one (you're not the only one.)

| A3 |

           E   *C#m*
You're gonna lose that girl, (yes, yes, you're gonna lose that girl.)

          F#m   *B7*
You're gonna lose that girl.

          F#m   *D*
You're gonna lose (yes,yes, you're gonna lose that girl.)

C1
G / C / G
I'll make a point of taking her away from you,(watch what you do,) yeah,

C / F
The way you treat her what else can I do?

Inst. | E | G# | F#m | B7 | E | G# | F#m | B7 ||

A4
E / C#m
You're gonna lose that girl, (yes, yes, you're gonna lose that girl.)

F#m / B7
You're gonna lose that girl.

F#m / D
You're gonna lose (yes,yes, you're gonna lose that girl.)

C2
G / C / G
I'll make a point of taking her away from you,(watch what you do,) yeah,

C / F
The way you treat her what else can I do?

B3
E / G#
If you don't take her out tonight,

F#m / B7
She's gonna change her mind, (she's gonna change her mind.)

E / G#
And I will take her out tonight,

F#m / B7
And I will treat her kind. (i'm gonna treat her kind.)

A5
E / C#m
You're gonna lose that girl, (yes, yes, you're gonna lose that girl.)

F#m / B7
You're gonna lose that girl.

F#m / D / A / E
You're gonna lose — that girl.

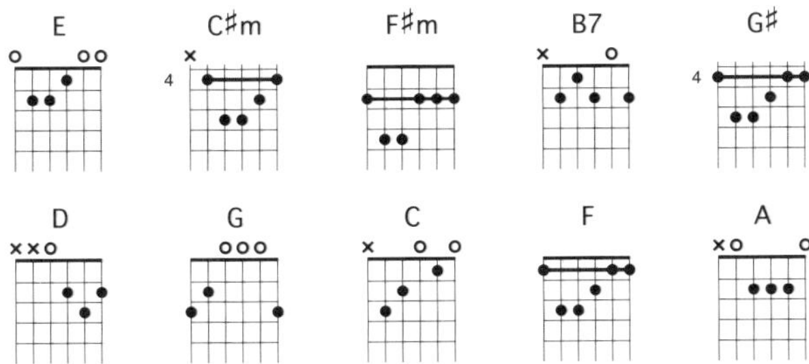

You've Got To Hide Your Love Away

Words & Music by
John Lennon & Paul McCartney

|A1|
G   Dsus4 Fadd9 C G
Here I stand, head in hand,

C   Fadd9   C
Turn my face to the wall.

G   Dsus4 Fadd9 C   G
If she's gone I can't go on

C   Fadd9   C   D
Feeling two foot small.

|A2|
G   Dsus4 Fadd9 C G
Everywhere peo - ple stare,

C   Fadd9   C
Each and every day.

G   Dsus4   Fadd9 C G
I can see them laugh at me,

C   Fadd9   C   D   D/C   D/B   D/A
And I hear them say.

|B1|
G   C   Dsus4   D Dsus2 D
Hey you've got to hide your love away,

G   C   Dsus4   D Dsus2 D
Hey you've got to hide your love away.

|A3|
G   Dsus4 Fadd9 C   G
How can I   ev — en   try?

C   Fadd9   C
I can never win.

G   Dsus4 Fadd9 C   G
Hearing them, see — ing them

C   Fadd9   C   D
In the state I'm in.

|A4|

G   *Dsus4*   *Fadd9*   *C*   *G*
How could she   say   to   me

C   *Fadd9*   *C*
Love will find a way?

G   *Dsus4*   *Fadd9*   *C*   *G*
Gather round, all   you   clowns,

C   *Fadd9*   *C*   *D*   *D/C*   *D/B*   *D/A*
Let me hear you say.

|B2|

G   *C*   *Dsus4*   *D*   *Dsus2*   *D*
Hey you've got to hide your love away,

G   *C*   *Dsus4*   *D*   *Dsus2*   *D*
Hey you've got to hide your love away.

Inst. | *G*   *Dsus4*   *Fadd9*   *C*   *G* | *C*   *Fadd9*   *C* |
        | *G*   *Dsus4*   *Fadd9*   *C*   *G* | *C*   *Fadd9*   *C* | *G*   ‖

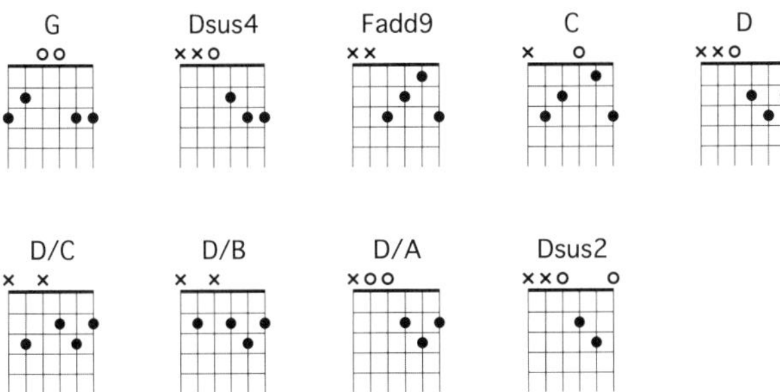

Your Mother Should Know

Words & Music by
John Lennon & Paul McCartney

Inst. | *Am* | *Am* ‖

A1
Am   *Fmaj7*
Let's all get up and dance to a song

            A7/E   *Dm*
That was a hit before your mother was born.

G7   *C*   *C/B* *A7*
Though she was born a long, long time ago

                     D7
Your mother should know,

G7   *C*
Your mother should know,

E7
Sing it again.

A2
Am   *Fmaj7*
Let's all get up and dance to a song

            A7/E   *Dm*
That was a hit before your mother was born.

G7   *C*   *C/B* *A7*
Though she was born a long, long time ago

                     D7
Your mother should know,

G7   *C*
Your mother should know.

Inst. | *E* | *Am* | *Fmaj7* | *Fmaj7* | *Fmaj7/G* | *C* | *E7* ‖

A3
Am   *Fmaj7*
Lift up your hearts and sing me a song

            A7/E   *Dm*
That was a hit before your mother was born.

G7   *C*   *C/B* *A7*
Though she was born a long, long time ago,

                     D7
Your mother should know,


```
G7                        C
Your mother should know.

A7                       D7
Your mother should know,

G7                        C
Your mother should know.
```

Inst. | E | Am | Fmaj7 | Fmaj7 | Fmaj7/G | C ‖

```
E7
Sing it again.
```

A4
```
Am                    Fmaj7
Da-da-da-da-da, da-da-da-da

              A7/E        Dm
Da-da-da, da-da-da-da, da-da-da-da.

G7                            C         C/B     A7
Though she was born a long, long time ago,

                  D7          G7
Your mother should know, (your mother should...)

                  C       A7
Your mother should know, (yeah.)

                  D7          G7
Your mother should know, (your mother should...)

                  C       A7
Your mother should know, (yeah.)

                  D7          G7
Your mother should know, (your mother should...)

                  C
Your mother should know, (yeah.)
```

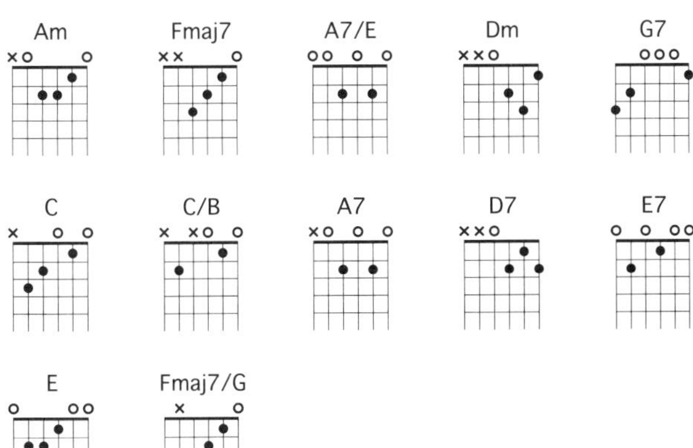

Hello Little Girl

Words & Music by
John Lennon & Paul McCartney

INTRO
> *E7*   *A* *F#7* *Bm7*
> Hello little girl,
>
> *E7*   *A* *F#7* *Bm7*
> Hello little girl,
>
> *E7*   *A* *F#7* *Bm7* *E7*
> Hello little girl,

A1
>   *A*   *E*
> When I see you everyday
>
>   *D* *E7* *D* *E*   *A*
> I say, mm-mm,   hello little girl.
>
>   *A*   *E*
> When you're passing on your way
>
>   *D* *E7* *D* *E*   *A*
> I say, mm-mm   hello little girl.

A2
>   *A*   *E*
> When I see you passing by
>
>   *D* *E7* *D* *E*   *A*
> I cry, mm-mm,   hello little girl.
>
>   *A*   *E*
> When I try to catch your eye
>
>   *D* *E7* *D* *E*   *A*
> I cry, mm-mm,   hello little girl.

B1
> *A*   *F#7*   *Bm7*   *E7*
> I send you flowers, but you don't care,
>
> *A*   *F#7*   *Bm7*   *E7*
> You never seem to see me standing there.
>
> *A*   *F#7*   *Bm7* *E7*
> I often wonder what you're thinking of,
>
> *A*   *F#7*   *Bm7*   *E7*
> I hope it's me and love, love, love.

A3   So I hope there'll come a day

  A ... *E*

When you'll say, mm-mm   you're my little girl.

D   *E7*   *D*   *E*   *A*

Inst. | *A*   *E* | *D*   *E* | *D*   *E* | *A* ||

B2   It's not the first time that it's happened to me,

A   *F#7*   *Bm7*   *E7*

It's been a long lonely time.

A   *F#7*   *Bm7*   *E7*

And it's funny funny to see

A   *F#7*   *Bm7*   *E7*

That I'm about to lose my mi-mi-mind

A   *F#7*   *Bm7*   *E7*

A4   So I hope there'll come a day

  A ... *E*

When you'll say, mm-mm   you're my little girl.

D   *E7*   *D*   *E*   *A*

Mm-mm   you're my little girl.

F#7   *Bm7*   *E*   *A*

Mm-mm   you're my little girl.

F#7   *Bm7*   *E*   *A*

Oh yeah, you're my little girl.

F#7   *Bm7*   *E*   *A*   *C#m7*   *Bb*

Do do do do do

A   *A6/9*

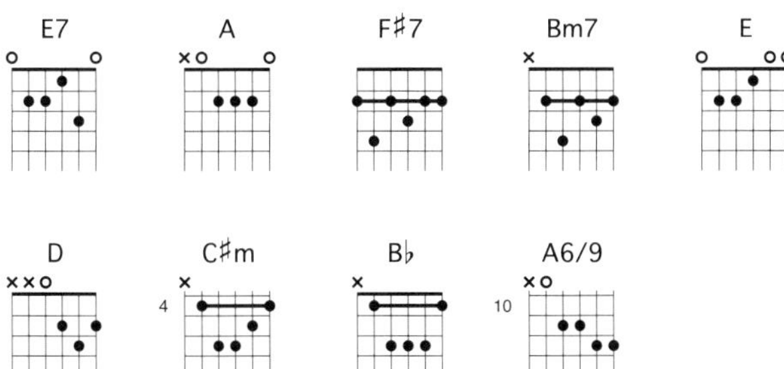

I've Got A Feeling

Words & Music by
John Lennon & Paul McCartney

Inst. ‖ A   D/A │ A   D/A ‖

A1
> A   D/A   A   D/A   A   D/A
> I've got a feeling, a feeling deep inside. oh yeah,

>   A   D/A
> oh yeah, that's right

> A   D/A   A   D/A   A   D/A
> I've got a feeling, a feeling I can't hide oh, no, no

>   A   D/A   A
> Oh no,   oh no

> A7   E   G   D
> Yeah,   yeah,

>   A   D/A   A   D/A
> I've got a feeling, yeah.

A2
> A   D/A   A   D/A
> Oh please believe me, I'd hate to miss the train

>   A   D/A   A   D/A
> Oh yeah, yeah,   oh yeah.

> A   D/A   A   D/A
> And if you leave me, I won't be late again,

>   A   D/A   A   D/A
> Oh no,   oh no, oh no.

> A7   E   G   D   A   D/A
> Yeah   yeah   I've got a feeling, yeah.

> A   D/A
> I've got a feeling.

B1
> E
> All these years I've been wandering around,

> G7
> Wondering how come nobody told me

> D7
> All that I was looking for was somebody

>   A7
> Who looked like you.

[A3]
A   *D/A*   *A*   *D/A*
I've got a feeling, that keeps me on my toes,

    A   *D/A*   *A*   *D/A*
Oh yeah,   oh yeah.

A   *D/A*   *A*   *D/A*
I've got a feeling, I think that everybody knows,

    A *D/A*   *A*   *D/A*
Oh yeah,   oh yeah,   oh yeah.

A7   *E*   *G* *D*   *A*
Yeah, yeah.   I've got a feeling, yeah.

Inst. ‖ *A* *D/A* | *A* *D/A* ‖

[C1]
A   *D/A*
Everybody had a hard year,

A   *D/A*
Everybody had a good time,

A   *D/A*
Everybody had a wet dream,

A   *D/A*
Everybody saw the sunshine,

    A   *D/A*   *A* *D/A*
Oh yeah, (oh yeah) oh yeah, oh yeah.

[C2]
A   *D/A*
Everybody had a good year,

A   *D/A*
Everybody let their hair down,

A   *D/A*
Everybody pulled their socks up,

A   *D/A*
Everybody put their foot down,

Inst. ‖ *A7* | *A7* | *A7* | *A7*   ‖

|C3| *A*   *D/A*
Everybody had a good year,

A   *D/A*
Everybody had a hard time,

A   *D/A*
Everybody had a wet dream,

A   *D/A*
Everybody saw the sunshine,

|C4| *A*   *D/A*
Everybody had a good year,

A   *D/A*
Everybody let their hair down,

A   *D/A*
Everybody pulled their socks up,

A   *D/A*
Everybody put their foot down,

Oh yeah.

Inst. | *A7* | *A7* | *A7* | *A7*   ‖
         | *A7* | *A7*   ‖

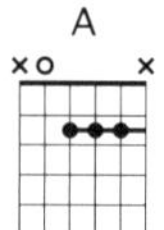

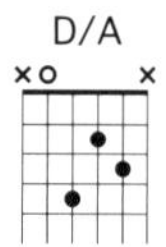

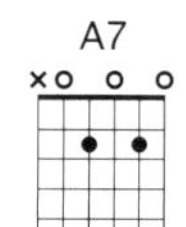

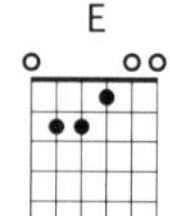

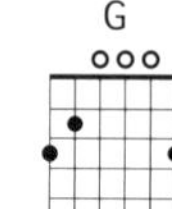

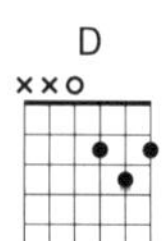

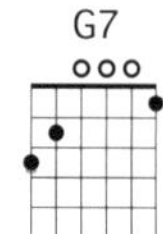

In Spite Of All The Danger

Words & Music by
Paul McCartney & George Harrison

Inst. | E   ‖

A1
B7   *E*
In spite of all the danger,

In spite of all that may be,

E7   *A*
I'll do anything for you,

                              B7
Anything you want me to,

                    E   *A*   *E*
If you'll be true to me.

A2
                              E
In spite of all the heartache

That you may cause me,

E7   *A*
I'll do anything for you,

                              B7
Anything you want me to,

                    E   *A*   *E*   *E7*
If you'll be true to me.

B1
          A
I'll look after you

              E   *E7*
Like I've never done before,

          A
I'll keep all the others

              B7
From knocking at your door.

                          E
[A3] In spite of all the danger,

In spite of all that may be,

E7   *A*
I'll do anything for you,

       B7
Anything you want me to,

    E *A* *E*
If you'll be true to me.

Inst. | *E* | *E* | *E* | *E7* | *A* | *A* |
     | *E* | *E* | *B7* | *A* | *E* | *B7* ‖

                          E
[A4] In spite of all the heartache

That you may cause me,

E7   *A*
I'll do anything for you,

      B7
Anything you want me to,

    E *A* *E* *E7*
If you'll be true to me.

      A
I'll do anything for you,

      B7
Anything you want me to,

    E *A* *E*
If you'll be true to me.

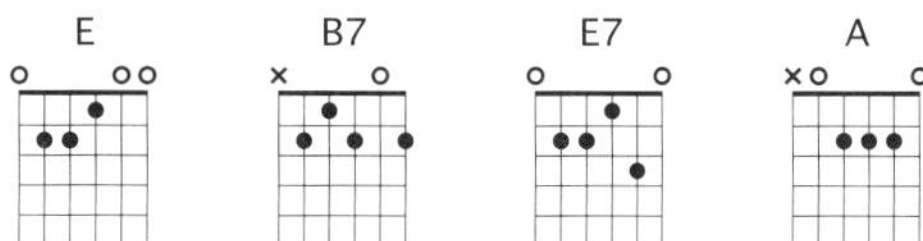

Like Dreamers Do

Words & Music by
John Lennon & Paul McCartney

|B2|
    A   *C#7*
And I waited for your kiss,
           Bm   *E7*
Waited for the bliss
                   A
Like dreamers do.

|C2|
      D   *E*
And I,
         A
I, I, I, I,
         Bm   *B7*
Oh I'll be there, yeah,
           E7
Waiting for you, you, you, you, you, you.

|A3|
A   *F#m*
You, you came just one dream ago,
       Bm   *C#m* *E*
And now I know that I will love you.
    A   *F#m*
Oh I knew when you first said hello,
       Bm   *C#m* *E*
That's how I know that I will love you.

|B3|
    A   *C#7*
And I waited for your kiss,
           Bm   *E7*
Waited for the bliss
                   A
Like dreamers do,
Adim   *A*
Oh like dreamers do,
Adim   *A*
Like dreamers do.

Inst. | *Adim* | *F C#7 F# D7* |
| *G D#7 G# E7* | *A* | *A6/9* ||

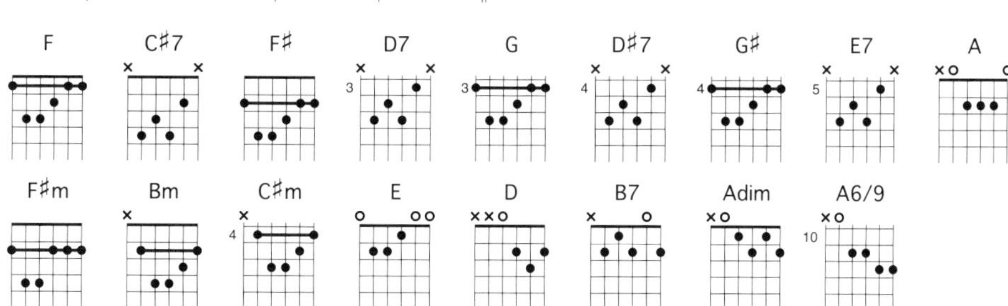

Old Brown Shoe

Words & Music by
George Harrison

Inst. | *C7* | *C7* | *C7* | *C7* ||

          C7
A1 I want a love that's right but right is only half of what's wrong.

          Dm7
  I want a short haired girl who sometimes wears it twice as long.

       F   *F7*   *Ab*   *Ab7*
B1 Now I'm stepping out this old brown shoe, baby, I'm in love with you.

       F   *Eaug*   *Am*
  I'm so glad you came here, it won't be the same now, I'm telling you.

Inst. | *C7* | *C7* ||

          C7
A2 You know you pick me up from where some try to drag me down.

          Dm7
  And when I see your smile replace every thoughtless frown.

    F   *F7* *Ab*   *Ab7*
B2 Got me escaping from this zoo, baby, I'm in love with you,

       F   *Eaug*   *Am*
  I'm so glad you came here, it won't be the same now when I'm with you.

    G   *F*
C1 If I grow up I'll be a singer wearing rings on every finger,

    G   *F*
  Not worrying what they or you say. I'll live and love and maybe someday,

    F#dim   *G*   *G7*
  Who knows, baby, you may comfort me.

Inst. | *C7* | *C7* | *C7* | *C7* | *Dm7* | *Dm7* | *Dm7* | *Dm7* |
| *F* | *F7* | *Ab* | *Ab7* | *F* | *Eaug* | *Am* | *Am* ||

C2
   G   *F*
I may appear to be imperfect, my love is something you can't reject,

G   *F*
I'm changing faster than the weather if you and me should get together,

F#dim   *G*   *G7*
Who knows, baby, you may comfort me.

A3
               C7
I want that love of yours, to miss that love is something I'd hate.

             Dm7
I'll make an early start, I'm making sure that I'm not late.

B3
  F   *F7*   *Ab*   *Ab7*
For you sweet top lip I'm in the queue, baby, I'm in love with you,

F   *Eaug*   *Am*
I'm so glad you came here, it won't be the same now when I'm with you.

     F   *Eaug*   *Am*
I'm so glad you came here, it won't be the same now when I'm with you.

Inst. ‖: *C7* | *C7* | *C7* | *C7* :‖   *... fade out*

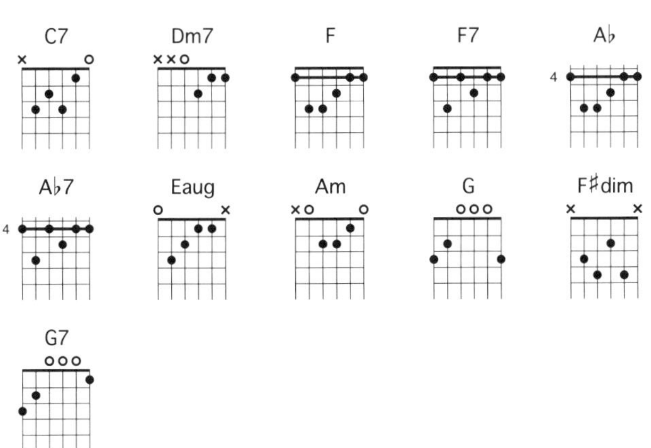

THE BEATLES

201•CHORD SONG BOOK

발 행 일 2016년 7월 1일
저 자 YJ(정영준)
편 집 유경아
디 자 인 하다
영 업 현석호
관 리 남영애
발 행 인 최우진
발 행 처 (주) 스코어
등 록 2012년 6월 7일 제313-2012-196호
I S B N 979-11-5780-062-9
주 소 서울시 마포구 동교로 13길 34(121-896)
전 화 02)333-3705
팩 스 02)333-3748
www.allmu.co.kr
www.openhousebooks.com